THE LEGEND OF THE MICK

THE LEGEND OF THE MICK
Stories and Reflections on Mickey Mantle

JONATHAN WEEKS

LYONS
PRESS

Essex, Connecticut

An imprint of Globe Pequot, the trade division of
The Rowman & Littlefield Publishing Group, Inc.
4501 Forbes Blvd., Ste. 200
Lanham, MD 20706
www.rowman.com

Distributed by NATIONAL BOOK NETWORK

British Library Cataloguing in Publication Information available

Library of Congress Cataloging-in-Publication Data

Names: Weeks, Jonathan, author.
Title: The legend of the Mick : stories and reflections on Mickey Mantle /
   Jonathan Weeks.
Description: Essex, Connecticut : Lyons Press, [2023] | Includes
   bibliographical references.
Identifiers: LCCN 2022041040 (print) | LCCN 2022041041 (ebook) | ISBN
   9781493070176 (trade paperback) | ISBN 9781493070183 (epub)
Subjects: LCSH: Mantle, Mickey, 1931-1995—Anecdotes. | Baseball—United
   States—History—Anecdotes. | Baseball players—United
   States—Anecdotes.
Classification: LCC GV865.M33 W44 2023 (print) | LCC GV865.M33 (ebook) |
   DDC 796.357092 [B]—dc23/eng/20220929
LC record available at https://lccn.loc.gov/2022041040
LC ebook record available at https://lccn.loc.gov/2022041041

Contents

Dreams brimming over,
childhood stretched out in legs,
this is the moment replayed on winter days
when frost covers the field,
when age steals away wishes.
Glorious sleep that seeps back there
to the glory of our baseball days.

—Marjorie Maddox, *Rules of the Game: Baseball Poems*, 2009

INTRODUCTION

Like other Yankee icons before and after him, Mickey Mantle has been the subject of numerous volumes of literature. He wrote and/or contributed to several biographies during his lifetime. But multiple sources agree that he wasn't the most accurate historian. In her acclaimed work, *The Last Boy: Mickey Mantle and the End of America's Childhood*, author Jane Leavy explains, "[Mantle] is a blend of memory and distortion, fact and fiction, repetition and exaggeration. . . . In a life so publicly led, the accretion and reiteration of fable and detail are as thick as 50 years of paint jamming an old windowsill."

Mantle's career on the diamond was a contrast between what actually happened and what might have been. Hampered by an endless string of injuries, he missed hundreds of games during his 18 seasons in the majors. His unnaturally high strikeout and walk totals prompted him to famously joke that he "played seven years without ever hitting the ball." In spite of the pain, and the surgeries, and the missed opportunities, he assembled an impressive batch of statistics. To the present day, he still holds the all-time record for home runs by a switch-hitter.

Mantle was among the most revered and decorated players in baseball history, capturing seven World Series rings and three MVP awards. Not only was he the face of the Yankees, but he was the face of the game itself—rakishly handsome and perpetually smiling. Tom Molito, a marketing executive and author who developed a friendship with Mantle during his later years, colorfully remarked, "Mickey Mantle was the All-American Boy. He was Babe Ruth, Jack Armstrong, and Red Grange wrapped up in one. His platinum blonde hair complemented his natural muscular build and boyish good looks. All that was missing was the cape with the big 'S.'"

Though he publicly fit the image of the wholesome "boy next door," Mantle was a complex individual with a number of tragic flaws. Haunted by childhood trauma and frustrated by his inability to reach his full potential as a ballplayer, he became a chronic alcoholic and incorrigible womanizer. He could be generous and accommodating, but there were times when he was unforgivably rude. By his own admission, he was rarely around when it counted for his wife and four sons—all of whom developed substance abuse issues of their own.

In spite of the many setbacks he encountered on and off the field, Mantle acknowledged his own good fortune. He escaped a life of drudgery in the Oklahoma mining trade by forging a successful career in baseball. "I could have ended up in a hole in the ground, and I ended up being Mickey Mantle," he once said. "There must be a god somewhere."

Mantle's flaws—his humanness—make him eminently more appealing. Toward the end of his life, he sought treatment for his drinking problem. He apologized to his sons for being neglectful and reconciled with his estranged wife. He advised young fans not to follow his example. Similar to his experience on the ballfield, he never got to realize his full potential as a recovering alcoholic. In 1995, he learned that his liver had been irreparably damaged by cirrhosis and hepatitis C. In the wake of a transplant procedure, doctors discovered that cancer had spread throughout his body. He died in August of 1995.

Today, Mantle's life story is still absorbing to many. He has maintained a sizable fan base over the years. Often acknowledged as the godfather of the trading card industry, his cardboard likeness still commands a high price. Even now, more than a quarter-century after his passing, it seems that people still want a piece of "The Mick."

ON MANTLE

PLAYERS AND WRITERS

"There is no sound in baseball akin to the sound of Mantle hitting a home run, the crunchy sound of an axe biting into a tree, yet magnified a hundred times in the vast, cavernous echo-making hollows of a ballfield."

—Arnold Hano

"No man in the history of baseball had as much power as Mickey Mantle. No man. You're not talking about ordinary power. Dave Kingman has power. Willie Mays had power. Then when you're talking about Mickey Mantle, it's an altogether different level. [It] separates the men from the boys."

—Billy Martin

"Until I saw Mantle peel down for his shower in the clubhouse at Comiskey Park one afternoon, I never knew how he developed his brutal power, but his bare back looked like a barrelful of snakes."

—Dave Lancaster

"Mickey Mantle is the strongest hitter in the game. He's the only one who hits the ball so hard, he knocks the spin off it. Catching a liner from him is like catching a knuckleball. It flutters all over."

—Jim Busby

"He didn't train and didn't take good care of himself. He just assumed that he would die at an early age of Hodgkin's disease, as had his father and others on his father's side. So he lived it up at night. He'd wrap those knees every single day and then go out and do the job. Amazingly, he could still run and hit despite the pain. . . . He was truly a marvel to watch."

—Joe DeMaestri

"Mickey Mantle's greatness was built on power and pain. He exuded the first and endured the second."

—Roy Fitzgerald

"On two legs, Mickey Mantle would have been the greatest ballplayer who ever lived."

—Nellie Fox

Mantle on Mantle

"While you're playing ball, you're insulated. All the ballparks and the big crowds have a certain mystique. You feel attached, permanently wedded to the sounds that ring out, to the fans chanting your name, even when there are only four or five thousand in the stands on a Wednesday afternoon."

"I am proud to have been a Yankee. I was in there with some of the greatest outfielders of all time: Willie Mays, Hank Aaron, Ted Williams, Joe DiMaggio, Stan Musial, Duke Snider—I was among them, a Hall of Famer. To think of it sends chills up and down my spine. Since I was four years old, it's all I ever worked for."

"Perhaps if I had been around when Babe Ruth was playing, he would have been my idol. I was like him in many ways. No, not the home runs. I mean the staying out all night. And boy, how often I've thought about being on the same team with him."

"After I hit a home run, I had a habit of running the bases with my head down. I figured the pitcher already felt bad enough without me showing him up rounding the bases."

"Sometimes I think if I had the same body and the same natural ability and someone else's brain, who knows how good a player I might have been."

"If I had played my career hitting singles like Pete [Rose], I'd wear a dress."

"There never was any talk about what I would be in life. Dad and I knew I was going to be a ballplayer."

PART I:
A CHRONOLOGICAL JOURNEY THROUGH MANTLE'S LIFE AND CAREER

Humble Beginnings

The Mantle clan originally hailed from a region of the English West Midlands known as "Black Country"—named for its coal mines and iron foundries. Seeking a more agreeable way of life, the family moved to America in the mid 19th century. Elvin "Mutt" Mantle (Mickey's father) was born in Osage County, Oklahoma, in 1912. His mother, Mae, died in childbirth when he was eight years old. Charlie, Mutt's father, raised four kids with the help of various family members. He never remarried.

When Mutt was still a teenager, he tied the knot with an older divorcee named Lovell Richardson. She had two children from a previous marriage. While Mutt was described as quiet and easygoing, Lovell was widely regarded as outspoken and domineering. Mickey—the first of four sons born to the couple—came into the world on October 20, 1931. He was named after Mutt's favorite baseball player, Hall of Famer Mickey Cochrane. The boy's training began before he could even walk, when Mutt and Charlie got in the habit of propping him up in the corner of the living room and rolling balls to him across the floor.

Mutt worked on a road crew in Spavinaw, Oklahoma, but ended up losing his job during the Great Depression. He turned to farming on an 80-acre plot of land before a prolonged drought drove him into the mining trade. By the time the 1940s arrived, the family had grown significantly with the addition of four more children. The Mantles took up residence in Commerce, where living space was limited. Their single-story house had only four rooms and measured 25 by 30 feet.

The tract of land that came to be known as Commerce had originally been allocated to the Cherokee Nation. In the early 20th century, a settler named Amos Hatton founded a mining camp there. The rich mineral deposits attracted many workers and, in 1908, a railway was built connecting the camp to adjacent communities. The town received its name in 1914, when the seams were acquired by the Commerce Mining and Royalty Company. In 1926, Commerce became one of many stops along US Route 66. By the late 1950s, the mineral supply was drying up and the highway was falling into a state of disrepair.

When Mickey was in his early teens, his grandfather fell ill with Hodgkin's disease. Believing he might recover in a more rustic setting, Mutt moved the family to a farm on the outskirts of town. The fresh air didn't help as Charlie's health declined rapidly. In the wake of his passing, the Mantles eventually returned to Commerce, which had a population of around 2,400.

When Mickey began playing sports as a boy, Mutt refused to sit with Lovell at the games. She was fiercely protective of her sons and prone to angry outbursts. She once punched an opposing football coach after one of Mickey's brothers was injured during a game. Mickey's wife, Merlyn, described Lovell as a cool and emotionally detached woman who rarely offered verbal expressions of love. She was also known to use corporal punishment on her children when they misbehaved.

As a boy, Mickey was quiet but spirited. He had a number of phobias, including a fear of heights and bugs. He was a chronic bed wetter until his teen years—a secret he later revealed to talk show host Dick Cavett on national television. His parents often attended Friday night barn dances, leaving the children in the care of Mickey's half sister, Anna Bea. During his preschool days, Mickey was repeatedly molested by his teenaged sibling—sometimes in front of her friends. He was so deeply embarrassed and ashamed, he held onto the secret until his twilight years, revealing it only to his wife. "I thought I understood more clearly than I ever had why his ego was so fragile," Merlyn later said. "He was a loner who loved a crowd when they cheered from a distance. He never respected women. He demonstrated it in the ladies he chose for his one-night stands and in the crude way he talked and acted in front of women when he drank."

Mutt took a keen interest in his son's sporting activities. Like his father before him, he played at the semipro level as a pitcher and catcher. Moderately talented, his skills went into decline after he broke his leg sliding into a base. He lived vicariously through his son, pushing the boy unreasonably hard at times. Even so, Mickey always spoke highly of his dad. "What [kept] me driving hard, from the time that I was ten, to hit the ball better and farther was first of all my own love for the game and then my love for my father," the Yankee slugger once said. "I knew from the time I was small that every small victory I won, and every solid hit I made or prize I was awarded, brought real joy to my father's heart."

Mickey's first baseball outfit—handmade by his mother—was comprised of material cut from Mutt's old uniform. Mickey wore it for the first time at the age of five—the same year he was taught by his father and grandfather to hit from both sides of the plate. Using a decrepit old shed as a backstop, they developed special ground rules, which the slugger explained in a 1953 magazine article. A grounder or popup was an out. A drive off the side of the house counted as a double. A ball hit onto the roof was a triple, and anything

Mantle's boyhood home is located at 319 South Quincy Street in Commerce, Oklahoma. It had only two bedrooms and measured a mere 672 square feet. The tin barn on the property supposedly served as a backstop while Mickey's father and grandfather taught him how to switch-hit. (Courtesy of Lisa Ann Photography on Visual Hunt)

that sailed over the roof onto neighboring properties was a home run. "I'm probably the only kid who made his old man proud of him by breaking windows," he joked.

A baseball prodigy, Mantle broke plenty of windows growing up. He was so talented by the time he reached the majors, he dazzled even the most hardened skeptics. During his up-and-down 1951 debut, Casey Stengel fittingly said: "He has more speed than any slugger and more slug than any speedster—and nobody has ever had more of both of 'em together. This kid ain't logical. He's too good. It's very confusing."

LIFE-THREATENING INJURY

Mutt Mantle had high hopes for Mickey during the boy's developmental years. Money was in short supply, but baseball was considered essential. While the other Mantle children received socks or other trivial gifts for Christmas, Mickey always ended up with a new baseball glove. He later confided to a friend that he cried every year because he never got any toys to play with.

Lovell Mantle was an avid baseball fan. She religiously followed the St. Louis Cardinals, listening to the radio broadcasts while doing housework. During supper, she regaled family members with detailed game accounts. Her passion was contagious, and Mickey grew up rooting for the Cards.

When Mickey was 10, he joined a Pee Wee League team in Douthat, which is located just north of Commerce. He started out as a catcher, but was ill suited to the position. "When he squatted down behind the batter wearing that protector that was too big for him, you couldn't see his feet," Lovell recalled. "About all you could see of him—except for his arms—were those two little eyes sticking out of the protector like a scared turtle looking out of its shell." Despite his diminutive stature, Mickey helped guide the team to a league championship.

Mutt wanted his son to continue as a catcher (following in his own footsteps), but Mickey was eventually moved to other infield stations. Mutt had a low tolerance for mistakes on the field and was known to become highly irritated when his instructions were ignored. One day, he got out of work early and found Mickey batting right-handed against a right-handed pitcher. After being subjected to Mutt's long-winded tirade, Mickey never repeated the mistake.

Though Mutt was generally even-tempered, Mickey recalled an incident from his childhood in which he received a beating. During the 1930s, water and ice were delivered to homes in commercial trucks. One day, Mickey grabbed hold of the wooden beams supporting the water tank and rode the underside of the truck while it was in motion for about half a block. When he returned home, his father was so angry, he swatted Mickey several times with a piece of baling wire. "It was just about the only time he ever whipped me," Mantle asserted. "[It] was about the last time he ever *had* to whip me, too."

Mutt was dead-set against football, but Mickey joined the Commerce squad in his freshman year of high school. His exceptional speed and natural athleticism made him an ideal running back. According to multiple sources, he scored 10 touchdowns in seven games during his debut season. Even then, he suffered from leg problems and would sometimes limp off the field.

Shortly before his 15th birthday, Mantle was kicked in the shin during practice. Allan Woolard—the Commerce football coach—didn't believe it was a serious injury, but he was mistaken. By the following day, the leg was grotesquely swollen and had turned an angry shade of red. Even worse, Mantle was spiking a temperature of almost 104 degrees.

Mutt and Lovell rushed their boy to a nearby hospital in Picher, where he was diagnosed with osteomyelitis—a rare and potentially fatal infection that, if left untreated, results in a loss of blood to the affected area. Mantle's half-brother, Ted, had developed the same condition during his boyhood, and maggots had been used to strip away the infected flesh. Though the procedure sounds barbaric, it was not uncommon at the time. Amputation was another unpleasant option. When the doctors in Picher told Mickey's parents that they wanted to cut off the boy's leg, Lovell ordered them to pursue another course of treatment.

Fortunately, a new drug called penicillin had proved effective in clinical trials and was coming into widespread use. Mickey received multiple injections every day for over a week. His complexion, which had become jaundiced and pale, returned to a healthier hue. Likewise, the swelling in his leg dissipated and he was able to leave the hospital—temporarily at least.

There were numerous follow-up visits, including a trip to the Crippled Children's Hospital in Oklahoma City, which was located about 200 miles southwest of Commerce. Mantle spent more than five weeks under the direct care of physicians and nurses over a 13-month period. It served as foreshadowing for the troubles that lay ahead.

Opportunity Beckons

In 1947, Mantle was invited to play for a Junior League team known as The Whiz Kids. He was so small in stature, owner/manager Barney Barnett had trouble finding him a uniform. Though Mantle put up mediocre numbers in a handful of scattered appearances, Barnett saw great potential. In the offseason, he set Mickey up with a cemetery job. After many hours spent digging graves and hauling gravestones, the budding slugger added some bulk to his frame.

In the summer of 1948, Barnett spoke to scout Tom Greenwade about a number of prospects. Mantle was included in the discussion. A top minorleague pitcher before his arm went dead, Greenwade spent two decades evaluating talent for the Browns, Dodgers, and Yankees. In addition to Mantle, he was responsible for the discovery of Elston Howard and Bobby Murcer. He was also instrumental in the signing of Jackie Robinson.

Greenwade first saw Mantle play in Alba, Missouri. At that time, the future Yankee icon was being groomed as a shortstop. Greenwade wasn't blown away by the youngster's performance, but he took note of some qualities that might warrant future consideration. In some retellings of the story, Greenwade convinced Mantle's high school principal to leak a false rumor that his bout with osteomyelitis had left him with permanently damaged legs. This allegedly prompted scouts from the Indians and Cardinals to pursue other prospects.

In the spring of 1949, a Ban Johnson League umpire named Kenny Magness mentioned Mantle in an informal conversation with Greenwade. The veteran talent hawk decided to give the kid another look. By then, Mickey was hitting the ball with power and demonstrating remarkable speed. Existing rules prevented scouts from speaking with underage prospects, so Greenwade inquired about Mantle's high school status before approaching him. As it turned out, Mickey was scheduled to graduate that afternoon but the ceremony had been postponed until the evening, when he was slated to play in Coffeyville, Kansas. According to various accounts, Greenwade (accompanied by Commerce football coach Johnny Lingo) talked the superintendent of schools into giving Mantle his diploma while excusing him from commencement activities.

Mickey went 3-for-4 at Coffeyville with a pair of home runs—one from each side of the plate. Greenwade claimed he didn't know Mantle could switch hit until then. Sufficiently impressed, he entered into tentative negotiations with the slugger's father. In an attempt to keep the signing price down, he told Mutt that he still needed to take a look at another prospect before arriving at a decision.

The next game was in Baxter Springs. The evening was wet and dreary, but Mantle played exceptionally well, prompting Greenwade to make an official bid. His initial proposal was less than what Mickey could have made playing semipro ball while working in the Commerce mines. Greenwade justified the offer by pointing out Mantle's deficient skills at shortstop and below-average physical stature. The Yankees typically drove a hard bargain in those days, knowing full well that they were the team of choice among a majority of young players. After a bit of haggling, Mutt convinced Greenwade to add a modest signing bonus with a monthly salary of $140. It took less than a half-hour to close the deal. At the age of 17, Mickey was officially on his way to a career in professional baseball.

There is another small piece of the story that has rarely been included in accounts of Mantle's early career. According to Yankee farm director Lee MacPhail, the budding star was invited to a Yankee tryout camp in Branson, Missouri, prior to his high school graduation. He failed to impress the scouts on hand. "I know Tom was a little disappointed in his showing there," MacPhail said, "but you could see all the tools that he had. Tom was a very good judge of talent, so it was only understandable that he hoped Mickey would do better." Interestingly, Mantle's father brought him to another camp being held by the St. Louis Browns during his senior year of high school. Fate intervened when a drenching downpour resulted in the cancellation of scheduled activities.

AN AUSPICIOUS DEBUT

After coming to terms with Mantle, the Yankees assigned him to Independence, Kansas, where their Class D affiliate was located. While he was excited to be joining the most successful franchise in the majors, he was nervous about leaving home. He knew he would miss his family and friends. He also worried about not having his father around to provide input and instruction.

Mantle found his new manager, Harry Craft, to be cold and detached at first meeting. But as the season wore on, he grew accustomed to Craft's hands-off style. A center fielder during his playing days, Craft helped the Cincinnati Reds to consecutive World Series appearances in 1939 and 1940. Although he was an exceptional fielder, his mediocre hitting eventually drove him out of the majors at the age of 27. He finished his career in the Yankees' farm system, becoming a manager in 1949—the year of Mantle's pro debut.

The new surroundings were a lot to take in, and Mantle almost wilted under the pressure. "I suppose small town kids who go away for the first time still get homesick," he told a biographer in later years. "But I have never met anyone who was home-sicker than I was my first few days in Independence.... For a time, I seriously thought I would give up the whole deal and go back to playing ball in Commerce." He didn't, of course, and the Yankees were better off because of it.

The Independence squad was composed mostly of teenagers, and Mantle soon blended in. A high-spirited bunch, they kept Craft on his toes with their juvenile behavior. On long bus rides, they shot each other with squirt guns. During hotel stays in out-of-the way places such as Chanute, Kansas, and Ponca City, Oklahoma, they stirred up trouble by filling paper bags with water and dropping them from upstairs windows onto the heads of pedestrians. They also engaged in melon wars, cutting the fruit into small pieces and flinging it at one another. Craft tolerated the behavior to an extent, but was not above reprimanding players he felt had crossed the line.

During homestands, Mantle and his cohorts frequented a soda shop known as "Pop's Place," which was located in the busiest section of town. After enjoying a snack, they would stand outside on the street corner razzing each other and ogling passing women. Mantle struck up a friendship with future major leaguer Lou Skizas—the team's starting third baseman. One day, on a ride to Bartlesville, Oklahoma, Mickey began demonstrating how to grip a knuckleball. Skizas asked him to throw one while the two were playing catch during warmups. The ball had so much movement, Skizas was unable to get his glove on it. It hit him squarely in the face, breaking his nose and putting him out of action for a few days.

Mantle was not a good fit for the position of shortstop. Though he had quick reflexes and decent range, he struggled with pop flies and his throws to first base were often wild. By season's end, he had committed 47 errors in 89 appearances. There were times when he sulked on the bench, feeling embarrassed and dejected, but Craft had a way of keeping his spirits up.

The team played well behind Craft, finishing first with a 71-53 record. Mantle was a major contributor with 29 extra-base hits, 63 RBIs, and a .313 batting average. The squad breezed through both rounds of the playoffs, making quick work of the Iola Indians in the finals. Though it was a highly successful season for Mantle on the whole, he clearly wasn't ready for the majors.

MOVING UP THE LADDER

In the fall of 1949, Mantle took a job in the Commerce mines with his father, who had worked his way up to a supervisory position. To ensure his son's safety, Mutt assigned him to the electrician's shop, which was located aboveground. Mantle was settling nicely back into small-town life when he received a postcard ordering him to report to the Ottawa County draft board for a physical. Mickey and his dad dreaded the possibility of putting his promising baseball career on hold, but they needn't have worried. In the end, the injury that had nearly killed him spared him from military duty. In the wake of a full examination and X-ray of Mantle's right leg (which had been afflicted with osteomyelitis), he was given a 4-F classification.

The fall of 1949 was significant in another respect as Mantle ended up meeting his future bride. While attending a high school football game in Picher, one of Mickey's friends arranged a triple date with some of the local team's majorettes. Mantle was originally paired with a girl named Lavanda Whipkey, but when she declined a second date, he set his sights on her friend, Merlyn Johnson. In those days, Mantle wasn't a smooth operator. During an outing with Merlyn to a movie theater in Picher, he accidentally locked his keys in the car and left the engine running. He called his dad for help, but ultimately it was a local police officer who opened the car door with a wire hanger. In spite of the embarrassing mishap, Merlyn and Mickey continued to see each other regularly after that.

When the spring of 1950 arrived, Mantle attended a Yankee training camp located in the Ozark Mountains near Branson, Missouri. He spent his idle time with teammates hunting frogs and fishing for bass on Lake Taneycomo—a manmade reservoir located on the White River. He carried fond memories of the experience into his later years, remarking in his 1985 autobiography, "I'm not kidding—it was one of the most fun times I ever had. Not a single care in the world from the middle of March until mid-April."

After a strong showing in camp, Mantle was assigned to the Joplin Miners—a Class C team affiliated with the Western Association. A number of his Independence teammates also made the cut, including his good pal, Lou Skizas. Pleased with Harry Craft's performance in 1949, the Yankees offered him the managerial post in Joplin. It was the first in a long line of promotions that ultimately carried him back to the major leagues. Mantle was greatly pleased to be playing for Craft again.

The ballpark in Joplin was somewhat small and run-down. There was an orphanage situated beyond the right field fence, and Mantle recalled that the children would watch the games from the windows. Over the course of the season, he hammered a number of shots over the fence onto the adjacent property. One of his blasts shattered a window. According to Mantle, the children hung a bedsheet over the broken pane with a message that read, "Thanks For the Ball, Mickey!"

Mantle became very popular while playing for Joplin. A local restaurant began giving out free steaks every time the Miners hit a home run, and Mantle's team-leading 26 clouts fed quite a few fans for free. Not everyone was enamored with Mickey's talents, however. At a local house party one night, he was punched in the face immediately upon stepping through the door. The blow caught him completely off guard, allegedly breaking his nose. He never found out who assaulted him, figuring it must have been someone holding a jealous grudge.

The Miners went off on a tear in the early going, building a 20-game lead over their closest competitors. To keep things interesting, league officials switched to a split-season format, dividing the campaign into separate halves and scheduling a playoff series between the winners of each half. Mantle was chosen to participate in the Western Association All-Star Game, which took place in Muskogee, Oklahoma. It turned out to be an embarrassing experience as he committed four errors and was hit in the face with a throw from his third baseman.

Though the Miners compiled the best overall record in the Western Association at 90-46, they lost to the Springfield Cubs in the playoffs. Mantle's .383 average that year—the highest single-season total of his professional career—easily earned him a batting crown. As if that wasn't cause enough for celebration, the Yankees invited him to New York. On September 17, 1950, his picture appeared in the *Oklahoman* with a caption that read, "Mickey Mantle, 18 year-old Commerce product who burned up the Western Association with Joplin this season, may become one of the all-time greats of the New York Yankees."

A TASTE OF THE BIG APPLE

When Mantle arrived in the Bronx as a non-roster invitee, the Yankees were locked in a close pennant race with the Tigers and Red Sox. They finished strong, winning 8 of their last 11 games and wrapping up the pennant by the end of September. There was very little in the way of celebration since the club was so accustomed to winning.

Having been recruited as a shortstop, Mantle paid close attention to Phil Rizzuto, who was putting the finishing touches on an MVP season.

After observing his graceful fielding and exceptional range firsthand, Mickey decided that he could never be a suitable replacement. Rizzuto later admitted to feeling somewhat threatened when Mantle first appeared, but he kept up a good front. Asked by a reporter what he thought of the new Yankee prospect, he said with a wink, "A little big for a shortstop, don't you think?"

Casey Stengel was very accommodating to Mantle, singing his praises to the New York press. Stengel had begun his career in the Dead Ball Era and developed a reputation as an eccentric. In an oft-told tale, he allegedly hid in an outfield drainage hole one day and popped out just in time to catch a flyball. Before managing the Yankees, he played for both of the other New York teams. He was a World Series star for the Giants and Robins, compiling a .393 postseason batting average.

Stengel's big-league managerial career began in Brooklyn during the mid-1930s. When the team failed to contend, he was dismissed. During a six-year stint with the woeful Boston Braves (officially known as "The Bees" from 1938 through 1940), he used humor to deflect tough questions about the club's abominable performances. His comical quotes made him popular with sportswriters. He was less popular with players, many of whom came to resent his endless shuffling of players in and out of the lineup.

By the time he took over the Yankees in 1949, Stengel had just one winning season to his credit—a fact that greatly concerned members of the Gotham press corps. Justifying his presence in New York, he told them, "I didn't get the job through friendship. The Yankees represent an investment of millions of dollars. They don't hand out jobs like this because they like your company. I know I can make people laugh and some of you think I'm a damn fool, [but] I got the job because the people here think I can produce for them."

He did produce . . . big time.

In 12 years at the Yankee helm, Stengel guided the club to a record 10 pennants and seven World Series titles, distinguishing himself as an outstanding judge of talent along the way. Recognizing Mantle's vast potential, he took the shy, star-struck teenager under his wing. But he wasn't the nurturing type. Describing Stengel's managerial style, outfielder Gene Woodling commented, "There were a lot of field managers as good as Casey, but Casey was better than other managers at understanding his players' attitudes. He figured out how to stir us up so that we were so angry—and I wanted to kill him sometimes—that we'd go out and beat the other team's fanny. . . . All that fun stuff was for the press and fans, but he was a tough man to play for. You didn't horse around with him. He was all business. Which isn't to say he wasn't compassionate. You could go to him with problems." Mantle later claimed that Stengel was like a father to him, but their relationship was complicated. Though Mickey could have used a little more nurturing, Stengel frequently chose the tough-love approach. During one of the slugger's periodic dugout tantrums, Casey handed him a bat and invited him to smash himself over the head with it.

Mantle's early days in New York were very lonely. He missed his father and his Joplin teammates. He needed someone he could relate to. That someone arrived in the form of Bill Skowron.

After a doubleheader against the Browns at Sportsman's Park on September 17, the Yankees traveled to Chicago to play the White Sox. Skowron, a 19-year-old college kid who carried the nickname of "Moose," had been invited to Comiskey Park for a tryout. During batting practice, he impressed Stengel by depositing a couple of pitches into the upper deck. This prompted an invitation to stick around as a non-roster player for the remainder of the season.

Over the next couple of weeks, Mickey and Moose became fast friends, sharing a room together at the Concourse Plaza Hotel. They established a daily routine, taking batting and fielding practice before games. After the regular players hit the showers, they attended evening workouts supervised by Yankees coaches. In their spare time, they binged on pizza, went to movies, and got lost on the subway.

Though he formed a strong bond with Skowron, Mantle got off on the wrong foot with the club's preeminent star. As the story goes, he was playing Pepper with a few of the younger players during practice when one of his hits struck Joe DiMaggio squarely in the shin. This prompted an icy glare from the "Yankee Clipper." Mantle admitted to being highly intimidated by DiMaggio. "With [Joe], I couldn't even mumble hello," he said. "He had this aura. It was as if you needed an appointment just to approach him. Then it was a question of getting enough courage to speak."

After the Yankees swept the Phillies in the World Series, Mantle was invited to an instructional camp in Phoenix along with the team's other top prospects. Though Mantle earned an official roster spot in 1951, Skowron spent the next three seasons in the minors. In his absence, Hank Bauer—a former US Marine with a commanding presence—befriended Mickey, helping him through what would prove to be a very rocky year.

SPRING PHENOM

Mantle spent the winter of 1950-51 working in the Commerce mines. He provided conflicting accounts of what tasks he was assigned to. In his 1985 autobiography, he claimed to have worked underground on a pump crew. But an earlier recollection placed him aboveground as a jack of all trades.

Life in the mines was dangerous and stressful. Workers developed a twisted sense of humor. Mantle recalled a bizarre ritual in which crew members would hit each other with a wooden paddle. Those who endured five or six solid whacks without crying out in pain were entitled to use the paddle against their aggressors. The risk of cave-ins was a looming hazard. When the sound of loose rocks or gravel was detected, alarms were activated and crews would scramble to evacuate. The men gradually became desensitized, resorting to tactless practical jokes such as throwing stones at the helmets of coworkers when their backs were turned. This resulted in a lot of false alarms.

Over the course of the winter, Mutt Mantle's failing health became increasingly evident. He began to steadily lose weight. He also suffered from chronic fatigue and soreness. But a life of hard labor had taught him to carry on in spite of his afflictions.

Mickey and Merlyn developed an exclusive relationship. Charmed by her wholesome small-town values, Mutt began pressuring his son to make a serious commitment. He worried that a bachelor's lifestyle would negatively impact Mickey's baseball career. Whether it was out of true love or a sense of allegiance to his father (or likely a combination of both), Mickey purchased a ring with money borrowed from his half brother, Ted. He gave it to Merlyn shortly before Christmas.

Mantle's invitation to spring training arrived in February. Since there was no money or train ticket included, he assumed he would have to cover the cost himself. Short on funds, he continued to work in the mines. His failure to report prompted a second summons to camp. Concerned that he might be holding out, the Yankees eventually wired him the money.

It was a long drive to the train station, and both of Mickey's parents made the trip. Though he had gotten a taste of major-league life a few months earlier, he found himself overwhelmed by sadness, fear, and anxiety. "I kept swallowing hard and drinking more water than I ever needed before," he recalled. He was still choking back tears an hour into the trip.

When Mantle arrived in Phoenix, he discovered that the Yankees had an army of rookies on hand, among them Skowron, Gil McDougald, and Bob Cerv. Casey Stengel was still in the process of asserting control over the club and sometimes held team meetings that lasted for more than an hour. Many players walked away confused and/or resentful—especially the established stars who didn't feel that they needed to be told what to do.

At the end of the 1950 campaign, Joplin manager Harry Craft had drafted a scouting report recommending that Mantle be switched from shortstop to third base or the outfield. Stengel was inclined to agree, but since the club already had a regular third baseman and a wealth of capable outfielders, it was a question of where to put him. Mickey's incredible skills convinced Stengel that he needed to be somewhere in the lineup. He was clocked running the bases at 13 seconds—a figure so astonishing that Casey repeated the trial several times believing that his watch was broken. Mantle's exceptional speed earned him the nickname, "The Commerce Comet."

In a story Mantle retold on multiple occasions, he made his first exhibition appearance in center field. Indians infielder Ray Boone hit a line drive straight toward him. He raced in a couple of steps and flipped his sunglasses down. The sudden change from bright light to shade left him disoriented and the ball hit him squarely in the forehead, breaking his glasses. After trotting in to get another pair from the batboy, he realized that all of his teammates were laughing at him.

There were better moments ahead. During a game against the USC college team, Mantle hit a pair of tape-measure homers. One of them sailed over the left field wall and landed on the roof of a distant house. The other was originally believed to have traveled in excess of 600 feet. After the game, Mantle was mobbed by a throng of enthusiastic college students seeking autographs.

As Mickey's popularity grew, an unexpected problem arose. Hailed as the second coming of Babe Ruth, a number of writers began to question why he had been exempted from military duty. It created enough of a stir that the Yankees asked the Oklahoma draft board to perform another physical examination.

The exam took place in Tulsa. After an exhibition swing through Texas and Kansas City, Mickey met up with his dad. He noticed that Mutt looked alarmingly pale and thin, but when he inquired about it, he received a dismissive response—something to the effect of "don't worry about it, I feel fine." Together, they made the long drive to the military induction center in Tulsa. The results were the same. Even in a dormant state, osteomyelitis was considered a chronic condition that was sufficient grounds for deferment.

Mantle remained unsure of his status with the Yankees late into the spring. He would have been satisfied to play for the club's Texas League affiliate in Beaumont, where Harry Craft had been reassigned, but on the other hand, he didn't want to disappoint his father. One day, Mickey's friend Nick Ferguson called him on the phone pretending to be Beaumont's GM and instructed him to report immediately. Mantle fell for the ruse, politely conceding. He was greatly relieved when Ferguson told him it was just a prank. Shortly afterward, he learned that he had earned a spot on the Yankees' Opening Day roster.

GROWING PAINS

The 1951 regular season began with a series of rainouts at Washington. When the team returned to New York, outfielder Hank Bauer noticed that Mantle was not adhering to the standard Yankees dress code, which included a dress shirt and tie. Realizing that he probably couldn't afford a new set of clothes, Bauer took Mickey to an upscale men's apparel store and bought him a pair of suits. He proved to be quite helpful to the rookie slugger on a number of other occasions that year.

Sportswriter Jim Murray once quipped that Bauer "had a face like a clenched fist." A hard-nosed, no-nonsense kind of guy, he had fought in the Pacific Theater during World War II and earned a number of medals for valor. During his 12 years with the Yankees, he emerged as a team leader and clutch performer, capturing seven World Series rings.

With all the media hype surrounding him, the pressure on Mantle to perform was intense. Though Joe DiMaggio's skills were obviously in decline, he was still adored by New York fans. Mantle was viewed by many as an interloper out to steal "Joltin' Joe's" thunder. Subjected to boos and catcalls whenever he failed to deliver in the clutch, Mickey began to doubt himself and throw tantrums in the dugout. Bauer offered reassurance and support, helping him avoid the pitfalls of life on the brightly lit New York stage.

Mantle made his regular-season debut against the Red Sox at Yankee Stadium in front of 44,000 fans. It was the largest crowd he had ever seen. In an amusing story that may or may not be embellished, Yogi Berra met him on the dugout steps and asked him if he was nervous. When Mickey answered "no," Berra teased him by asking why he was wearing his jockstrap on the outside of his uniform. "I took off for right field like my ass had caught fire and didn't stop grinning until they finished playing the National Anthem,"

Mantle said. Batting third in front of DiMaggio, he matched the Yankee Clipper's performance that day with a single and RBI in four at-bats.

At the end of his first week, Mantle's batting average stood at .320. But that was as high as it would get all year. He played fairly well in May and then fell into a bit of a funk. He was pressing too hard and swinging at pitches outside the strike zone. As the New York crowds got on his case, he began to dread coming to Yankee Stadium, where disgruntled fans were sometimes waiting at the players' entrance to harass him.

In a doubleheader against the White Sox on June 19, Mantle went 4-for-8 with a pair of homers. The outstanding performance was followed by another slump. Though he wasn't totally ineffective, gathering 45 RBIs in the first half, he clearly wasn't living up to expectations. And he had lost his confidence to boot.

On July 15, Mantle received some very discouraging news. While Yankee players were taking the field for warmups at Detroit, Casey Stengel asked the clubhouse attendant to bring Mickey back in. The Yankee skipper had tears in his eyes when he told Mantle that he was being sent to the minors for more conditioning. "All we want you to do is just go down to Kansas City and get a couple of home runs, a couple of hits," Stengel said. "And the first thing you know, you'll get your confidence back, and we'll bring you right back up." Mantle appreciated the fact that Casey had waited until the clubhouse was empty before speaking with him.

In Mantle's first game with the Kansas City Blues, he beat out a bunt for a base hit. Upon returning to the dugout, manager George Selkirk scolded him, pointing out that the only reason he was there was to find his power swing. It was a slow process, and Mantle nearly quit the game altogether. At one point, he called his father complaining that he didn't think he could cut it as a ballplayer. Mutt made the 160-mile trip from Commerce to Kansas City. Though Mickey expected a pep talk of sorts, he got something entirely different.

Upon entering Mickey's hotel room, Mutt began irritably throwing his belongings into a suitcase. When Mickey asked what he was doing, Mutt told him that he was taking him back home to Commerce. "I thought I raised a man," he snarled. "You're nothing but a coward, a quitter. You might as well be a miner like me, so just get your stuff and let's get ready to go." The hard-line strategy worked as Mickey agreed to tough it out.

Mantle hit .361 in 40 games for Kansas City with 11 homers and 50 runs batted in. Before returning to New York in late August, he was called by the draft board to Fort Sill, Oklahoma, for another physical. To no one's surprise, he was deemed unfit for military duty yet again. He resumed his major-league career on August 24 against the Indians, collecting a hit and a walk in five plate appearances. The following day, he smashed a two-run homer off of 20-game winner Mike Garcia. He finished the season strong, hitting close to .300 in his last 20 games. Proving he had what it took to overcome adversity, he remained a regular in the Yankee lineup for the next 17 years.

OCTOBER DISASTER

Though the 1950s are often viewed as a "golden era," it was actually a troubled time for many. In June of 1950, the North Korean People's Army staged the first military offensive of the Cold War by invading their neighbors to the south. Within a week, the United States had entered the conflict on South Korea's behalf. That same year, Wisconsin senator Joseph McCarthy claimed that dozens of communists had infiltrated the US State Department. An ongoing series of accusations and investigations followed, bringing the country to the brink of panic.

The 1951 baseball season was played in a climate of fear and paranoia as Chinese and North Korean forces captured the South Korean capital of Seoul. In response to the perceived threat of communism, the United States began testing weapons in the Nevada desert. A one-kiloton bomb known as "Able" was the first air-dropped nuclear device to be detonated on American soil. Hundreds of subsequent tests were conducted over the course of the decade.

Baseball underwent a significant organizational change in 1951 with the appointment of Ford Frick as commissioner. A former sportswriter for the *New York American*, Frick had served as public relations director of the NL before ascending to the league presidency in 1934. During his 30-plus years as a major-league executive, he played a vital role in the establishment of the National Baseball Hall of Fame and the integration of the sport.

The 1951 regular season produced a number of memorable moments as St. Louis Browns owner Bill Veeck staged a wild publicity stunt, sending a 3-foot-7 circus performer named Eddie Gaedel to the plate against Tiger hurler Bob Cain. Instructed not to swing at anything, Gaedel walked on four pitches. The pennant races were tight with the Giants battling the Dodgers to a first-place tie. A rare three-game playoff was scheduled to crown the champions of the National League. It ended with Bobby Thomson's memorable walkoff homer in the third meeting. Years later, the Giants were accused of conducting a sign-stealing operation in the second half of the season. Thomson didn't deny that signs had been stolen, but insisted he had received no advance notice of pitcher Ralph Branca's offerings during his iconic at-bat.

The AL pennant race was a shootout between the Yankees, Red Sox, and Indians. The Yankees set the pace in September while their rivals crumbled down the stretch. Boston and Cleveland combined for a 4-16 record in their last 10 games, allowing the Yankees to capture a third consecutive American League title.

With Stengel's platoon system in effect, Yogi Berra and Phil Rizzuto were the only players to appear in more than 140 games for the Yankees. Berra had a fine season, claiming the first of three MVP awards. Meanwhile, an aging Joe DiMaggio was hampered by injuries, slumping to .263 at the plate—the lowest mark of his storied career. In the pitching department, Eddie Lopat and Vic Raschi both gathered 21 victories while Allie Reynolds stole the spotlight with a pair of no-hitters. The second one was a pennant-clinching effort against the Red Sox.

After his tune-up in Kansas City, Mantle more closely resembled the highly touted prospect he had been made out to be. Satisfied with his progress, Stengel elevated him to first-string status in the postseason. The Giants' early-October heroics drained a bit of energy from the city's ninth "Subway Series" (six of which had been won by the Yankees to that point). Prior to Game 1, Red Smith of the *New York Herald Tribune* wrote, "After that final playoff game in the Polo Grounds, this sport can hold no more surprises, offer no excitement or entertainment that wouldn't seem pale by comparison."

Over 65,000 fans attended the series opener at Yankee Stadium. Most of the highlights were provided by the Giants as Reynolds faltered on the mound, allowing eight hits and five runs in six innings. Mantle hit in the leadoff spot, drawing two walks off of starter Dave Koslo. He never made it as far as second base. The Yankees' only run came on a second-inning double by AL Rookie of the Year Gil McDougald. He was driven home on a single by infielder Jerry Coleman. There were no other tangible Yankee threats in the 5–1 loss.

In Game 2, Mantle recorded his first career postseason hit with a bunt single. He came around to score on successive hits by Rizzuto and McDougald. The Yankees were leading, 2–0, when disaster struck. Willie Mays, playing in his rookie season, led off the fifth inning with a popup to short right-center field. DiMaggio, slowed by a bad heel, was not nearly as mobile as he had been in earlier years. Acutely aware of that fact, Mantle sprinted into DiMaggio's territory. When he got there, he was surprised to find Joe D. already camped out under the ball. Forced to make an abrupt stop, Mantle's spikes caught the rubber cover of an irrigation outlet. There was a loud snap as the ligaments in his knee tore loose. He crumpled to the ground in agony. DiMaggio told him not to move and assured him that a stretcher was on the way. It was one of few conversations that took place between the two men that season.

Forced to sit out the rest of the series, Mantle underwent surgery on the day of Game 3. While climbing out of a cab in front of Lenox Hill Hospital in Manhattan, he leaned heavily on his father, who promptly collapsed to the pavement. The two were admitted to the same hospital room. Though Mickey's procedure was a success, Mutt was in bad shape. A battery of tests revealed that he was dying of Hodgkin's disease—a cancer of the lymphatic system. The news, though disheartening, came as no surprise to Mickey, who had lost his grandfather and an uncle to cancer.

Summarizing his October experiences, Mantle once remarked, "All of my early memories about the World Series are woven around my family and glad times laced by pain and sadness. That became a kind of pattern of mine and I never questioned my luck, good or bad. I was just a mouse in a maze. I'd get the cheese and then the electric shock."

Mantle's 1951 surgery was the first of several that would be required to preserve his career. In his absence, the Yankees won the World Series in six games. Rizzuto hit .320 with five runs scored. McDougald drove in a team-high seven runs. And DiMaggio blasted the final home run of his extensive postseason career. Though the Yankees offered Joltin' Joe a handsome salary to play one more season, he officially announced his retirement in December. It left an opening in center field that Mantle would capably fill for more than a decade.

Good Times, Bad Times

Mutt Mantle's diagnosis shook Mickey to the core. In his book *The Last Hero: The Life of Mickey Mantle*, author David Falkner writes, "The news was devastating to Mantle. He was not yet twenty years-old, and his father was the emotional pillar of his life and career. He could not accept that Mutt would die. He hung on to his father as never before, as though Mutt still had much more to give."

To make his father as comfortable as possible, Mickey bought the family a seven-room house using his World Series bonus as a down payment.

Honoring Mutt's wishes, he made plans to marry Merlyn on the day before Christmas. The ceremony took place at the Johnson family home, which was decorated with flowers and candles for the occasion. Merlyn later remarked that Mutt was the happiest person in the room aside from herself.

Following a brief vacation with friends in Hot Springs, Mickey and Merlyn drove Mutt to the Mayo Clinic in Rochester, Minnesota, for exploratory surgery. It was a 500-mile trip on wintry roads. Doctors confirmed that Mutt's condition was incurable and advised the newlyweds to take him home so that he could die peacefully.

By the time February arrived, Mantle's knee had healed sufficiently to participate in spring training. After he left for St. Petersburg with Merlyn, Mutt decided to seek treatment at the Spears Chiropractic Hospital, a disreputable Denver facility run by a doctor who had been referred to as a "quack" in *Collier's* magazine. Mutt never returned to Commerce alive.

With Mantle still hobbling a bit, Stengel platooned him with Jackie Jensen in center field during the spring. The regular season began with Jensen in center and Mantle in right. When Jensen got off to a 2-for-19 start at the plate, he was traded to Washington in a deal involving five other players. Bob Cerv took over briefly until Mantle grew strong enough to claim the center field job for himself. Though the Yankees got off to a slow start in April, Mickey hit .317 during the month with six extra-base hits and seven RBIs.

On May 6, Stengel called Mantle at his New York apartment with dreadful news. His father had passed away in Denver. Describing the thoughts that went through his head, the slugger wrote in his memoirs, "What had happened to him in the thirty-nine years of his life, with all the scrambling and disappointments and frustrations? Where did it get him? He needed me and I wasn't there. I couldn't make it up to him." (NOTE: Mantle was mistaken about his father's age. He actually lived slightly beyond the age of 40.)

Merlyn offered comfort and support, but Mickey resisted her efforts. In the first of many episodes that left her hurt and bewildered, she was instructed to stay in New York while Mickey attended the services. "I never did know why I wasn't invited to the funeral unless he just wanted to be with his family," she told biographer Jane Leavy.

Although the Mantles weren't religious, the funeral was held at the First Christian Church in Commerce. Mutt was laid to rest beside his father and brother in a miners' cemetery on Route 66 outside of town. After the other mourners left the graveside, Mickey hung around by himself for a while, wondering where he would end up without Mutt's guidance and cursing himself for never telling his father that he loved him. In later years, he remarked that such a display of affection between the two men would have been unthinkable.

Despair might have gotten the best of Mantle had he not developed a close friendship with Billy Martin—New York's fiery second baseman. Martin had come from a broken home in a poor section of Berkeley, California. He developed a passionate interest in sports during his teen years, joining the Oakland Junior Oaks baseball club while boxing on the side at the amateur level. His boldness and determination helped earn him a spot on the Oaks senior squad—a Triple-A Pacific Coast League affiliate managed by Casey Stengel.

Casey took a shine to Martin, personally grooming him for the majors. Under "The Old Professor's" tutelage, Martin became a competent infielder. In October of 1949, his contract was sold to the Yankees. Stengel called him to New York the following year. Known for his competitive spirit and mercurial temper, Martin developed a reputation for delivering in the clutch. Cleveland GM Frank Lane once said, "[Billy's] the kind of guy you'd like to kill if he's playing for the other team, but you'd like 10 of him on your side."

Mantle and Martin roomed together during the 1952 campaign, becoming virtually inseparable. Their wives developed an amicable bond as well. When the Yankees were in New York, the two couples walked around the city, attended movies, and enjoyed many dinners together. During road trips, Mantle and Martin partied like frat boys. A number of photos exist of the two clowning around together in various settings.

Sufficiently distracted from the loss of his father, Mantle enjoyed a fine offensive campaign, leading the team in doubles with 37. He finished second in homers and RBIs. If there was room for improvement, it was in his patience at the plate. He tied for the American League lead in strikeouts. Even so, his efforts kept the team in contention throughout the summer.

WORLD SERIES HERO

The year 1952 brought sweeping changes for America and the rest of the world. In February, King George VI of England died in his sleep, leaving the throne to his daughter, Elizabeth. A few months later, King Farouk of Egypt was ousted in a military coup. On the US front, Republican candidate Dwight D. Eisenhower won the presidential election, ending a string of Democratic victories dating back to the early 1930s. Though the balance of power was shifting elsewhere, it was business as usual in New York as the Yankees captured their fourth consecutive pennant.

Complementing a breakout season by Mantle, Yogi Berra powered the Yankee offense for the fourth straight year with 30 homers and 98 RBIs. Allie Reynolds and Vic Raschi were the most reliable members of the pitching staff, combining for 36 wins while junkballer Eddie Lopat missed close to a dozen starts due to shoulder issues. Former Braves ace Johnny Sain (acquired in a late-August trade the previous year) picked up some of the slack, posting an 11-6 record.

In the National League, the Dodgers avenged their 1951 playoff collapse by finishing 4 1/2 games ahead of the second-place Giants. The 1952 World Series was the fourth installment of the storied Yankee-Dodger rivalry. This time around, the Brooklyn lineup was stacked with superstars from top to bottom. Powered by four eventual Hall of Famers (Jackie Robinson, Pee Wee Reese, Roy Campanella, and Duke Snider), the Dodgers led the league in runs per game while compiling the third-highest collective batting average. Energizing the pitching corps, Rookie of the Year Joe Black paced the staff with 15 wins and 15 saves.

The Dodgers had come away empty-handed in each of their previous October showdowns against the Yankees, generating a lot of resentment among fans in Flatbush. Before the start of Game 1, Mantle recalled riding the team bus to Ebbets Field. Yankee supporters were lined up all along Second Avenue, holding signs and cheering loudly. When the bus turned onto Flatbush Avenue in Brooklyn, hostile Dodger fans treated the visitors to streams of verbal abuse. "You didn't know whether to feel sorry for the Dodgers or to view them as you would a dangerous, wounded animal," Mantle commented.

A local beat-writer polled players on the eve of the series opener to get their predictions. Brooklyn pitcher Billy Loes said that the Yankees would win in seven games. When manager Chuck Dressen called him out for making the remark, Loes explained that he had been misquoted. He had actually picked the Yankees to win in six. *New York Herald Tribune* reporter Red Smith agreed with Loes's assessment. "The simplest argument to support a belief that the Yankees will win is to point out that they always do," he wrote. "Since the beginning of time, no Brooklyn team has won a world championship. . . . It does not of course follow that what has happened in the past must on necessity continue to happen. Yet one suspects that the knowledge of what has always happened must have some effect upon the players and the games."

The series was a seesaw affair with both teams picking up a pair of wins in the first four meetings. Hitting out of the third slot in the Yankee order, Mantle went 3-for-5 in Game 2. He scored the Yankees' first run of the afternoon on a fourth-inning sacrifice fly by Berra. In the eighth inning of Game 4, he tripled off of reliever Johnny Rutherford and came home when the throw to third got away. Pee Wee Reese was charged with an error on the play as the Yankees went on to win, 2–0.

Fans in Brooklyn got a glimpse of Mantle's prodigious power during Game 6. The Yankee slugger reached base in three of his five plate appearances that afternoon. The Dodgers led, 1–0, entering the top of the seventh before a Berra homer and RBI-single by Vic Raschi put the Yanks ahead. Batting left-handed against Loes, Mantle led off the eighth inning with a deep drive into the left-center field bleachers—the first homer of his postseason career. It held up as the game-winning hit in a 3–2 nail-biter.

Game 7 was another tightly contested match. Making his third start in the span of a week, Joe Black was running out of gas. After cruising through the first three innings, he gave up a run in the fourth and another in the fifth. The score was tied at 2 in the top of the sixth when Mantle launched a 3–1 pitch over the scoreboard in right field. It traveled an estimated 450 feet, landing on Bedford Avenue. For the second straight day, the budding Yankees star had delivered the game-winner. "I knew I had been a factor in this one," he said years later. "I was still 13 days shy of my 21st birthday and my heart was almost orbiting the earth."

In spite of Mantle's heroics, Game 7 is best remembered for a heads-up defensive play made by Billy Martin. The Dodgers threatened in the bottom of the seventh, loading the bases with one out. Reliever Bob Kuzava retired the dangerous Duke Snider on a weak popup to third base. With two outs and the runners in motion, Jackie Robinson hit a wind-blown fly to the first base side of the infield. Kuzava and Joe Collins both lost the ball in the sun. Describing what happened next, biographer Glenn Stout wrote, "[Martin] looked at Collins, saw the puzzled first baseman frozen, and took off on a mad sprint, charging toward the ball, desperate, gaining speed with each step, his hat falling off and his arms outstretched as the ball fell from the sky. Then, with a final lunging step, he grabbed the ball at his shins." Had Martin failed to make the play, at least two runs—possibly three—would have scored.

Though the World Series MVP award would not be handed out until 1955, Mantle—with his series-high five runs and 10 hits—would have been a prime candidate. On October 17, he was honored with a parade in

Commerce, which featured marching bands from all over Ottawa County. Mickey rode in the backseat of a convertible with Merlyn, waving to the appreciative crowds. It had been a magical season. He only wished that his father could have been around to witness it.

BALKY KNEES AND MOON SHOTS

In the offseason, Mantle arranged to have a house built in Commerce across town from his mother. Merlyn was pregnant with their first child, and Mickey wanted to stay connected to family. Things weren't going quite as well for Billy Martin, who had celebrated the birth of his daughter, Kelly Ann. His wife, Lois, was asking for a divorce, and he called Mantle to tell him he would be spending the winter in Kansas City. The two good friends didn't see each other again until spring training.

Though Mantle's right knee had been surgically repaired in 1951, it remained unstable. He developed early-arthritis in the joint, and his knee-cap frequently filled with fluid. He made valiant attempts to play through the pain, but was forced to sit out regularly. Teammates observed that he often returned to the dugout after plate appearances with tears in his eyes. And Merlyn said that he would lie on the couch after ballgames groaning plaintively for hours at a time. As the knee began to deteriorate even further over the years, trainers were forced to swaddle him in foam bandages from ankle to thigh. They wrapped him so tightly that it cut off the circulation and mummified the skin underneath. Opponents noted that he sometimes appeared at the plate with blood soaking through his uniform. Yankee short-stop Tony Kubek recalled, "I used to say to him, 'For God's sake, don't play. Let that thing heal.' But he'd say, 'Tony, maybe there's a guy out there with his kid and it might be the only ticket he can afford all season, and he brought his kid here to see me. So I better be out there.'"

Mantle roomed with outfielder Irv Noren at the Edison Hotel during spring training in 1953. Noren, who also suffered from knee issues, remembered the two of them having difficulty even getting out of bed in the morning. After struggling to their feet, they would limp around the room trying to work out the stiffness. Noren appeared to be on his way to a promising career with the Yankees before his ailing legs began to seriously hamper his abilities. He played for four different teams in his last five seasons.

The Yankees' pitching staff was strengthened considerably in 1953 by the return of Whitey Ford, who had spent the previous two seasons in the Army. A native of New York City, the handsome, articulate southpaw fit in well with the other late-night carousers in residence. During a team meeting one day, Stengel cast an accusatory glare in the direction of Mantle, Ford, and Martin. "Some of you are getting whiskey slick," he said grouchily. From that point on, Mickey and Whitey referred to each other as "Slick." Members of the press dubbed the Yankee trio "The Dead End Kids."

Despite his fondness of the nightlife, Ford became one of the greatest pitchers in Yankee history, setting a franchise record with 236 wins. He added 10 more in the World Series—an all-time record. The handle of "Slick" fit him exceptionally well given his coolness under pressure. "I don't care what the situation was [or] how high the stakes were," said Mantle. "The bases could be loaded and the pennant riding on every pitch, it never bothered Whitey. He pitched his game. Cool, crafty, nerves of steel." In spite of their vastly different backgrounds, Mantle and Ford maintained a lifelong friendship, sharing their experiences in a 1977 joint autobiography. Fittingly, they were inducted into the Hall of Fame together in 1974.

By the time the Yankees began their exhibition schedule in 1953, Merlyn was well into her third trimester. During a game against the Dodgers at Ebbets Field, Mickey was on his way to the plate when he heard the following announcement: "Now batting, Number 7. Mickey Mantle. Mickey doesn't know it yet, but he just became the father of an eight-pound, 12-ounce baby boy." They named the child Mickey Elvin, in honor of Mantle's father. Though the middle name was different, they added the title of "Jr." According to Merlyn, it was a full month before the Yankees gave her husband a leave of absence to meet his new son. "When you sign up to be a baseball wife, you forfeit your right to bitch about not having your husband at the hospital when you go into labor," she later wrote. "That's part of the game—a phrase every baseball wife needs to keep handy."

The season held more setbacks for Mantle. Around the All-Star break, he sprained his left knee and it became inflamed. He continued to play anyway, favoring the other knee, which had been operated on twice. While making a throw in the outfield, he tore ligaments in the "bad" knee. Against Stengel's better judgment, he returned for the stretch run wearing a heavy brace. He sat out a total of 24 games that year.

Even in a diminished capacity, Mantle began to build his own legend by crushing home runs of the Ruthian variety. One of his most celebrated shots came on April 17 at Griffith Stadium in Washington, which was known for its deep dimensions (so deep, in fact, that the Senators regularly finished near the bottom of the AL rankings in home runs). Mantle's victim was Chuck

Stobbs—a left-handed swingman with four effective pitches in his arsenal. The ball sailed over the back wall of the bleachers roughly 60 feet above the playing field and nicked the side of the scoreboard before landing in the backyard of a neighboring home a block away. Marveling at the distance, Senators manager Bucky Harris commented, "I just wouldn't have believed that a ball could be hit that hard. I've never seen anything like it."

Yankee publicity director Red Patterson allegedly traced the flight of Mantle's homer and paid a neighborhood kid $5 for the ball. His unscientific measurements placed the blast at 565 feet—one of the longest bombs in major-league history. It wasn't Mantle's only colossal drive of the season. A week earlier, he had hit a monstrous homer over the 100-foot-high grandstand at Forbes Field during an exhibition game. He was told afterward that Babe Ruth and Ted Williams were the only other players to have accomplished the feat.

Mantle had awesome power from both sides of the plate. Though only 164 of his 536 career homers came from the right side of the plate, some of his longest shots came as a right-hander. (Courtesy of The National Baseball Hall of Fame)

Having missed close to a month of action, Mantle's regular-season totals were only slightly above average. Though he was chosen for the All-Star team, he failed to lead the American League in any major statistical category. Still, his 105 runs scored and 92 RBIs were personal-high marks (to that point). His season ended on a low note as he managed just four hits in his last 19 at-bats. But without a comparable replacement on the bench, he remained in the lineup throughout the postseason.

FIVE IN A ROW!

In 1953—a year of hope for many—the Korean War came to an end after three long years. Ruthless Soviet dictator Joseph Stalin died at the age of 74, ushering in a more temperate era of Russian leadership under Nikita Khrushchev. Great strides were taken in the world of medical research as American virologist Jonas Salk successfully tested a polio vaccine.

In the world of baseball, Brooklyn's "Boys of Summer" enjoyed one of the finest seasons in franchise history. Hall of Famer Roy Campanella set records for catchers with 41 homers and 142 runs batted in. He wasn't the only one tearing the cover off the ball as the Dodgers homered in 24 straight games—a feat previously unmatched by any major-league squad. Six Brooklyn players scored at least 100 runs, helping the club coast to its third pennant in a five-year span.

Meanwhile, in the Bronx, Whitey Ford finished his first full season with 18 wins—tops on the Yankees staff. The pennant race remained relatively close until late May, when the Bombers rattled off a string of 18 consecutive victories, falling one short of a record set by the 1906 White Sox. By mid-September, the New Yorkers had wrapped up their fifth consecutive pennant.

The postseason began on a controversial note. Celebrating the Yankee victory, Mantle, Martin, and Ford enjoyed a wild night of drinking in New York's Latin Quarter. When the bill arrived, they signed owner Dan Topping's name. All three of the so-called Dead End Kids were summoned to GM George Weiss's office in the morning. Ford was conspicuously absent, but Mantle and Martin reported as directed. Weiss and Topping reminded them that they had committed forgery—a serious crime punishable by incarceration. In the end, all three players were fined $500.

On the day of the opener at Yankee Stadium, Harry Truman and Dwight D. Eisenhower both went on record saying that they hoped the Yankees would lose. Commemorating the 50th anniversary of the Fall Classic, baseball icon Cy Young threw out the ceremonial first pitch. Even in his 80s, he might have fared better than Dodger starter Carl Erskine, who walked the bases full and gave up four runs before recording the final out of the first inning. The Yankees disappointed both US heads of state with a 9–5 Game 1 victory.

Mantle hit just .208 in the series, but put up impressive numbers in other departments. His seven RBIs were second to Billy Martin. And he was one of four players to collect multiple homers. The first one was a timely blast. Facing spitballer Preacher Roe in the eighth inning of Game 2, he launched a two-run shot into the left field bleachers. It held up as the deciding blow. In Game 5, he hit a grand slam off of Russ Meyer, giving the Yankees a commanding 6–1 lead. "The grand slam was a big moment in my life because baseball wasn't a game to me as the spectator understands it," he later said. "It was my job and my living and all I knew. Without it, I was going to be digging fence posts back in Commerce or carrying a pick down to the zinc mines."

Mantle's worst game of the Series came against Carl Erskine at Ebbets Field. After the debacle in the opener, Brooklyn manager Chuck Dressen sent his staff ace back to the mound in Game 3. Erskine turned in one of the finest performances in postseason history, setting a single-game record with 14 strikeouts (later broken by Sandy Koufax). Mantle whiffed four times that afternoon, as did first baseman Joe Collins. Limited to pinch-hitting duty, aging Hall of Famer Johnny Mize repeatedly barked at both players in the dugout, admonishing them for swinging at balls in the dirt. After Don Bollweg became Erskine's 13th victim in the top of the ninth, Casey Stengel summoned Mize to bat for Vic Raschi. Mize struck out on three pitches then skulked back to the dugout. Neither Mantle nor Collins dared speak a word to the veteran slugger, but Mickey later admitted that he felt vindicated.

Though Mantle and Mize maintained a cordial relationship, Mickey described the former Cardinals star as a curmudgeon and a penny-pincher. One day, after Whitey Ford had held up the team bus while finishing a game of pinball, Mize reprimanded the hurler for his tardiness. Unaffected, Ford settled into the seat next to Mize and said sarcastically, "What's on sale today, John?"

After tying the Series at two games apiece, the Dodgers fell apart, committing four errors and allowing 15 runs in the next two meetings. For the Yankees, it was their fifth consecutive championship—a record that has stood the test of time. Asked by reporters why the Dodgers had been beaten, team captain Pee Wee Reese remarked, "I wish I could think of something real brilliant, but I'm afraid I'm not up to it. . . . I think that we didn't play as good ball as we're capable of playing. In fact, we played lousy at times." Reliever Clem Labine offered credit where it was due. "Nobody can sell me on [the Yankees] being lucky," he said. "A team that wins as often as they do has to have something more than luck."

After the Series victory, the Yankee brass forgave Mantle, Martin, and Ford for the forgery incident and waived the fine.

COMING UP SHORT

Mantle was quite busy during the offseason in 1953-54. Shortly after the Yankees victory over the Dodgers, he flew to Cuba with Merlyn for a vacation. They lounged on the beach, sampled regional cuisine, and gambled in the casinos. Upon returning to Commerce, Mickey did some PR work for Harold Youngman, a highway construction mogul who lived in nearby Baxter Springs. For fun, the Yankee slugger coached an amateur basketball squad known as "Mickey Mantle's Southwest Chat All-Stars." The team, which included Mickey's twin brothers, Ray and Roy, played a pair of exhibitions against the Harlem Globetrotters. Mickey participated in a couple of games himself, but ended up in the hospital after twisting his right knee. Another procedure was performed, leaving him with a temporary limp.

Having separated from his wife, Billy Martin became a winter resident of Commerce. Youngman, who served as a sort of personal advisor to Mantle for many years, was more than happy to have two Yankee stars on his payroll. In their spare time, Mickey and Billy hunted, fished, and got drunk at a local watering hole known as "The 400 Club." In later years, Mantle admitted, "Billy and I were bad for each other. We were always on the go—rushing out the door, telling Merlyn we were going fishing, but instead heading straight to a bar."

One night, Mickey came home late and found himself locked out of the house. After punching out a garage window to get inside, he discovered that Merlyn had cleaned out her closet and left with Mickey Jr. A trip to a local emergency room for stitches was followed by a drunken encounter with Merlyn's father at the Johnson family home. While pulling out of the driveway, Mantle clipped a telephone pole and wound up in a ditch.

The hunting trips involved a fair share of drama as well. According to Mantle, there was a run-in with an Oklahoma Game Commission officer, who caught Mickey and Billy shooting at ducks on private property. Mantle claimed that the officer ran for the safety of his vehicle when Martin threatened to shoot at him. No legal charges were ever filed.

Martin didn't play with the Yankees in 1954. He ended up being drafted into the Army. In his absence, Mantle roomed with infielder Jerry Coleman. There were a few other notable changes in New York as Bill Skowron made his Yankee debut, splitting time at first base with Joe Collins. Third baseman Bobby Brown returned to the club following a long military stint in Korea. He played his last game in June, leaving baseball to become a full-time doctor. After a successful career in cardiology, he was appointed president of the American League—a post he held for 10 years.

The AL had a new look in 1954 as the St. Louis Browns were sold in the offseason. They moved to Baltimore and became the Orioles, losing 100 games under veteran manager Jimmy Dykes. A new rule prohibited players in both leagues from leaving their gloves on the field between innings. The policy change prevented meddlesome players like Eddie Stanky from filling the mitts of opponents with dirt, spit, and tobacco.

In almost any other season, the Yankees would have captured a sixth consecutive pennant. They posted a record of 103-51-1, never losing more than three in a row. Proving that they were miles above the cellar-dwelling clubs, they won 35 of 44 meetings against Baltimore and Philadelphia. The high point of the season was a 13-game winning streak that stretched from July 3 through July 18.

Yogi Berra proved to be the driving force of the Yankee offense yet again, putting up MVP numbers with 56 extra-base hits, 125 ribbies, and a .307 batting average. Not to be completely outdone, Mantle established new personal-highs in multiple categories, including runs scored (129), and home runs (27). His 102 runs batted in were also a career-best mark (to that point).

The Yankee pitching staff was outstanding. Right-hander Bob Grim captured Rookie of the Year honors with 20 victories and a 3.26 ERA. It would prove to be the greatest season of his career as arm troubles later forced him out of the rotation and into the bullpen. Whitey Ford enjoyed another fine campaign, finishing among the league leaders in strikeouts, shutouts, and wins. Aging hurlers Eddie Lopat and Allie Reynolds (in their late 30s by then) combined for a 25-8 record while Johnny Sain assumed the role of a closer, picking up 26 saves (though the statistic was not official at the time).

The Yankees tied for first place on July 20, but it was the last time they would occupy the top slot as the Indians enjoyed the greatest season in franchise history, winning 111 games—the most by any team since the

"Murderers' Row" Yankees of 1927. On paper, the Tribe didn't look like a pennant-winning club. In fact, a majority of their starting players put up mediocre numbers at the plate. The glue that held the Indians together was a marvelous pitching staff anchored by Hall of Famers Bob Feller, Early Wynn, and Bob Lemon. By season's end, Cleveland's five-man rotation had combined for a 93-36 record. It was enough to leave the Yankees eight games behind in the standings.

In the National League, Willie Mays claimed the first of two MVP awards, helping the Giants capture the pennant. Though the New Yorkers entered the World Series as heavy underdogs, they orchestrated a shocking sweep. The tone was set in the eighth inning of Game 1 at the Polo Grounds. With the score tied at 2, Indians slugger Vic Wertz drove a pitch into the deepest recesses of center field. Mays, who was playing shallow, sprinted toward the wall with his back to home plate and made a stupendous over-the-shoulder catch. He then spun and relayed the ball back to the infield, holding Al Rosen and Larry Doby on base. The Giants rallied for a 5–2 win in 10 innings. Mays's catch has often been referred to as the greatest defensive play in baseball history. The Giants wrapped up the Series three days later at Cleveland. It was the first time since his arrival in the majors that Mantle had no impact on postseason events.

THE DODGERS' REVENGE

A landmark year for American pop culture, 1955 brought the television debuts of *The Mickey Mouse Club, Gunsmoke,* and *The $64,000 Question.* Disneyland and McDonald's both opened their doors to the public. In a more serious development, the civil rights movement took a giant leap forward when an NAACP secretary named Rosa Parks refused to give up her seat to a white passenger on a segregated bus. A subsequent public transportation boycott in Montgomery, Alabama, brought about the arrest of organizers Martin Luther King Jr. and Ralph Abernathy.

In a loosely related happening, the Yankees added Elston Howard to their roster, finally integrating the team after a long holdout. Howard provided 12 years of reliable service at multiple defensive stations, making the All-Star team in nine straight seasons and winning the AL MVP award in 1963. When his playing days were over, he spent another decade as a Yankee coach.

With great skills come great expectations. At the start of the 1955 campaign, fans and sportswriters were greatly divided on their opinions of Mantle.

Arthur Daley of the *New York Times* ranked him third among active center fielders behind Willie Mays and Duke Snider. Shirley Povich of the *Washington Post* was of a similar mind-set, commenting, "[Mantle] hits the ball farther, runs faster, bunts better than anyone in baseball, but apparently lacks the high resolution to make the most of his skills." Other writers pointed out qualities in past Yankees greats that Mantle appeared to be lacking, such as charisma, fortitude, and sophistication. One reporter even questioned the level of Mickey's I.Q.

Fans were extremely hard on the 23-year-old Oklahoma native, booing him regularly when he took the field and peppering him with insults. It was undeserved. Mantle enjoyed one of his finest seasons, leading the league in multiple statistical categories. On May 13, he slugged three homers in a game, carrying the Yankees to a 5–2 win over the Tigers.

Despite the periodic abuse he was subjected to, Mantle was named to the All-Star team for the fourth straight year. Other Yankees to make the squad included Yogi Berra, Whitey Ford, and Bob Turley—a right-handed hurler acquired from Baltimore in the offseason. Facing Hall of Famer Robin Roberts in the first inning, Mantle launched a three-run homer to deep center field. The American League jumped out to a 5–0 lead, but couldn't hold it as Stan Musial delivered a walkoff homer in the bottom of the 12th.

The Yankee pitching staff was inundated with fresh faces. Ford was the undisputed ace while Turley, Tommy Byrne, and Don Larsen all carried sizable workloads. Allie Reynolds and Vic Raschi—staples of the early-1950s dynasty—were both gone. Johnny Sain was sold to the Athletics in early May after running his ERA up to 6.75. Eddie Lopat hung on until July 30, when his 4-8 record prompted a trade to Baltimore.

In Brooklyn, the Dodger lineup remained virtually intact from the previous World Series bid. Roy Campanella, Gil Hodges, and Duke Snider all reached the 100-RBI mark while collecting no fewer than 25 homers apiece. Returning from a two-year military absence, right-hander Don Newcombe posted a stellar 20-5 record. Clem Labine was as reliable as they come out of the bullpen, winning 13 games and saving 11 more as the Dodgers built a comfortable 13 1/2-game lead over the second-place Braves.

The Yankees had a tougher time of it in 1955, spending most of September in second place before catching up with the Indians. They won 10 of their last 12, capturing the pennant by a slender three-game margin. Mantle suffered a typical late-season injury, tearing a muscle in the back of his right thigh while beating out a bunt. He played in just two regular-season games after September 16. Before the mishap, he had been poised to become the first Yankee to hit 40 home runs since Joe DiMaggio in 1937. He finished with 37, claiming the first of four home-run crowns.

Describing the state of the Yankee-Dodger rivalry in 1955, Turley recalled, "There was no hatred between the [two clubs]. A lot of us had good friends on the Dodgers. We all liked Campanella, Hodges, Snider ... there was a mutual respect between the teams. I don't think we thought we were better, especially with Mantle hobbling. We knew how good they were."

The Yankees won the first two games of the World Series without Mantle in the lineup. In the third meeting, Casey Stengel decided to test the ailing center fielder's leg, inserting him into the cleanup slot. He looked good in his first at-bat of the Series, clubbing a long homer off of Johnny Podres. But he grounded into a rally-killing double play in the sixth inning. He finished the afternoon at 1-for-4 as the Dodgers won handily, 8–3.

Game 4 was largely forgettable for Mantle as he struck out twice and grounded out twice. His only hit was a routine single off of reliever Don Bessent in the fifth inning. He wound up being stranded at second base. By the end of the game—an 8–5 Yankee loss—Mickey's thigh injury had flared up again, seriously limiting his mobility. His only other appearance of the Series came in the finale, when he produced an inning-ending infield popup as a pinch-hitter.

Trailing 3 games to 2, the Yankees rebounded with a convincing 5–1 win as Ford tossed a four-hitter and struck out eight opponents. Game 7 is best remembered for a spectacular catch made by Cuban-born outfielder Sandy Amoros. Inserted as a defensive replacement in the bottom of the sixth, Amoros robbed Yogi Berra of a game-tying double, then fired the ball back to relay man Pee Wee Reese, who threw to first base to complete a rare 7-6-3 double play. The Dodgers held on for a 2–0 win, setting off a wild celebration in Flatbush. Church bells rang, factory whistles blew, and fans danced in the streets. Effigies of Yankee players hung from lampposts. On Wall Street, skyscrapers opened their windows and released confetti into the evening sky.

In a classy move, Berra visited the Brooklyn clubhouse after the game, congratulating players and clowning around with Amoros, whom he pretended to beat up. In the years that followed, Mantle was asked many times if he was glad that the Dodgers had finally shaken the Yankee curse. Although he answered "no" publicly, he later admitted, "Maybe in a tiny, hidden corner of my heart I was kind of happy for them, and especially for Sandy Amoros. That was his one shining moment in the big leagues." Amoros lasted just four more seasons in the majors before fading into obscurity. He closed out his 11-year Cuban league career with a highly respectable .281 batting average (though some sources consider his Cuban stats to be unreliable).

After the tough Game 7 loss, Mantle sat in the corner of the Yankee clubhouse with his head in his hands. Casey Stengel kindly offered words of encouragement, assuring the dejected slugger that championships were lost by teams, not individuals. "I want you to be a tough loser," he advised. "That shows you want to win. Don't go blaming yourself for losing the series."

In spite of Casey's pep talk, Mantle's drinking problems escalated during the offseason. Merlyn, who was pregnant with their second son, David, had spent the entire 1955 campaign in Oklahoma. In her absence, Mickey had grown accustomed to doing whatever he pleased. He spent much of the fall and winter cavorting with assorted friends. On Christmas Eve, Merlyn came home from her parents' house to find Mickey standing outside with a group of drunken house guests. Having misplaced his house key, he flew into a rage and shoved Merlyn, who was just two days away from delivering the baby by then. Mickey's twin brothers, Ray and Roy, were appalled by his behavior and promptly informed their mother of the incident. Lovell administered a verbal lashing that Mickey didn't soon forget. Merlyn said it was the first time he had ever embarrassed her in front of friends. The $2,500 mink stole he gave her for Christmas helped settle the rift between them.

THE GREATEST SEASON

In early January, the Yankees extended a $32,000 contract offer to Mantle. Though it paled in comparison to Yogi Berra's annual salary, it was roughly equivalent to the earnings of the other two center fielders Mantle was often associated with—Willie Mays and Duke Snider. Finding the terms agreeable, Mickey signed with New York in late January.

During spring training, Mantle had a candid discussion with assistant GM Bill DeWitt about how he might improve his reputation as a player. DeWitt advised him to be more accommodating to writers—even on days when he didn't feel like talking to them. To enhance his offensive skills, Mantle began to exercise more patience, holding up on pitches that were well outside the strike zone. He altered his batting stance, standing farther from the plate and deeper in the batter's box to help him identify the offerings of opposing hurlers. Upon observing his progress, Shirley Povich wrote, "This is Mickey Mantle's year. This is the one when he'll burst into full magnificence, hit more and longer home runs than anybody else, lead the league in batting, perhaps, and certainly get more extra base hits than anybody else."

On April 17, President Eisenhower officially opened the season by throwing out the ceremonial first pitch at Griffith Stadium in Washington. Mantle appeared more than ready to fulfill Povich's prophecies, blasting a pair of homers. The first one was a titanic shot that cleared the 30-foot fence in left-center field. It sailed out of the stadium, traveling around 500 feet in the air before settling on the roof of a neighboring house. The second clout, which came with a pair of runners aboard, was a line drive that hit a tree outside the ballpark and landed more than 430 feet from home plate. There is no telling how much farther it would have carried unimpeded. Mantle's performance that day landed him on the front page of all the New York daily newspapers.

The Yankees slugger's most memorable hit of the season came on May 30 at New York. Facing Pedro Ramos of the Senators, he lifted a pitch into the right field façade, which was located more than 100 feet above the playing field. The ball missed clearing the roof by a matter of inches. Mathematical estimates placed the homer at a whopping 620 feet—a distance equaled only by Babe Ruth. The landmark blast earned Mantle a spot on the covers of *Time* and *Newsweek*.

Less than halfway through the season, Mantle was on pace to hit 69 homers, which would have shattered Ruth's long-standing single-season record. Reporters followed his daily exploits closely and hounded him with questions. Growing weary of frequent comparisons to the all-time greats, he told a group of writers one day, "I'm not Ruth, Gehrig, Foxx, Williams, or whoever they say. I'll just be satisfied with having a good year and that's about it."

As could only be expected, there were minor injuries over the course of the season. In a game against the Red Sox, he tweaked his hamstring beating out a bunt. He was visibly limping by the end of the day, but remained in the lineup. During the first week of May, he pulled a groin muscle. Two days later, he fouled a ball off of his foot during batting practice. His right toe was so badly swollen that the trainer had to cut a hole in his shoe to relieve the pressure. He played anyway, producing a home run and single. By season's end, he had appeared in 150 games—the highest total of his career to that point.

With Merlyn back in Oklahoma looking after David and Mickey Jr., Mantle kept a suite at the Hotel St. Moritz, which was located in an upscale area of Midtown Manhattan. Having attained full-blown celebrity status, he ate in the most popular restaurants and rubbed elbows with some of the brightest stars of the era. One of his favorite hangouts was a steakhouse known as Danny's Hideaway, which was frequented by the likes of Elizabeth Taylor and Rock Hudson. He also became a regular at Toots Shor's—a legendary eatery catering to the high-profile New York sports crowd.

Mantle finished first in All-Star voting—no small feat considering the players he was up against. Mays and Snider were both on the ballot along with Stan Musial, Ted Williams, and Hank Aaron (among many others). Mantle played all nine innings of the All-Star Game, cracking a long homer off of Milwaukee ace Warren Spahn. The shot proved to be virtually meaningless in a 7–3 AL loss.

Mantle's home-run production dropped off considerably in the second half. Though he went deep 13 times in August, he managed just seven blasts during the month of July and five in September. He finished the season with

A familiar sight that thrilled fans at Yankee Stadium for nearly two decades—
Mantle in the on-deck circle (Courtesy of The National Baseball Hall of Fame)

52—a personal record that would stand until the home-run race of 1961. His .353 batting average and 130 RBIs made him the 10th major-league player of the 20th century to win a Triple Crown. He was the only player to accomplish the feat during the 1950s.

Mantle's extraordinary slugging statistics during the magical 1956 campaign overshadowed other notable aspects of his performance. Despite ongoing knee miseries, he was successful in 10 of 11 stolen base attempts. He also finished among the top three center fielders in putouts, assists, and fielding percentage. Though he had been widely labeled as an underachiever to that point, there was no longer any question as to what he was capable of accomplishing on the field.

BACK ON TOP

In 1956—a remarkable year for technology—IBM invented the first computer hard drive. Unlike the machines of today, it weighed close to a ton and measured 16 square feet. A major milestone was reached in the area of communications as the transatlantic telephone cable system became operational. Portable black and white televisions hit the market, making iconic shows such as *I Love Lucy*, *The Price Is Right*, and *Father Knows Best* readily available to the masses. In music news, Elvis Presley topped the Billboard charts with his bluesy rock 'n' roll ditty, "Heartbreak Hotel." And in the world of boxing, Rocky Marciano retired as the only undefeated heavyweight champion—a distinction he holds to the present day.

In baseball, the Dodgers overcame a mediocre first-half start, capturing their sixth pennant in a 10-year stretch. The race for the NL flag came down to the last day of the season, when staff ace Don Newcombe survived a slugfest against the Pirates, earning his 27th victory. He ended up claiming the inaugural Cy Young Award along with NL MVP honors.

In the Bronx, Mantle's Triple Crown performance made the accomplishments of teammates seem ordinary. Yogi Berra logged his fourth consecutive 100-RBI season while pitchers Whitey Ford and Johnny Kucks combined for a 37-15 record. The Yankees spent a total of 165 days in first place, finishing with a nine-game lead over the second-place Indians.

The seventh installment of the storied Yankee-Dodger rivalry went the full distance. It was the last postseason matchup between the two clubs while the Dodgers were stationed in Brooklyn. President Eisenhower and Secretary of State John Foster Dulles both attended the opener at Ebbets Field. The Yankees squared off against right-hander Sal Maglie, who was known for his menacing scowl and penchant for throwing at hitters—a habit that earned him the nickname of "The Barber." He looked vulnerable early on as Mantle crushed a two-run homer over the right field screen in his first at-bat. Maglie pitched carefully to The Mick after that, holding him to a strikeout and a pair of walks. Ford crumbled on the mound for the Yankees in a 6–3 loss.

Newcombe was shaky in Game 2, getting pulled in the second inning after coughing up six runs. But the Dodgers chased starter Don Larsen from the game, tying the score in the bottom of the frame. It was a rough day for the Yankee staff as Brooklyn hitters kept hacking away, adding seven more runs before the last out was recorded. The Yankees limped back to the Bronx with a two-game deficit on their hands.

Though Mantle's bat remained relatively quiet in Games 2 and 3, he began to heat up in the fourth contest, launching a homer off of Ed Roebuck. In the fifth meeting, he victimized Maglie again with a solo shot that held up as the game-winner. His heroics were overshadowed by a landmark pitching performance from Larsen. Evaluating the underachieving right-hander's career, Mantle remarked: "It [sic] kind of begs the obvious to say that Larsen was an odd candidate for immortality. He was one of the great night owls—a happy-go-lucky guy who drifted from team to team and would never win more than 11 games in a season." In spite of his shortcomings, Larsen was absolutely untouchable in his second start of the series, retiring all 27 batters he faced. In the second inning, Jackie Robinson hit a hard smash that bounced off of third baseman Andy Carey. Shortstop Gil McDougald alertly grabbed it and fired to first in time to nail Robinson. In the fifth, Gil Hodges hit a towering shot to deep left-center field, but Mantle caught up with it in time to make an over-the-shoulder grab. He later said it was one of the best catches he ever made. The remainder of the afternoon passed somewhat uneventfully for Larsen, whose perfect game remains the only one in the history of the Fall Classic.

The rest of the series was anticlimactic by comparison. The Dodgers tied things up with a 1–0 win in Game 6 and the Yankees romped to a 9–0 victory in the finale at Brooklyn. Capturing the somber mood in Flatbush, organist Gladys Gooding serenaded fans with a rendition of "Auld Lang Syne" as they filed toward the exits. It was the last World Series game played at Ebbets Field.

FIGHT CLUB

Cashing in on the slugger's fame, Mantle's agent, Frank Scott, created a small corporation, Mickey Mantle Enterprises. Scott kept the money rolling in with a variety of bookings that included after-dinner speeches, autograph signings, and assorted endorsement deals. In August 1956, Mantle even cut a record with Teresa Brewer, who was one of the most popular female performers of the 1950s. The novelty song they collaborated on, "I Love Mickey," featured Brewer's vocals with Mantle speaking back to her. Though it wasn't a smash hit, it spent three weeks in the *Billboard* Top 100, peaking at number 87.

In the spring of 1957, Harold Youngman—one of Mantle's business partners—offered him a 25 percent stake in a hotel located at the end of the Oklahoma Turnpike in Joplin, Missouri. The star outfielder jumped at the opportunity, lending his name to the Mickey Mantle Holiday Inn, which had more than 50 guest rooms along with a restaurant and banquet hall. It also featured the Mickey Mantle Suite, where guests could spend the night in a bed the Yankee icon had actually slept in. The hotel netted Mantle substantial profits until it was sold to a group of New York investors in the mid-1960s.

Instead of rewarding Mantle for his Triple Crown effort with a smooth round of contract negotiations, Yankee GM George Weiss made him jump through hoops. When Mantle asked for twice the amount in his 1956 contract, Weiss threatened to go public with reports from private detectives regarding his assorted misbehaviors (which included a number of extramarital affairs). Weiss was so confident that he held the upper hand, he threatened to trade Mantle to the Indians for budding slugger Rocky Colavito and pitcher Herb Score, who had set a rookie strikeout record in 1955. Feeling that their tight-fisted GM had crossed a line, Yankee owners Del Webb and Dan Topping stepped in with a $60,000 offer, which Mantle readily accepted.

Mantle's growing wealth only served to steer him more toward extracurricular activities. Unlike the highly paid Joe DiMaggio, who had rarely picked up the tab for postgame celebrations, Mantle regularly treated teammates to dinners, drinks, and cab rides. According to biographer Tony Castro, the FBI began keeping files on Mickey and some of his Yankee cohorts, who were said to patronize brothels and associate with gamblers. The most notorious incident of the 1957 campaign prompted a significant roster purge.

On May 16, a group of Yankees and their wives went out on the town to celebrate Billy Martin's 29th birthday. The revelers included Mantle, Whitey Ford, Yogi Berra, Hank Bauer, and pitcher Johnny Kucks. After eating at

Danny's Hideaway, they went to the Waldorf-Astoria to see singer Johnnie Ray perform. From there, it was on to the Copacabana, where Sammy Davis Jr. was making the last of several appearances.

When the performance began, a group of drunken bowlers from Washington Heights began directing racial epithets toward the stage. After Bauer told them to pipe down, they took to insulting the players' wives. To this day, no one seems to know precisely what happened during the ensuing brawl, which left a 42-year-old deli owner named Edwin Jones with a fractured jaw, broken nose, and concussion. Jones later filed a lawsuit against Bauer, who was blamed for laying him out cold.

The story was all over the newspapers for months afterward. Bauer denied throwing any punches and Berra backed up the claim, famously commenting, "No one did nothing to nobody." Testifying in front of a grand jury, Mantle provided a moment of comic relief when he flippantly remarked, "I think Roy Rogers rode through the Copa and Trigger kicked the man in the head." Though the case was thrown out due to lack of substantial evidence, Yankees executives were not pleased, fining each player $1,000 (with the exception of Kucks, whose salary was significantly lower than the others).

Weiss had long believed that Martin was a bad influence on Mantle. Seizing the opportunity, he orchestrated a major deal with the A's, sending Martin to Kansas City along with Woodie Held, Bob Martyn, and Ralph Terry in exchange for three players. One of Weiss's acquisitions was a flame-throwing right-hander named Ryne Duren, who became one of the top relievers in the American League for a short span.

Martin never attained the same level of success elsewhere. He ended up being traded five times between November 1957 and June 1961. According to Mantle, he held a long-standing grudge against Casey Stengel. "He knew that Weiss was the one who traded him because he was out gunning for him anyway," Mantle explained, "but Billy still felt Casey must've agreed to it. He said that was the one time he needed Casey and Casey didn't help him. And even though he had always been Casey's favorite player, he couldn't forgive him because he got traded away from the Yankees." Martin went on to a highly successful managerial career, guiding four different clubs into the playoffs. He steered the Yankees to a pair of pennants and one World Series title during the 1970s.

In 2020, a former Copacabana bouncer named Joey Silvestri claimed to have punched Jones while restoring order on that fateful night in May of 1957. "The fight wasn't a fight," Silvestri told a *New York Times* reporter.

"It was two punches—over." Shortly after Jones was rendered unconscious, members of the Yankees entourage were escorted out the back kitchen entrance. "Hank Bauer and Billy Martin have always been maligned, when they're really the good guys," Silvestri asserted. "They were protecting Sammy Davis that night. If that happened today, they'd build a monument to them."

The Copacabana was not the only site of a Yankee brawl in 1957. During a game against the White Sox on June 13, starter Art Ditmar threw a pitch at Hall of Famer Larry Doby's head. The ball sailed to the backstop and Ditmar ran to cover home plate. After exchanging words with the Yankee hurler, Doby punched him. A wild melee followed as Moose Skowron jumped on Doby and Walt Dropo—a 6-foot-5, 220-pound bruiser—came to Doby's aid. Enos Slaughter's uniform was nearly torn from his body. A famous snapshot taken near the end of the fracas shows Slaughter on his way back to the Yankee dugout with his shirt in tatters, his bare chest exposed, and his hat on backwards. Four players were ejected, among them Billy Martin, who ended up being traded a couple of days later.

Mantle was unhappy to see Martin go, commenting that it was like losing a brother. But he enjoyed an exceptional season nevertheless, posting a career-high .365 batting average. His stellar performance was upstaged by Red Sox slugger Ted Williams, who captured the AL batting crown with a lofty .388 mark. Williams also cracked more homers and compiled a higher on-base percentage. But Boston's third-place finish made him a slightly less viable candidate for MVP. Mantle received six first-place votes to Williams's five, claiming the award for the second straight year.

UNFAMILIAR FOES

In the early part of the 20th century, the Boston Braves were a star-crossed franchise. After winning a World Series in 1914, they waited more than three decades to make another appearance on the October stage. A subsequent move to Milwaukee initiated a series of important lineup changes. By 1957, the club was among the most powerful in baseball. Hank Aaron and Eddie Mathews did a majority of the slugging that season, combining for more than 70 homers and 200 RBIs. The pitching staff was anchored by Hall of Famer Warren Spahn, who was still piling up the wins at the age of 36. The Dodgers had a mediocre campaign, slumping to third place while the Cardinals hit a rough patch in August, ultimately finishing eight games out of the running. For the first time in seven years, the National League sent a team from outside New York to the World Series.

There was trouble on the international front in 1957 as Viet Cong guerrillas began a terrorist bombing campaign in South Vietnam, ultimately killing hundreds of civilians and government officials. The Asian flu pandemic imposed a heavy death toll, claiming over a million lives worldwide. The Cold War continued to escalate as the Soviets launched a pair of artificial satellites (Sputnik I and II), kicking off a "space race" against the United States. In pop culture, Wham-O Frisbee products hit the shelves and Theodor Seuss Geisel (aka Dr. Seuss) published his best-known work—*The Cat in the Hat*. Moviegoers flocked to theaters to see a trio of celebrated classics, *The Ten Commandments*, *12 Angry Men*, and *The Bridge Over the River Kwai*.

Six Yankee hurlers finished with double-digit win totals in 1957. Whitey Ford was among them, though chronic shoulder issues limited him to 17 regular-season starts. The Bombers were a bit sluggish during the spring, spending a significant period of time in second place. But a 10-game winning streak before the All-Star break put them on top for good. Oddly enough, it was the humble Tigers who gave the Yankees the most trouble in head-to-head matchups, winning 10 of 22 meetings in spite of their fourth place status. In contrast, the defending world champions compiled an aggregate 28-16 record against pennant contenders.

With the departure of Billy Martin, Casey Stengel created a second-base platoon that consisted of Bobby Richardson, Gil McDougald, and Jerry Coleman. Coleman was the primary starter in the postseason. Looking every bit as capable as "Billy the Kid," he had a spectacular World Series, tying for the team lead in hits and doubles while hitting at a robust .364 clip.

Evaluating the competition, Mantle said: "There was no way we could take the Braves lightly. They had a great ballclub . . . the city of Milwaukee had gone wild over them. The players couldn't pick up a check anywhere— free groceries, free laundry, free beer." Even so, the Yankees were heavily favored to win.

No one was terribly surprised when Ford stifled the Braves in the opener. Milwaukee's only run came on an RBI-single by infielder Red Schoendienst in the seventh inning. The Yankees had better luck against Spahn, tagging him for three runs on nine hits. Mantle didn't figure into the scoring, but he had a good day at the plate, going 2-for-4 with a pair of singles.

Refusing to roll over, the Braves took three of the next four games. This included a dramatic come from behind victory in the fourth meeting. Milwaukee led, 4–1, entering the ninth, but a three-run homer by Elston Howard sent the game into extra innings. In the bottom of the 10th, Mathews drilled a two-run walkoff shot that tied the Series at two games apiece.

Mantle put forth his best effort in Game 3, gathering two hits and a pair of walks. In the fourth inning, he gave the Yankees an impregnable lead with a two-run homer off of reliever Gene Conley that landed in the bullpen in right-center field. The blast came in the wake of a baserunning mishap. After drawing a first-inning walk, Mantle stumbled and fell while taking a lead off of second base. Braves starter Bob Buhl tried to pick him off, but the throw sailed high into center field. Schoendienst leaped for the ball and then landed with his full weight on Mantle's right shoulder. It hampered the slugger's swing for the rest of the series. He went 0-for-5 in Game 4 and was limited to one pinch-running assignment in the next two meetings. He finished the series with a middling .263 batting average.

The hero of the 1957 affair was a right-handed pitcher named Lew Burdette. An incorrigible prankster who once put a snake in an umpire's pocket and posed as a lefty for his 1959 Topps baseball card, Burdette had an expansive repertoire that included a sinker, slider, and sidearm curve. After winning 17 games for the Braves during the regular season, he padded his totals against the Yankees, adding three complete-game victories. Recapping the events of Game 7, *New York Times* correspondent John Drebinger reported, "For good measure and by way of giving his team additional security, Del Crandall, Burdette's catcher, dropped a home run into the left field stands in the eighth. But that shot was not needed. For by then, Selva Lewis Burdette Sr.—30 year-old right-hander and one-time farmhand in the Yankee chain, was putting the finishing touches to one of the most astounding exhibitions of sustained pitching mastery in more than a half century of World Series competition."

Explaining the key to Burdette's success, one of his staff mates remarked, "The Yankees were an impatient, fastball-hitting team and he kept them off balance with his motions and his sinkers and sliders. He'd always make the big pitch." Mantle was of a similar mind-set, commenting, "The way he dominated us proved two points that I believed in. One is that, unlike the regular season, pitching isn't 75 percent of the World Series, but 90 percent. The other is that the so-called book on hitters means very little in such a short competition."

THE 1958 MVP SNUB

By the end of the 1957 campaign, life in Commerce had become difficult for Mantle and his family. "There was no privacy," the slugger wrote in one of his autobiographies. "If [neighborhood kids] weren't out on the lawn yelling and wanting autographs, they'd be waiting for my car, hoping to get me to sign their scrapbooks or pictures or toy bats as I walked into the house. Merlyn felt we were living in a zoo." Strangers knocked on the door with business propositions while casual acquaintances routinely showed up asking for money. Looking for a more peaceful place to spend the offseason, Mantle eventually bought the family a four-bedroom house in the Preston Hollow section of Dallas, Texas.

During the fall of 1957, Merlyn was pregnant with the couple's third son. Mickey had gotten in the habit of spending Thanksgiving week hunting with Billy Martin and Harold Youngman on a Texas ranch owned by another friend. Though Merlyn began experiencing discomfort shortly before his departure and believed she might be going into labor, Mickey left anyway. She ended up in a Joplin, Missouri, hospital, where she delivered the baby. By the time Mickey returned in Youngman's private plane, Merlyn was distraught. "You could have waited a few more days before taking off like that!" she sobbed.

Mantle's 1957 World Series injury required surgery, and he was still not fully recovered by the time spring training arrived. When George Weiss proposed a salary cut, Mantle considered holding out. But after reading a newspaper article stating that Weiss had threatened to trade him again, the Yankee outfielder promptly boarded a flight to St. Petersburg. The two parties eventually came to terms on a $5,000 pay increase.

Mantle's shoulder bothered him considerably during the spring, and he got off to a slow start. Through the first three months of the season, he was hitting just .268 with 14 homers and 33 RBIs. He made the All-Star team anyway, gathering more votes than any of the other center field candidates. On the day after the All-Star Game, he was summoned to testify before a US Senate subcommittee regarding Major League Baseball's antitrust exemption.

The term *antitrust* refers to any contract that illegally restrains trade and promotes anticompetitive behavior. Under antitrust statutes, price-fixing, monopolies, and acts intended to prevent free commerce are prohibited by the US government. In 1922, Major League Baseball was deemed exempt by the Supreme Court. After more than a quarter of a century, the Senate Judiciary Committee decided to reevaluate the status of that exemption.

Rather than assembling a team of legal experts to debate the matter, subcommittee chairman Senator Estes Kefauver invited a number of baseball insiders to take the stand. Ted Williams, Stan Musial, and Casey Stengel (all fresh off All-Star appearances) were summoned along with Mantle and Yankees owner Del Webb. When it was his turn to speak, Stengel—known for his creative use of the English language—rambled on for what seemed like an eternity, talking in circles and confusing virtually everyone in the room.

Called to the stand immediately after his long-winded manager, Mantle inadvertently prompted a moment of hilarity. When Senator Kefauver asked the slugger if he "had any observations with reference to the applicability of the antitrust laws to baseball," he answered, "My views are just about the same as Casey's." The room instantly filled with uproarious laughter.

When the regular season resumed, Mantle went off on a tear, hitting .333 from the beginning of July to season's end. He was especially effective against left-handed moundsmen, raking them for a .377 batting mark. After the last pitch of the regular season had been thrown, the Yankee icon was a statistical leader in more than half a dozen major categories.

The annual MVP vote has produced some questionable results over the years. Ted Williams finished second to Joe DiMaggio in 1941 despite his .406 batting average and on-base streak of 69 games. In 1950, baseball writers overlooked Stan Musial's league-leading .346 batting average and Ralph Kiner's 47 home runs (also a league-high), handing the award instead to a relief pitcher named Jim Konstanty, who never had another exceptional season. In 1958, MVP voters seemed to forget that Mantle was alive. Though he led the league in home runs (42), runs scored (127), walks (129), and total bases (307), he didn't receive a single first-place vote. Instead, the award went to Jackie Jensen of the Red Sox, whose only notable accomplishment that year was winning the RBI crown. If members of the Baseball Writers Association of America hadn't cast seven first-place votes for Cy Young Award winner Bob Turley, Mantle might have had a better chance. Instead, he missed a shot at becoming the first player to win the award in three consecutive seasons.

REWRITING THE SCRIPT

In 1958 the Giants and Dodgers both moved to the West Coast after more than seven decades of tenancy in the Big Apple. It was a sad year for New York baseball. Playing in unfamiliar surroundings, the Dodgers posted a miserable 71-83 record while the Giants finished a distant third—12 games out of the race. Meanwhile, the Braves got dynamic performances from the usual sources as Hank Aaron and Eddie Mathews both reached the 30-homer mark. Warren Spahn and Lew Burdette combined for 42 victories, guiding the team to its second consecutive pennant.

The world was entering a new era in 1958 as Egypt and Syria bonded to form the United Arab Republic. Scrambling to catch up with the Soviet space program, President Eisenhower signed the National Aeronautics and Space Act into law. NASA—the newly formed federal agency—launched the first American satellite into orbit. In another technological breakthrough, electrical engineer Jack Kilby invented the first integrated circuit—a device that would revolutionize the computer industry.

In the Bronx, right-hander Bob Turley enjoyed the most productive season of his career, compiling the best winning percentage in the American League with a 21-7 record. His 19 complete games were also a league-high mark. In the Yankee bullpen, Ryne Duren saved 19 games while averaging more than 10 strikeouts per nine innings. Duren had a 100-mph fastball and questionable control. During warmups, he got in a habit of deliberately throwing pitches over the heads of his battery mates to intimidate on-deck hitters. Aside from a couple of days in April, the Yankees remained in first place all season, finishing with a 10-game lead over the second-place White Sox.

The World Series opened at County Stadium in Milwaukee. Warren Spahn squared off against Whitey Ford in a battle of Cooperstown greats. Moose Skowron put the Yankees on the board in the fourth with a solo homer, but the Braves answered with a pair of runs in the bottom of the frame. Hank Bauer's two-run blast in the fifth gave the Yankees a lead that held up until the bottom of the eighth. After a leadoff walk to Mathews and a double by Aaron, Ford's day on the mound was finished. Summoned from the bullpen, Duren coughed up the tying run on a sacrifice fly by Wes Covington. The game went into extra innings and ended with a walkoff single by Milwaukee outfielder Bill Bruton.

The second contest was a blowout. Turley had a miserable start, facing just five batters while getting charged with four earned runs. Reliever Duke Maas coughed up three runs of his own as Milwaukee jumped out to a 7–1 first-inning lead. It was an industrious day at the plate for Mantle, who slammed a pair of homers off of Burdette. The second one was a two-run blast that traveled well over 400 feet. It hardly made a difference as the Braves breezed to a 13–5 win. In the clubhouse after the game, a TV correspondent stuck a microphone in Casey Stengel's face and asked if his team was choking. Stengel swore at the reporter then deliberately turned around to scratch his behind, effectively ruining the audio and video feed.

With the thunderous chants of Milwaukee fans still ringing in their ears, the Yankees returned to the Bronx, where Duren and Don Larsen combined for a six-hit shutout in Game 3. Hank Bauer was the man of the hour, driving in all four New York runs. The celebration was short-lived, however, as a defensive meltdown in the fourth meeting led to another Yankee loss. Left-fielder Norm Siebern, who won a Gold Glove that year, delivered one of the most appalling defensive performances in postseason history, misplaying three flyballs that led to three Milwaukee runs. It wouldn't have made much of a difference as Spahn pitched a shutout. Mantle's fourth-inning triple was one of just two Yankee hits. After the game, Braves left fielder Wes Covington sympathized with Siebern. "That's a rough field to play with the sun and the fog or mist that seems to come in later in the afternoon," he said.

On the brink of elimination, the Yankees fought back in Game 5, batting around in the sixth inning against Burdette, who had beaten them in each of his last four postseason starts. Mantle went 2-for-3 with a walk and a run scored in the 7–0 romp. Empowered by the victory, the Bombers rallied in the 10th inning of Game 6 to even the Series. Duren, who had provided 4.2 strong innings of relief, was interviewed by a *Today Show* crew in the locker room. The segment had to be scrapped when Yogi Berra kept walking past the camera naked and scratching his buttocks.

In Game 7, Braves manager Fred Haney sent Burdette back to the mound on short rest. It turned out to be a mistake as the Yankees became the first team since 1925 to overcome a 3-games-to-1 Series deficit. Turley was called upon in relief for the second day in a row, picking up his second win. In Game 5, he had struck out 10 Milwaukee hitters, establishing himself as only the second pitcher in history to have a pair of double-digit strikeout performances in postseason play (the previous one coming in 1956). He was a resounding choice for Series MVP. "Being on the mound for the final out in the World Series was the most exciting moment of my career," he later remarked. "Most of the Yankees had won so often, they acted as if nothing had happened." The lack of enthusiasm bothered Mantle as well. "I was a little envious of the Braves, who were still heroes to their fans," he said. "New Yorkers expected us to win. There had been no celebration, no ticker-tape parades, and not much in the way of free beer and bratwurst." The victory in 1958 was New York's sixth and final championship of the decade.

A YEAR TO FORGET

After capturing eight pennants in a nine-year span, the Yankees finally crumbled, spending the entire 1959 season chasing the competition. Bob Turley was one of several disappointments, following up his signature campaign with a lackluster 8-11 effort. Hank Bauer posted one of the lowest single-season batting averages of his career at .238. And Moose Skowron sat out a majority of the second half with a fractured wrist.

Though Mantle played in 144 games, the only statistical category he led the league in was strikeouts. "I'd like to forget 1959 altogether as far as baseball goes," he wrote in his memoirs. "We finished third, 15 games behind the White Sox and 10 behind the second place Indians. And as our fortunes sank, my moods became darker. I'd sit with my head hanging, deep in the dumps, knowing I wasn't contributing as much as I wanted to. . . . I was miserable."

By the time July arrived, Mantle was really pressing at the plate, and fans began riding him hard. His melodramatic dugout tantrums prompted Casey Stengel to mockingly purchase a Joe Palooka punching bag for him to take his frustrations out on. One night in Baltimore, he picked up a water cooler and smashed it to pieces as Orioles fans egged him on. Still, the season held a couple of milestones as he slugged his 250th career homer and drove in his 800th run. He was also named to the All-Star team for the eighth straight year.

Looking to raise money for players' pension funds, Major League Baseball held a second All-Star Game in 1959—a practice that continued through the 1962 slate. Mantle played in all but one of those contests, gathering two hits and five walks in 19 plate appearances.

Mantle observed an alarming change in Stengel during the 1959 campaign. The 68-year-old Yankee manager began showing up at the ballpark hung over with increasing regularity, sometimes allowing his coaches to run things for him while he napped on the bench. As the Yankees sank in the standings, owner Dan Topping publicly criticized "the Old Professor" for overusing the platoon system. Many players were in agreement. Shortstop Tony Kubek recalled: "In later years, Casey's platooning probably became rougher on the young players. He was more difficult with them. I played five different positions before settling at shortstop, but even then I figured he platooned me less than some of the others." Infielder Bobby Richardson griped, "If I started a game, I'd be pulled out almost immediately for a pinch hitter. If I did bat once in a game, I was so tense that I tried too hard." True to form,

Stengel tried to make light of his managerial shortcomings with humorous remarks. In one of his most famous quotes, he joked, "The secret of successful managing is to keep the five guys who hate you away from the ones who haven't made up their minds."

As the Yankees limped to the finish line, the White Sox ended a long-standing curse, capturing their first pennant since the ill-fated 1919 season (during which eight members of the team conspired to throw the World Series). Managed by Hall of Famer Al López, the 1959 Chicago squad, nick-named the "Go-Go Sox," employed a "small-ball" strategy—bunting, stealing, and sacrificing in an era when those strategies had become virtually obsolete. They met their match in the postseason as the Dodgers claimed their first West Coast championship, clinching the World Series in six games.

A NEW HOPE

Mantle's fourth son, Danny, was born in March 1960. By then, the family had taken up residence in Dallas, where Mickey had purchased a bowling alley. As usual, he was forced to haggle with George Weiss over his annual contract. He had little bargaining power this time around since his 1959 offensive numbers were well below average. Weiss's initial bid included a massive pay cut. When Mantle asked if there had been some mistake, Weiss assured him that $55,000 was the best the Yankees could do. After a 10-day holdout, Mantle flew to St. Petersburg for a second round of negotiations. In the end, he accepted a $10,000 salary reduction. Reporters were waiting for him when the deal was done. "They got what they wanted," the slugger recalled, "a shattered ballplayer trying to put up a brave front. And to face them was the bitterest pill of all."

Mantle had a lackluster spring along with the rest of the team as the Yankees finished near the bottom of the Grapefruit League standings. The salary dispute haunted Mantle through the first few months of the regular season. He found it difficult to focus at times, making embarrassing mental mistakes. One day, after striking out, he failed to notice that the ball had eluded the catcher and rolled to the backstop. He returned to the dugout instead of running to first base. On another occasion, he hit an infield grounder with a runner on first and one out. Mistakenly believing there were two outs, he stopped running after a couple of steps. Fans treated him to a hearty chorus of boos as Casey Stengel replaced him with Bob Cerv. The jeering continued periodically in the weeks that followed, and Mantle vented his frustrations more than once by gesturing rudely toward fans.

While Mantle struggled to find his swing, Roger Maris reluctantly stepped into the spotlight. A soft-spoken, publicity-shy right fielder, Maris had spent four seasons in the minors before joining the Indians in 1957. The Yankees had courted his services as early as 1958, but Cleveland executives refused to send him to a contender, shipping him to Kansas City instead. This worked out well for the Bombers, who frequently conducted business with the A's. In the winter of 1959-60, Weiss organized a blockbuster deal, sending four players—among them Hank Bauer and Don Larsen—to Kansas City in exchange for Maris and Joe DeMaestri. DeMaestri faded quickly into obscurity, but Maris had a major impact in New York.

By season's end, Mantle and Maris were drawing comparisons to Ruth and Gehrig. Mel Allen referred to the hard-hitting duo as "the Gold Dust Twins." Another writer called them "the Buzz-Saw Team." In typical prosaic fashion, Stengel declared: "The fellow in right does the job if the other fellow can't."

In spite of his league-leading 40 homers, Mantle was still feeling the effects of his 1957 World Series injury, which he likened to having a bag of cement dropped on his shoulder. According to Stengel, the slugger developed a permanent hitch in his swing. Mantle's .246 average from the left side (against right-handed pitchers) in 1960 served as compelling evidence that something was wrong. A story began to circulate that he intended to give up switch-hitting, but he promptly dismissed it. "It isn't true," he told a group of writers. "What I said was that if ever I was traded to Washington or Boston, I might consider hitting right-handed all the time. Everyone knows how tough it is to hit homers at Griffith Stadium and Fenway Park. Otherwise, though, I wouldn't think of changing." In the final analysis, it might not have been such a bad idea. He compiled a much higher batting average as a right-handed hitter during his career.

THE ONE THAT GOT AWAY

After a lethargic first-half start, the 1960 Yankees finished eight games ahead of the second-place Orioles. Maris landed among the league leaders in multiple offensive categories, including home runs (39) and RBIs (112). In the end, he captured the AL MVP by a narrow margin over Mantle. The two generated better power numbers than any comparable slugging tandem in the American League.

In the National League, the Pirates returned to the October stage after a seemingly interminable absence. Prior to then, the last World Series game at

Forbes Field had featured the likes of Ruth and Gehrig. The new Pittsburgh lineup was carried by future Hall of Famers Roberto Clemente and Bill Mazeroski, with first baseman Dick Stuart (aka "Dr. Strangeglove") playing a strong supporting role. The pitching staff was bolstered considerably by Roy Face—a durable forkballer who regularly appeared among the NL saves leaders.

Statistics from the 1960 World Series are misleading. Though the Yankees established new postseason records for runs (55), hits (91), and team batting average (.338), they lost in seven games. Mantle ruminated over this for many years, bitterly referring to it as the biggest disappointment of his career.

A majority of the Yankee onslaught took place during Games 2, 3, and 6. During those lopsided contests, the Pirates were outscored by a margin of 38–3. But the resilient Bucs refused to lie down, pushing the Bombers to the brink of elimination. Flexing their own muscles, they roughed up New York pitchers for 10 runs in Game 7. The last at-bat of the Series turned out to be one of the most celebrated moments in baseball history.

Trailing, 7–4, the Pirates exploded for five runs in the bottom of the eighth. The big blow was a three-run homer by Hal Smith that never should have happened. With a runner on first and nobody out, center fielder Bill Virdon hit what appeared to be an easy double play ball to Tony Kubek at short. It took a bad hop and nailed Kubek, who collapsed to the ground clutching his throat. He was rushed to the hospital as the Pirates rallied to take the lead. After the Yankees had tied the score in the top of the ninth, Mazeroski (known more for his sparkling glovework around second base) established himself as an October hero, lifting a homer over the ivy-covered wall in left-center field. He loped around the bases like a jubilant kid, pinwheeling his arms and waving his batting helmet. At home plate, he was mobbed by a throng of frenzied fans. It was the first walkoff homer in a seven-game World Series.

Mazeroski's golden moment was commemorated 50 years later with the dedication of a 12-foot bronze statue outside of PNC Park in Pittsburgh. The former infielder—84 years old by then—was humbled by the tribute, commenting: "How could anyone ever dream of something like this?" It was a fair question. Though Mazeroski was a 10-time All-Star and eight-time Gold Glove Award recipient, he averaged just eight home runs per year during his time in the majors.

Stengel later regretted that he hadn't brought flamethrower Ryne Duren in to face Mazeroski. Instead, he chose to go with breaking-ball specialist

Ralph Terry, who hung a fat pitch in the middle of the strike zone. In another grievous oversight, the Yankee skipper chose not to use Whitey Ford in Game 1. Had Ford appeared in the opener, he would have been available for three starts. Stengel's lapse in judgment was glaringly exposed when Ford tossed a pair of shutouts, beginning a streak of 33.1 consecutive scoreless innings (a postseason record that has survived into the 21st century).

According to Mantle, Stengel's advancing age coupled with the pressure of finishing first every year gradually altered his personality. Instead of pulling players aside to discuss mistakes, he embarrassed them in front of the whole team. And his remarks to the press grew increasingly caustic.

The 1960 affair was Mantle's greatest World Series—on paper at least. Appearing in all seven games, he set personal-high marks with three homers, 11 RBIs, and eight runs scored. Additionally, he batted .400 with a robust .545 on-base percentage. Despite those flashy numbers, it was an October he would have liked to forget. "Even now, 34 years later I get upset when I think about it," he told a biographer in 1994. "There were undercurrents on that Yankee team that were not apparent until later. Maybe the back room maneuvering caught up with us in October."

THE 1961 HOME-RUN RACE

Shortly after the World Series loss to the Pirates, Casey Stengel learned that he would not be receiving a contract extension. A press conference was held at Casey's request to make it official. Asked if he had been fired, the veteran manager told the horde of assembled journalists, "Write anything you want—quit, fired, whatever you please. I don't care." He attributed his dismissal to ageism, famously remarking, "I'll never make the mistake of being seventy again."

Reminiscing over Stengel's departure, Whitey Ford wrote in his 1977 autobiography, "Maybe Casey started getting a little uptight as the seasons went by because we couldn't keep on winning every year and people started second-guessing him more.... But I don't remember us older guys on the ballclub getting too uptight. We were just getting older like Casey was.... And we didn't know why the hell everybody else was getting so nervous."

Stengel's replacement was a former catcher named Ralph Houk, who had appeared in 91 games with the Yankees between 1947 and 1954. He was appointed manager of New York's American Association affiliate in 1955, guiding the club to three consecutive playoff appearances. He returned to the Bronx as a first base coach in 1958. Describing Houk's on-field persona, shortstop Joe DeMaestri commented, "Having played many years for the Yankees, Houk really liked his players. And even if you went out there and did something stupid and got kicked out of a game, he'd fight for you. Everybody liked him because of that. He was a player's manager."

One of Houk's first acts as Yankee skipper was to discontinue the platoon system. Every member of the Yankee infield (with the exception of catcher Elston Howard) appeared in at least 140 games at one primary position. Whitey Ford was given a heavier workload—a role he gladly accepted. And Roger Maris was moved to the third slot in the batting order. The results were dramatic as the Yankees won 109 games—their highest single-season total since 1927.

With Mantle hitting behind him, Maris saw more good pitches than ever before. Opposing hurlers figured it was better to work on Maris than to put him on base with Mantle coming to the plate. Even so, Maris still managed to draw 94 walks—none of them intentional. In comparison, Mantle led the league with 126 free passes—nine of which were premeditated.

There was little indication in the early going that the two Yankee sluggers would battle each other for the most coveted record in sports. Maris got off to a slow start, finishing the month of April with just one home run to Mantle's seven. But by the end of June, both players were on pace to challenge Babe Ruth's long-standing single-season mark of 60 homers. From that point on, the daily activities of New York's "M & M Boys" became front-page news.

A veteran of 10 major-league seasons, Mantle had learned how to handle reporters, offering short, humorous answers to their persistent queries. In sharp contrast, Maris was unaccustomed to being the center of attention. He was too frank with writers at times and grew increasingly resentful of having to answer the same questions day in and day out. This was glaringly evident in his combative responses.

At the beginning of August, the home-run race was in full swing with Mantle trailing by a narrow margin. By then, Maris had come to be painted as a villain—an arrangement that actually benefited Mantle. "[Mickey] was supposed to hit a thousand home runs," said third baseman Clete Boyer. "When he didn't, fans got on him. Roger took the pressure off Mickey. They never booed Mickey again. It became good guy, bad guy. The press, everybody wanted Mickey Mantle to break Babe Ruth's record."

Making matters worse, the relationship between the two men was inaccurately portrayed as hostile. "There was a lot written that we didn't like each other—that we argued a lot, or fought a lot or something," Mantle later said.

"That's the farthest thing from the truth … Roger was one of my closest friends and we used to just joke about all the headlines that said we were fighting and arguing and mad at each other."

Early in the season, Maris began sharing an apartment in Queens with Bob Cerv. Realizing the immense pressure that Maris was under, Mantle accepted an offer to move in with them. He became a constant source of advice and support in the months that followed. The arrangement was mutually beneficial, since the suite Mantle had been renting at the Hotel St. Moritz was exorbitantly expensive.

The American League expanded to 10 teams in 1961 as the Senators moved to Minnesota and became the Twins. The Los Angeles Angels made their AL debut along with a new Washington club (which turned out to be even worse than the previous one). To keep the schedule balanced, the season was extended from 154 to 162 games. Looking to preserve the integrity of Ruth's landmark achievement, commissioner Ford Frick announced that if the 60-homer mark was surpassed in more than 154 games, the new record would be listed separately in the books. The declaration served to increase Maris's stress level.

By mid-August, the M & M Boys were even at 45 homers apiece. As the competition dragged on into September, even Mantle began to show signs of wear, developing flu-like symptoms during a late-season road trip. Yankee broadcaster Mel Allen talked him into seeing a doctor named Max Jacobson, who catered to high-profile celebrities.

Known to patients as "Miracle Max" or "Dr. Feelgood," Jacobson became infamous for his "vitamin shots," which were laced with powerful central nervous system stimulants. The shot he administered to Mantle penetrated the slugger's hip bone, causing excruciating pain. Mickey reportedly grew delirious on the way home and ended up in Lenox Hill Hospital with a massive abscess that had to be drained and lanced. "I spent the last week and a half of the season watching from my hospital bed," he later wrote. "That made the pressure twice as bad on Roger, because there was only one guy that the reporters could come to."

With his hair falling out in clumps, Maris persevered, tying Ruth's record in his 158th game of the season. He launched his 61st homer on the first of October. Summing up his trying experience decades later, an embittered Maris said: "They acted as though I was doing something wrong—poisoning the record books or something. Do you know what I have to show for 61 home runs? Nothing. Exactly nothing."

Mantle and Roger Maris were dubbed the "M & M Boys" by members of the New York media. In 1961, they staged an epic slugging duel that ended with Maris breaking Babe Ruth's single-season record for home runs. Maris finished with 61 homers while Mantle, who missed the latter part of the season due to illness, hit 54—the highest single-season total of his career. (Courtesy of The Leslie Jones Collection: Boston Public Library)

Mantle's 54 homers in 1961 were a personal record. His numbers tapered off considerably in the seasons that followed. The doctor responsible for putting him out of action during the epic duel with Maris was exposed by a *New York Times* reporter and subsequently charged with fraud and unprofessional conduct. By 1975, Dr. Feelgood was no longer practicing medicine.

WATCHING IT FROM THE BENCH

For many Americans, the 1961 home-run race served as a diversion from unpleasant events happening around the globe. In Germany, a wall was built to prevent residents of Soviet-controlled East Berlin from escaping to the West. In Cuba, a CIA-funded invasion at the Bay of Pigs was an utter disaster, ultimately bringing the United States to the brink of nuclear war with the Soviet Union. In Israel, shadows of the Holocaust were still omnipresent as former Nazi leader Adolf Eichmann was sentenced to death for crimes against humanity. The surrounding media coverage led to a heightened awareness of the Jewish experience during World War II.

While Yankee fans were busy watching the M&M Boys, a number of other fine performances went virtually unnoticed. Whitey Ford enjoyed the most successful season of his career, gathering 25 victories and capturing the Cy Young Award. Ralph Terry rebounded nicely from his disastrous World Series performance the previous year, posting a 16-3 record and 3.15 ERA (among the top marks in the AL). Six Yankee players reached the 20-homer plateau as the Bombers outslugged every team in the majors on their way to another pennant.

Though the Cincinnati Reds were predicted to finish in the second division, outfielders Vada Pinson and Frank Robinson formed a potent one-two punch, combining for more than 50 homers and 200 RBIs. Four Cincinnati hurlers finished with double-digit win totals as the Reds captured their first NL championship in over 20 years.

Exhausted both mentally and physically from his harrowing ordeal during the regular season, Maris had a poor World Series, managing just two hits in 19 at-bats. Mantle—still weak from the abscess in his hip—was forced to sit out the first two games. After repeatedly pestering manager Ralph Houk for playing time, he made a lackluster appearance in Game 3, going 0-for-4 at the plate with a pair of strikeouts.

Before the fourth meeting, Mantle squabbled with Houk over his physical condition. The Yankee skipper consulted with team physician Sidney Gaynor, who insisted that there was no risk of permanent injury if Mantle played. Against his better judgment, Houk inserted the ailing slugger into the lineup. In the top of the fourth, Mantle hit a screaming liner off the wall in left-center field. It should have been an easy double, but he pulled up at first base in a cold sweat with blood trickling down his leg. When the gauze was removed from the wound, his hip bone was visible through a hole that was allegedly big enough to fit a golf ball in. The Yankees won, 7–0, behind the strong pitching of Whitey Ford, who broke Babe Ruth's long-standing postseason record of 29.2 consecutive scoreless innings.

With Mantle out for the remainder of the series and Maris barely making an impact, new October heroes were born. Outfielder Hector López drove in seven runs in four appearances. Utility man Johnny Blanchard blasted a pair of homers and compiled a .400 batting average, while first baseman Moose

Skowron hit .353 with five RBIs. Reflecting on his own minimal contributions in the Yankees' five-game Series victory, Mantle remarked: "It was really a proper ending. Two guys had hogged the headlines all year and now some of the others had a chance to shine." In his 1994 memoirs, he referred to the 1961 Yankees as his favorite squad. Likewise, Houk later commented that 1961 was his favorite year in baseball.

AFTERGLOW

Ralph Houk kept the Yankee lineup virtually intact in 1962 with the exception of left field, which had been patrolled primarily by an aging Yogi Berra, who could no longer handle the physical demands of catching at the age of 36. A year older and a bit less durable, Berra drew just 59 defensive assignments during the 1962 campaign—28 as an outfielder. In his place, Houk used Hector López, Jack Reed, and Joe Pepitone to fill the gaps. In the pitching department, Houk implemented a three-man rotation with Whitey Ford, Ralph Terry, and Bill Stafford carrying a majority of the workload. Right-handers Jim Bouton and Rollie Sheldon started 16 games apiece, but neither was terribly effective as indicated by their combined 4.69 ERA.

Shortly after the departure of Casey Stengel, GM George Weiss announced his retirement—an event Mantle said he celebrated by pouring himself a stiff drink. His replacement, Roy Hamey, was far more accommodating in negotiations, handing Mantle a $20,000 pay raise before the season was underway. The slugger's $90,000 salary was the highest he had ever drawn as a ballplayer.

It was a rough year for Roger Maris. Relentlessly harassed by Ruth and Mantle fans wherever he went, he remained distant and hostile to the writers who had unfairly colored him as an insufferable boor during his chase for immortality. He caught even more flack when he refused to pose for a picture with Rogers Hornsby during spring training. The snub was based on some comments the surly Hall of Famer had made during the heat of the 1961 home-run race, when he called Maris a "bush leaguer" and said that he had no right to break Ruth's record.

The defamation of Maris continued to work in Mantle's favor. "I could do no wrong," the Yankee icon remembered. "Everywhere I went, I got standing ovations. All I had to do was walk out on the field. . . . I became the underdog. They hated him and liked me."

In addition to a number of lucrative endorsement deals, the M & M Boys were paid $25,000 apiece to play themselves in the Columbia Pictures comedy/drama, *Safe at Home!*. Directed by Walter Doniger, the sequences involving Mantle and Maris were filmed over a three-day period at the Yankees' training camp in Fort Lauderdale. The set was packed with non-essential people throughout the shoot, and Doniger repeatedly had to prompt visitors to be quiet before filming. One member of the movie crew remarked sourly, "I've heard of guests on a movie set, but this is ridiculous." The two Yankee sluggers remained cordial until the very end, when they finally grew tired of answering relentless questions from a group of boisterous Little Leaguers who had been cast as extras. "I've never seen such a business," Mantle complained to Maris during a rare moment of solitude. "Seems you stand around all day doing nothing and then do about five minutes of the show." It wasn't the first movie appearance for the Yankee duo. Both had landed cameo roles in the Universal Pictures comedy, *That Touch of Mink*, starring Cary Grant and Doris Day.

Though his adventures in the batter's box overshadowed his defense, Mantle was an exceptional center fielder in his prime. He posted the highest fielding percentage among players at his position twice during his career. He finally won a Gold Glove in 1962. In this photo, he is chasing a ball in the gap. Yogi Berra is backing him up on the play. (Courtesy of The National Baseball Hall of Fame)

When the regular season began, Mantle came flying out of the gate, compiling a .333 batting average through May 15. Three days later, he pulled a hamstring in his right leg while attempting to beat out an infield hit. As he continued up the first base line, he tore ligaments in his left knee. He was out for a month, but returned in style, smashing a three-run pinch-hit homer off of Indians hurler Gary Bell. He scored 69 runs and stole seven bases (without getting caught) in the wake of the debilitating injury.

Despite sitting out 39 games, Mantle received his third MVP nod. It was a curious choice considering Harmon Killebrew's 48 homers and Leon Wagner's strong performance with the second-year Angels. Though Mantle posted the highest slugging percentage in the league, his detractors complained that he lagged behind the AL leaders in all three Triple Crown categories. Responding to their criticism, Yankee publicist Jackie Ferrell made reference to Mantle's resilience in the face of pain and adversity. "What did he lead the league in? Manhood, that's what," said Ferrell.

THE LAST HURRAH

After spending four years in the oddly proportioned LA Memorial Coliseum (which was jointly occupied by the LA Rams and USC Trojans), the Dodgers finally moved to their own home in Chavez Ravine in 1962. They spent close to three months in first place before stumbling in the final week of the season. A three-game series was necessary to break a tie with the Giants, who captured the pennant behind solid pitching performances from Billy Pierce and Juan Marichal.

In the American League, the Minnesota Twins made their first legitimate playoff bid since their days as the Washington Senators. Jim Kaat and Camilo Pascual—the club's top starters—combined for 38 wins, keeping the team in contention throughout the summer. In the end, the overachieving Twins fell five games behind New York.

As the Giants and Yankees were preparing for their seventh postseason showdown (the last of the 20th century), a major conflict was brewing between the United States and Soviet Union. In the wake of the Bay of Pigs episode, the Cuban and Soviet governments began secretly building missile bases capable of firing medium- and intermediate-range nuclear missiles at American targets. By early August, the US government began to suspect that something was amiss on the island of Cuba. For 13 days in October, the Russians engaged in a tense military standoff with American leaders. A diplomatic solution was finally reached on October 28—less than two weeks after the final pitch of the 1962 campaign.

The World Series opened at Candlestick Park in San Francisco, which was known for its swirling winds and foggy conditions. Whitey Ford was on-point in Game 1, going the distance in a 6–2 win. But Jack Sanford stifled the Yankee attack in the second meeting, evening the Series with a three-hit shutout. Mantle hit safely just twice in his first 12 plate appearances.

The Yankees scattered five hits in Game 3, making them count for a 3–2 win. Unfazed, the Giants tagged three New York hurlers for seven runs in the fourth contest. The victory came at a tremendous price as Marichal—a future Hall of Famer—injured his thumb attempting a bunt and was lost for the remainder of the series. For Mantle, it was the first of three consecutive hitless performances.

Game 5 was delayed due to rain. After regaining the series lead with a 5–3 win, the Yankees traveled to the West Coast, where torrential downpours pushed the start of Game 6 back by four days. Well rested by then, Billy Pierce tossed a three-hitter for the Giants. It was a rough day on the hill for Ford, who lasted just 4.2 innings and surrendered five runs—one of them on account of his own errant pickoff attempt.

The series finale was a pitchers' duel between Sanford and Ralph Terry. The only run of the game was scored on a double play ball hit by Tony Kubek in the fifth inning. Terry retired the first 17 batters he faced before yielding a single to Sanford in the bottom of the sixth. In the ninth, Matty Alou led off with a successful bunt. After a pair of strikeouts by Felipe Alou (Matty's older brother) and Chuck Hiller, Willie Mays launched a double into the right field corner. Out of respect for Maris's powerful arm, Alou held up at third base. Terry tried to handcuff the next batter—left fielder Willie McCovey—with an inside fastball, but the slugger adjusted his swing, ripping a hard liner toward a perfectly positioned Bobby Richardson, who put it away for the final out of the series. McCovey later said it was the hardest ball he ever hit. Marichal was in agreement, commenting, "I won't say he caught the ball. The ball caught him."

From a statistical standpoint, the 1962 October Classic was Mantle's worst. He finished with three hits in 25 at-bats, failing to drive in a single run. During the series-clincher, a Giants fan shouted at him from the bleachers, "I came out here to see which one of you guys was the better centerfielder. But it looks like I have to decide which one is worse. Hey, Mantle, you win!"

Mantle is seen here clowning around with (from left to right) catcher Johnny Blanchard and pitcher Bob Turley. Blanchard enjoyed his most successful season in 1961, slamming 21 homers in 93 games. Turley peaked in 1958, capturing the Cy Young Award and World Series MVP honors. (Courtesy of The Leslie Jones Collection: Boston Public Library)

The mouthy fan was comparing Mantle to Mays, who didn't fare much better than his AL counterpart, hitting just .250 with one RBI.

The 1962 campaign was like a farewell tour for Mantle in many respects. It was the last time he would capture a World Series ring, win an MVP award, and lead the league in a major slugging category. The Gold Glove Award he received was the first and only one of his career. Though he was just 31 years old by season's end, his body was breaking down on him rapidly. He had reached his peak as a player. And there was nothing left for him but a slow fade.

THE SHORT SEASON

The spring of 1963 began on a positive note for Mantle. On the strength of his MVP performance, he received another significant pay increase. Recognizing his value to the club and his ability to draw fans to the ballpark, the Yankees kept his annual salary at $100,000 for the remainder of his career.

A major trade in the offseason brought pitcher Stan Williams to New York in exchange for seven-time All-Star Moose Skowron. Williams—a big right-hander at 6-foot-5, 230 pounds—had won 43 games for the Dodgers over the previous three seasons. He would last just two years with the Yankees, posting an underwhelming 10-13 record. Skowron didn't fare much better with the Dodgers, hitting .203 in his LA debut before another trade landed him in Washington.

Filling the hole at first base, Ralph Houk made Joe Pepitone a full-time infielder. Brash, colorful, and supremely confident, Pepitone enjoyed all the perks of his affiliation with the most storied franchise in sports. To make his presence known to women at nightclubs, he would loudly announce to bartenders upon arrival, "If you get any phone calls for Joe Pepitone of the New York Yankees, he's right here." Though "Pepi" had some respectable seasons in pinstripes, he never blossomed into a superstar. "If he had just cared about *anything*, he could have been on top, among the very best," said Mantle. "His downfall? Strangely enough, he never took the game seriously."

Mantle logged three consecutive multi-hit games when the 1963 season began. He stayed relatively hot afterward. On May 22, he blasted a titanic shot off of Bill Fischer of the A's at Yankee Stadium. Had the ball not struck the façade in right field, it would have sailed clear out of the park. The memorable clout came in the wake of a multi-homer performance the previous day.

Through his first 36 games, Mantle was hitting .310 with 11 homers and 26 RBIs. But in a familiar pattern that had come to characterize his career, he suffered a major mishap in the outfield. In a June 5 game against the Orioles at Memorial Stadium, future Hall of Famer Brooks Robinson hit a deep fly to center field. Mantle raced after it at full speed. After the ball had cleared the seven-foot chain-link fence for a home run, Mantle's spikes got caught in the mesh, fracturing his third metatarsal. Though he had played through an assortment of injuries in the past, this one kept him out of action for two full months. Roger Maris carried the team until mid-July, when he was plagued by physical issues of his own.

Mantle recuperated at his home in Dallas before making a trip to Joplin, Missouri, where he visited the Holiday Inn he was part-owner of. He also made an appearance at the local Mickey Mantle League, which had been created to give youngsters who were not chosen for regional Little League teams a chance to play. Returning to the Yankees on August 4, he delivered a clutch pinch-hit homer against the Orioles. Over the next 28 games, he compiled a .309 batting average while drawing 12 walks. He finished the shortest season of his career (65 games) at .314 with 15 homers and 35 RBI.

A LESSON IN HUMILITY

With injuries limiting Mantle and Maris to a combined total of 155 appearances, manager Ralph Houk began using shortstop Tom Tresh and catcher Johnny Blanchard in the outfield. They hit at a mediocre .256 clip, but combined for 41 homers. Elston Howard was a standout both offensively and defensively, becoming the first Black player to win the AL MVP award. With the expansion of the strike zone, batting averages dropped considerably around the league. Only four everyday players exceeded the .300 mark at the plate. Benefiting greatly from this trend, the Yankees got sterling pitching performances from Whitey Ford and Jim Bouton, both of whom reached the 20-win plateau. Ralph Terry added 17 victories of his own as the Bombers built a 10 1/2-game lead over the second-place White Sox.

In the National League, Sandy Koufax enjoyed the first of three Triple Crown seasons, capturing Cy Young and MVP honors. A frequent victim of poor run support, number two starter Don Drysdale was charged with 17 losses in spite of a highly serviceable 2.63 ERA. Ron Perranoski was dominant in relief, notching 16 wins and 21 saves, as the Dodgers captured the NL pennant by six games over the St. Louis Cardinals.

Beyond the world of baseball, the Alcatraz Federal Penitentiary, which had housed some of the most notorious criminals of the 20th century, ceased operations. American astronaut Gordon Cooper made 22 complete orbits around the Earth, completing the longest manned spaceflight in history (to that point). In music, the Beatles recorded their first album, which included enduring classics such as "Love Me Do," "I Saw Her Standing There," and "Twist and Shout."

Newspapers appropriately billed the 1963 World Series as "Yankee Power vs. Dodger Speed." Eight New York players finished with double-digit home-run totals while the fleet-footed LA crew led the majors with 124 stolen bases. Though the Dodgers appeared to have a slight edge in the pitching department, oddsmakers favored the Yankees to win.

Mantle said that he was looking forward to hitting against Koufax. But he was less than enthusiastic about facing Drysdale. An intense competitor with a penchant for brushing back opponents, "Big D" had asserted his dominance over Mantle in a spring training game earlier that year. Realizing that Drysdale would be expecting him to swing away, Mantle reached safely on a bunt. As the ornery right-hander was covering first base, he deliberately stomped on Mantle's foot and barked at him not to pull the same stunt again. The Yankee slugger submissively agreed.

Batting against Koufax had its own set of disadvantages. Though he strenuously avoided throwing at hitters, his fastball topped out around 100 mph and his curve was known to break up to two feet. Hall of Famer Willie Stargell famously complained, "Trying to hit him is like trying to drink coffee with a fork."

In Game 1, Koufax set a new postseason record with 15 strikeouts, victimizing every player in the Yankee lineup at least once with the exception of Clete Boyer and Whitey Ford. "I had not seen stuff like that before," Bobby Richardson said. "By the third time up, I was honestly just trying to hit the first pitch so I wouldn't strike out again. Mantle was in the on-deck circle and when I walked past him, he said, 'No use even going up there.'" The Dodgers coasted along until the eighth inning, when Tresh slammed a two-run homer to deep left field. It was as close as the Bombers would get in a 5–2 loss. After the game, Yogi Berra quipped: "I can see how [Koufax] won 25 games. What I don't understand is how he lost 5."

Mantle's showdown with Drysdale came in the third meeting. By then, the Yankees were facing a two-game deficit. Putting them one step closer to elimination, Drysdale tossed a masterful three-hit shutout. Mantle went 1-for-4 with a pair of strikeouts. On a humorous note, he broke his spring training promise in the second inning, successfully beating out a bunt. There was no retaliation from the petulant Dodger hurler.

After an 0-for-3 showing against Koufax in the opener, Mantle faced him again in Game 4. It was another strong outing for the Dodger southpaw as he scattered six hits and struck out eight. New York trailed, 1–0, until the top of the seventh, when Mantle connected with a letter-high fastball, driving it into the outfield pavilion in left-center field. It was the first time in 34 innings that the Yankees had come from behind to tie the score. The celebration was brief as the Dodgers regained the lead in the bottom of the frame. The Yankees put runners on in the eighth and ninth, but couldn't produce a run as LA completed the sweep.

Humbled by the loss, Mantle remarked, "Humiliating may be too harsh a word, but I can't express how embarrassed we were. The Dodgers certainly deserved the win, but what couldn't be explained was how feeble we were. This kind of pratfall didn't happen to the Yankees."

Several weeks after New York's appalling World Series showing, Americans were jolted by devastating news. On November 22, President John F. Kennedy was shot by a sniper as he was riding in a motorcade through Dealey Plaza in Dallas, Texas. He was rushed to Parkland Memorial Hospital, where he was pronounced dead from multiple wounds. Suddenly, baseball didn't seem all that important anymore.

YOGI AT THE HELM

In late October 1963, Ralph Houk moved to the front office, replacing Roy Hamey as GM. The Yankees promoted Yogi Berra to the position of manager, beginning a turbulent yet successful new chapter in the catcher's career. During his playing days, Berra captured three MVP awards and made 15 consecutive All-Star appearances. His 10 World Series rings are the most by any player. He led the Yankees in RBIs every year from 1949 through 1955, and was behind the plate for three no-hitters—one of them a perfect game.

On a personal level, Berra was a happy-go-lucky guy with a positive attitude and an engaging smile. Viewed by many as a comedian, he became one of the most popular figures in baseball history. In the tradition of Casey Stengel, he was known for taking liberties with the English language. His enduring quotes, which came to be known as "Yogi-isms," have entertained fans for generations. Among the most famous are, "It ain't over 'til it's over," and "Ninety percent of the game is half mental."

Though the connection between Berra and the popular cartoon character Yogi Bear has never been definitively established, Berra tried to sue Hanna-Barbera Productions for defamation of character (he was later persuaded to drop the suit). With his short, paunchy appearance and bushy eyebrows, he looked a bit like a caricature himself. His homely facial features prompted him to memorably comment, "So, I'm ugly. So what? I never saw anyone hit with his face."

Mantle referred to Berra as "a gentle soul" and cited his primary managerial weakness as being too lenient. "He didn't have the heart to bawl out the players who deserved it. Plus, it was especially hard when he got around to me and Whitey [Ford]. We had played with him all those years and, when the chips were down, he could count on us to give him whatever help he needed. The thing is, he never demanded it. He was too proud. He'd come over to me in the dugout, still acting like the old teammate."

Ford had mostly positive things to say about Berra's brief time as manager. "I thought Yogi did a hell of a job," he wrote in his memoirs. "I thought he got screwed. You know, everybody counted us out of the pennant race after we blew the series with the White Sox in late-August. But we played like crazy in September and made it. Yogi was a good baseball man. He deserved to stay."

Ford was referring to a four-game series that took place at Comiskey Park from August 17 through August 20. The Yankees ended up getting swept, falling 4 1/2 games behind Chicago in the standings. On the ride to O'Hare Airport from the ballpark, Mantle inadvertently stirred up trouble for Berra. Mickey and some of his teammates had smuggled beer onto the bus, which was against the rules that Yogi had been lax about enforcing. As players sat ruminating over the disastrous turn the season had taken, infielder Phil Linz took out a harmonica and began playing it. New to the instrument, his crude rendition of "Three Blind Mice" quickly grated on Berra's nerves. In Mantle's retelling of the story, Yogi whipped his head around and growled, "Hey, Linz—stick that harmonica up your ass!" Linz stopped playing briefly and asked Mantle what Berra had said. Mantle replied impishly: "He said play it louder." When Linz resumed playing, Yogi stormed down the aisle and slapped the harmonica out of his hands. It struck Joe Pepitone on the knee, prompting a round of histrionics. By that point, players on the bus were laughing hysterically, which was inappropriate given the fact that they had just lost four in a row.

Mantle observed that something positive came of the incident. "In our eyes, it was the first time Yogi showed all of us his leadership qualities. It was the turning of the tide." Yankee executives saw things differently, believing that Berra had lost control of the team and had failed to win the respect of players. His job remained in jeopardy from that point forward. "I think the Yankee brass decided to fire me no matter what happened," Berra wrote in his 1989 autobiography. "I think they didn't think I could manage. I thought I could."

Mantle enjoyed his last great offensive campaign in 1964, launching 35 home runs and driving in 111 runs. As usual, he missed three weeks of action with various maladies. But he was a dangerous hitter whenever he was in the lineup, accruing a handsome .383 batting average with runners in scoring position. He feasted on White Sox pitching, hitting .400 in 14 games. Aside from the August sweep in Chicago, the Yankees compiled a 12-2 record against their Windy City rivals.

GOING OUT WITH A BANG!

In the turbulent year of 1964, North Vietnamese torpedo boats attacked the USS *Maddox* in the Gulf of Tonkin, prompting an official declaration of war. After a nine-month investigation of the JFK assassination, the Warren Commission released its findings, asserting that gunman Lee Harvey Oswald had acted alone. Albert DeSalvo, a former military police sergeant, ended a two-year reign of terror when he confessed to the infamous "Boston Strangler" murders. On a triumphant note, President Lyndon B. Johnson signed the Civil Rights Act into law, making it illegal to discriminate against others based on race, religion, sex, national origin, or skin color.

Berra's managerial debut was a success as he steered the Yankees to their fifth consecutive pennant. Though the Orioles and White Sox proved to be tough competitors, a remarkable 22-6 September stretch run (which included an 11-game winning streak) pushed the Bombers over the top. Mantle finished second in MVP voting to Orioles third baseman Brooks Robinson, who enjoyed the most productive offensive season of his career.

The National League race was a four-way dogfight between the Cardinals, Reds, Phillies, and Giants. In June, the Cardinals benefited from one of the most lopsided trades in history, acquiring future Hall of Fame outfielder Lou Brock from the Cubs in a deal involving five other players. Brock hit .348 in 103 games with St. Louis while Ken Boyer and Curt Flood both had spectacular campaigns, combining for nearly 400 hits. After sinking as low as eighth place in the first half, the Cardinals won nine of their last 11 games, clinching the pennant on the final day of the regular season.

Prior to 1964, the Yankees had faced the Cardinals four times in the World Series, winning twice. The new chapter of the rivalry featured a friendly clash between Yankee third baseman Clete Boyer and his older brother, Ken. (Cloyd—a third member of the clan—had pitched for the Cardinals during the early 1950s.) The sibling duo put up similar offensive numbers during the series, but it was the elder Boyer who came away with a ring.

Though few could have predicted it, the Yankees were on the verge of a lengthy pennant drought. Looking like a younger version of himself, Mantle was a force to be reckoned with in his October farewell, reaching base in every game while hitting .333. On the downside, the cumulative effect of multiple injuries made him a liability in the outfield. The Cardinals ran on him every chance they got, scoring several runs on account of his fading defensive skills.

The Yankees suffered a major blow when Whitey Ford—baseball's all-time postseason wins leader—came up with a lame arm after an unsuccessful appearance in Game 1. He was lost for the rest of the Series. Right-handed strikeout specialist Bob Gibson tossed five strong innings in the second meeting, but lost his effectiveness after that. The Yankees tagged him for four runs on eight hits, then padded their lead significantly against the St. Louis bullpen. Mantle scored two runs and drove in a pair as New York evened the Series with an 8–3 win.

The third contest was a tight pitching duel between Curt Simmons and Jim Bouton. With the game tied at 1 in the bottom of the ninth, St. Louis manager Johnny Keane called upon right-handed knuckleballer Barney Schultz to face Mantle. The veteran slugger got the best of the encounter, driving a pitch into the third deck in right field for the game-winner. The blast broke a tie with Babe Ruth for most postseason homers. It was also a called shot—of sorts.

Assigned to right field, Mantle's defensive woes persisted in the fifth inning of Game 3, when his miscue on a single by Tim McCarver led to the only St. Louis run of the afternoon. In the top of the ninth, he misjudged a line drive hit by Curt Flood and stumbled making the catch. Brooding over his misadventures in the outfield, Mantle told Elston Howard on his way to the plate that he intended to hit the first pitch thrown to him out of the ballpark. That's exactly how the game ended.

Taking advantage of shaky pitching and untimely errors, the Cardinals won the next two meetings, grabbing a 3–2 Series lead. But the Yankees refused to go quietly, tying the Series with an 8–3 win. The highlight of the game came in the sixth inning, when Mantle and Maris launched back-to-back homers.

Game 7 was an uphill battle for New York, as the Cardinals built a 6–0 lead by the end of the fifth inning. Mantle's 18th and final postseason homer was a three-run shot off of Gibson. Clete Boyer and Phil Linz went deep in the ninth, but the Yankees ultimately fell short. It was the third postseason failure for the Bombers in their last four tries, and it led to the firing of Berra.

Cardinals catcher Tim McCarver later credited second-string backstop Bob Uecker for the St. Louis win. "If [Uecker] had not been on the Cardinals, then it's questionable whether we could have beaten the Yankees. He kept everything so funny that we never had the chance to think of what a monumental event we were taking part in." Uecker's comedic exploits began during warmups before Game 1, when he fielded balls with a trombone he had borrowed from a local band that played at Busch Stadium. According to McCarver, Uecker was charged for damage to the instrument—a bill that St. Louis owner Gussie Busch refused to pay. In contrast, the Yankees appeared lifeless during the Series. "[They] were so blasé, so professional, it was disgusting," said Linz. "There was no display of emotion."

THE YANKEES IN DECLINE

Hoping to bring a championship back to New York, Yankee executives hired Cardinals skipper Johnny Keane to replace Yogi Berra. A lifetime minor leaguer, Berra's successor had played 15 seasons as a shortstop and third baseman, never progressing beyond the Double-A level. Described by Whitey Ford as a "straight and serious man," Keane believed that another pennant was a foregone conclusion. Before the season began, he told reporters, "I know this is a sound and powerful ballclub. A man would be a fool if he started changing things around." He had no idea that the Yankees were on the brink of collapse.

Mantle resented Keane from the start, commenting in his 1985 autobiography, "We were used to Casey and Ralph, who didn't even have a curfew, and Yogi, who didn't really enforce one. Now all of a sudden, here's this guy coming in like a drill sergeant with a curfew and everything." Whenever Keane suspected that Mantle had been out the night before, he worked the veteran slugger extremely hard during practice. One day, in the wake of a late-night bender, Mantle was forced to shag flyballs for well over an hour without a break. He grew so irritated that he rifled a throw directly at Keane's head. Fortunately, the Yankee skipper was able to dodge the incoming missile.

Mantle was certain that Keane was a bad fit for the club, commenting to a writer, "[He] might have been a good manager, but he wasn't right for the Yankees. He brought a coach with him and the two of them kept to themselves, almost as though we were on opposite sides. Instead of being our leader, he seemed to be working against us."

Plagued by past injuries, Mantle struggled all season long. Cortisone shots in his right leg provided only temporary relief, and he was moved to left field due to his limited range. The shoulder he had injured in the 1957 World Series continued to deteriorate as well. In and out of the lineup all year, he managed just 19 homers and 46 RBIs. His batting average was an uncharacteristic .255.

Mantle wasn't the only player sidelined with physical issues. Roger Maris sustained a broken bone in his wrist. When Keane tried to play him anyway, he threatened to quit the team. He missed a majority of the second half, barely making his presence known in 46 games.

There were other weak spots as well. Though Joe Pepitone provided stellar defense at first base, he failed to provide the offensive punch the Yankees needed, driving in a modest total of 62 runs. At 36 years of age, Elston Howard showed signs of slowing down, compiling a flimsy .233 batting average. His infield mates—Tony Kubek and Bobby Richardson—weren't much better, combining for a .237 batting mark.

Summarizing the Yankees' 1965 campaign, researcher Glenn Stout wrote: "When the usual injuries started piling up, the aging team became unsound and not very powerful. They grunted their way through spring training and into April, and this time there was no depth to fall back on, no Gil McDougalds available to fill in wherever needed, no Roger Marises available in a trade."

Among the few bright spots, pitcher Mel Stottlemyre—playing in his first full season—gathered 20 wins and led the American League with 18 complete games. He remained one of the most reliable members of the starting rotation for nearly a decade. Upon retiring in 1974, he moved on to a long, successful career as a Yankee coach.

Ford's World Series injury in 1964 was career-threatening. A major artery in his left arm was completely blocked, cutting off the circulation and leaving him without a pulse in his pitching hand. A procedure was performed in the offseason to restore the blood flow. Though he returned to the mound and won 16 games, he posted the highest ERA of his career. He also experienced periodic numbness in his fingers during starts. To counteract the effects, he got in the habit of warming his hand with a hot water bottle. A second operation after the 1965 campaign repaired the damage, but he was finished as a full-time pitcher by then. In his last two seasons with the Yankees, he posted a 4-9 record in 29 appearances.

As Mantle began to demonstrate obvious symptoms of decline, the Yankees stepped up their efforts to find a replacement. Bobby Murcer—another Oklahoma native who would successfully switch from shortstop to the outfield—batted .322 for Greensboro of the Carolina League before making his September debut. Roy White, a slick-fielding outfielder with exceptional speed, was called up from Columbus in the same week. Both would provide years of reliable service to the Yankees, but neither would enjoy the same level of success as Mantle.

The Yankees wallowed in sixth place throughout the second half, prompting members of the New York press to advocate for the return of Casey Stengel, who left the Mets in late August due to health concerns. No matter how much magic Casey had left in him, it's almost certain he could not have saved the Yankees from a second-division finish. They posted a 77-85 record—their first sub-.500 showing in 40 years.

On September 18, Mantle's 2,000th game in pinstripes was celebrated at Yankee Stadium. A sellout crowd was on hand to see the fading slugger receive a generous array of gifts that included a new car, a pair of quarter horses, and multiple vacation packages. Joe DiMaggio was recruited to introduce his former teammate, who received a roaring ovation as he walked out onto the field with his family. Multiple photos were snapped of Mantle shaking hands with Senator Robert F. Kennedy that day. One writer referred to the event as "an almost holy day for the believers who had crammed the grandstands early to witness the canonization of a new stadium saint."

A New Low

In November 1965, Mantle severely injured his shoulder playing a game of backyard football against his brothers. A visit to the Mayo Clinic confirmed the presence of calcium deposits and bone chips, which necessitated surgery. He recovered in time for spring training.

The 1966 regular season began on a sour note for the Yankees. After dropping a three-game series to Detroit at home, they traveled to Baltimore, where they lost two of three. A five-game losing streak followed from April 19 through April 25. It was the team's worst start since the Dead Ball Era, and the front office began to panic. When the club dropped to 4-16 on May 6, Johnny Keane was fired and Ralph Houk returned as manager.

Slowed by the offseason surgery, Mantle got off to a lukewarm start. His first homer didn't come until May 9. It was the latest he had ever waited to go deep in any season. He began to find his power stroke after that, gathering home runs in periodic clusters. Facing the Red Sox at Fenway Park on June 28 and 29, he logged a pair of multi-homer games. During a three-game set at Washington, he launched four more blasts, giving him eight in a six-day span.

On May 14 at Municipal Stadium in Kansas City, Mantle's 500-foot bomb cleared the playing field and hit a second fence near the ballpark's outer perimeter—a feat that had never been previously accomplished. There was also a memorable clout off of Bruce Howard at White Sox Park on July 29. Not only did it break a scoreless tie with the ChiSox, but it put Mantle in sixth place on the all-time home-run list ahead of Lou Gehrig. His last RBI of the season was the 1,400th of his career. He finished the campaign with 23 homers and 56 ribbies—not bad considering that he sat out more than 50 games.

With Whitey Ford effectively finished as a pitcher and Roger Maris still nursing a tender wrist, there was little to get excited about in the Bronx. Dan Topping and Del Webb had sold the team to CBS in 1964, but both men retained a 10 percent stake in the club. Webb dumped his remaining shares the following year while Topping held on as acting team president. Realizing that the ship was sinking fast, Topping resigned from his post in September of 1966 and sold the rest of his stock. In his absence, CBS executive Mike Burke assumed the title of president.

The team reached an all-time low on September 22, 1966, when only 413 fans turned up at Yankee Stadium for an inconsequential makeup game against the White Sox. Yankee broadcaster Red Barber fittingly remarked, "I don't know what the paid attendance is today, but whatever it is, it is the smallest crowd in the history of the stadium, and this crowd is the story, not the game." Barber asked the WPIX television crew to film the nearly empty stands, but his request was denied—twice. Apparently, team executives had instructed Perry Smith, the team's TV/radio supervisor, not to focus on the empty ballpark. Displeased with Barber's behavior, Burke called the longtime Yankee announcer into the front office after the game and fired him.

The Yankees finished 26 1/2 games out of the race with the worst record in the American League. Attendance figures were fifth in the AL and the lowest of the decade to that point. Even a second Mickey Mantle Appreciation Day couldn't help the Yankees outdraw their competitors in Baltimore, Anaheim, and Minnesota. Over the course of 16 seasons, Mantle had seen his team go from best to worst.

SEA OF STRANGERS
By the end of the 1967 campaign, the Yankee lineup was virtually unrecognizable. Tony Kubek and Bobby Richardson had both retired. Roger Maris

and Clete Boyer were traded. Whitey Ford pitched his last game on May 21. And Elston Howard bid farewell to the Bronx in August, becoming a member of the Red Sox. Mantle was the only star remaining from the dynasty of the 1950s.

Putting it bluntly, Mantle described the transformation as follows: "Most of the newcomers lacked the talents of my former teammates. . . . Until then, almost everybody came through our organization, all of us climbing the ladder, step by step. . . . Now we were getting ballplayers from everywhere. . . . The overall lack of talent made things a little easier for opposing teams."

To save his ailing knees, the Yankees installed Mantle at first base. He was little more than adequate by his own admission and never felt completely comfortable at the position. Recognizing his shortcomings, opponents tended to go easy on him out of respect for his career accomplishments. Dave Nelson—a speedy infielder who peaked at 51 steals in 1972—recalled an incident from the 1967 campaign in which he deliberately pushed a bunt in Mantle's direction. After easily beating it out, he was informed by his coach that it was against team policy to bunt on Mantle. Describing the events that followed, he told a writer, "So, then I walked back to first base and I'm standing next to Mickey Mantle. I'm looking at the guy's arms and they look like tree trunks and I'm saying 'Man, he's gonna pinch my head off' and then he pats me on the butt and says 'Nice bunt, rook.' And I look at him and say 'Thanks, Mr. Mantle.'"

Despite numerous physical problems, Mantle played in 144 games in 1967. He generated nearly identical power numbers to the previous year, although his batting average was much lower and he struck out nearly twice as often. One of the high points of the season came in a game against the Twins on July 4, when he smashed a pair of homers off of Jim "Mudcat" Grant, passing Mel Ott for sole possession of fifth place on the all-time home-run list. The Minnesota crowd cheered enthusiastically as he rounded the bases the second time.

The Yankees finished the season on a positive note, sweeping a four-game series from the A's at home and successfully avoiding a last-place finish. But there were few if any notable happenings in the Bronx to compete with national headlines. NASA launched the Lunar Orbiter 3 in an effort to find suitable landing sites for upcoming Apollo missions. Thurgood Marshall became the first Black justice appointed to the US Supreme Court. And the war in Vietnam was escalating with more than 475,000 troops in service. Amidst growing opposition to the conflict overseas, massive antiwar demonstrations were held in a number of cities. The world was changing and the Yankees were changing with it—not necessarily for the better.

END OF AN ERA

The addition of four expansion teams in the early 1960s seriously diluted the major-league talent pool. Alarmed by a surge in offense, owners from both leagues agreed to expand the strike zone in 1963. Over the next several seasons, the balance of power shifted dramatically in favor of pitchers. Never was this more apparent than in 1968, when a combined total of 339 shutouts were thrown. Bob Gibson set a modern record with a 1.12 ERA, while Denny McLain of the Tigers became the first hurler since Dizzy Dean to win more than 30 games. It was during this offensive implosion that Mantle embarked upon his final regular-season tour.

The Mantle of 1968 bore little resemblance to the slugger of old. Marty Appel, a former Yankee PR man assigned to answering Mantle's fan mail, remarked, "It was so sad to watch Mick in what would be his final season. No announcement was made, but there was a feeling. It was his fourth straight bad year. What was Mickey Mantle doing hitting .237? And who were these teammates? What was he doing batting behind Andy Kosco?"

Carl Yastrzemski was one of many opponents who noticed the deterioration of Mantle's skills. "I see him swing sometimes and even from the outfield you can see his legs buckle and the way he winces in pain," said the 1968 AL batting champ. "I wince, too. Because it's like seeing your kid in pain and you can feel the pain yourself. That's the way all ballplayers feel about Mantle."

The fact that Mantle was able to play in 144 games again given the woeful state of his physical health was a miracle in itself. As the Yankees crawled to a fifth-place finish in 1968, Mantle continued to blast his way into the record books. On May 6, he passed Ted Williams for fourth place on the all-time home-run list with #522. It came off of Indians fireballer Sam McDowell, who led the majors with 283 strikeouts that year. On September 19, a "gift" homer off McLain at Tiger Stadium lifted Mantle into third place. (Details of the memorable at-bat appear in another section of this book.) Mantle launched the final home run of his career the following day against the Red Sox. At one point during the game, a fan approached him in right field, shaking his hand and then dropping to the ground in an exaggerated gesture of worship.

The three-time AL MVP made his last appearance on September 28 at the age of 36. He finished with 536 homers and a .298 lifetime batting average. Throughout his career, he was his own worst critic. Though he never openly complained about his home-run totals, he was bitter about his cumulative batting mark. "Goddamn!" he said in later years. "To think you're a .300 hitter and end up at .237 in your last season then find yourself looking at a lifetime .298 average—it made me want to cry."

Over the fall and winter of 1968-69, Mantle entertained the possibility of playing one more season. He told inquisitive reporters repeatedly that he wouldn't announce his decision until spring training. Upon arriving in camp, he engaged in candid discussions with Ralph Houk and team president Mike Burke. He made his intentions publicly known at a press conference on March 1. "I'm not going to play baseball anymore," he said. "That's all I know. I can't play anymore. I don't hit the ball when I need to. I can't score from second when I need to. . . . I will never want to embarrass myself on the

Mantle's original Monument Park plaque was presented to him at a Yankee Stadium ceremony in June 1969. A new plaque was installed in August 1996—a year after his passing. The latter is pictured here. (Courtesy of jm cd 303 on Visual Hunt)

field or hurt the club in any way or give the fans anything less than they are entitled to expect from me."

Reacting to the sad but predictable news, journalist Dick Young wrote, "There is much more than muscle in Mantle. There is class and guts, and his own special kind of dignity. And there is enough pride for ten men. I suppose it was the pride, after all, that made him decide he'd had it." Joe DiMaggio sympathized with Mantle, remarking, "I know exactly how Mickey feels. They all told me I had a couple of years left when I quit, but I couldn't bounce back anymore." Mantle admitted to reporters that he was dreading playing another season. Describing his state of mind during the 1968 campaign, he said, "The body starts to go and the mind can't force it to respond. And before you realize it—*poof*—the enthusiasm is gone. It happens to all of us."

BUILDING A LIFE AFTER BASEBALL

In the winter of 1965, Mantle joined the Preston Trail Golf Club in Dallas—a private men's-only resort noted for its "bawdy boy's-club locker-room atmosphere." During one sweltering summer afternoon, Dallas Stars linemates Mike Modano and Brett Hull were said to have played 18 holes in their underwear. Mantle—as the legend goes—once completed the par-72 course naked while using his Cadillac as a golf cart (possibly after losing some kind of bet).

Mickey became a regular at the club, spending several hours on the links almost every day. Although his original handicap was 13, he pared it down to 8 in the years that followed. "He had the worst grip and worst set-up you ever saw," said one of Mantle's frequent golf partners. "You'd watch him take a cut at the ball and think, 'this clown can't beat anyone.' But he was the most competitive guy I ever played with. He got everything out of his game that he could." True to form, Mickey was known for his periodic tantrums. He sometimes snapped the heads off of clubs or threw them into water hazards after making bad shots. But of all the luminaries who have played at Preston Trail over the years (a list that includes Jack Nicklaus, Arnold Palmer, and Lee Trevino), Mantle remains the most revered. A shrine honoring him still stands in the clubhouse.

Mantle engaged in a number of business pursuits while playing for the Yankees—very few of which were successful. During the 1950s, he was part-owner of a bowling center in Dallas; a billiards hall in Waukesha, Wisconsin; and a hotel in Joplin, Missouri. By the time he retired in the spring of 1969, he had walked away from all three. A number of failed ventures followed—most notably a restaurant chain and a group of menswear outlets. The Mickey Mantle's Country Cookin' restaurants started in Texas and later expanded to Florida and Louisiana, losing an estimated total of $1 million before closing for good in the early 1970s. The men's apparel stores, which grew to 55 individual franchises, were forced to restructure when business began to flounder.

In 1968, advertising mogul George Lois convinced Mantle and New York Jets quarterback Joe Namath to lend their names to an employment agency called "Mantle Men and Namath Girls, Inc." The two cultural icons starred in a series of television ads and made a number of personal appearances to generate business. Though the company's clientele grew rapidly as a result of their efforts, an economic recession resulted in a decrease of available positions to fill. Lois eventually sold the agency and returned to advertising.

Mantle's steadiest income came from endeavors directly related to baseball. It seemed he was always in demand—even after he was finished as a player. On June 8, 1969, the Yankees officially retired his number in a ceremony at Yankee Stadium. More than 61,000 fans turned out to see Mantle deliver a stirring speech that ended with the words, "I've often wondered how a man who knew he was going to die could stand here and say he was the luckiest man in the world. But now I think I know how Lou Gehrig felt."

Later that summer, Mickey and his wife attended a White House reception hosted by President Richard Nixon, who was a self-proclaimed baseball fan. Billy Martin was also on the guest list that evening in addition to the wife of renowned Dodger executive Branch Rickey. During his 1972 reelection campaign, Nixon assembled hypothetical pre- and postwar All-Star teams. Mantle was included on the American League squad along with former teammates Yogi Berra, Elston Howard, and Bobby Richardson.

RETURN TO THE BRONX

In 1970, Mantle was invited to serve as a guest instructor at spring training in Fort Lauderdale. Upon completing his duties, he accepted a position as an *NBC Game of the Week* commentator. The Mets had been outdrawing the Yankees for several years and, in an attempt to boost sagging attendance figures, GM Lee MacPhail asked Mantle to rejoin the club in late August as a first base coach. Dissatisfied with his broadcasting job, Mickey accepted the offer, leaving NBC without formal notice.

Since the Yankees already had Elston Howard at first base, MacPhail's plan called for Mantle to coach the middle three innings while Howard handled the rest. Mickey had built a positive relationship with the former catcher over the years and found the arrangement to be extremely awkward. "He might have felt I was trying to grab his job away," said Mantle. "He never talked about it and I certainly didn't want him to think it."

Mickey lost the jersey he had worn during spring training, putting clubhouse attendant Pete Sheehy in a bind. Sheehy ended up removing the number 15 from Thurman Munson's used jersey and replacing it with a number 7. When Mantle reported to Yankee Stadium on August 30 for his first game as a coach, he found a memo in front of his locker outlining his itinerary. It included a press conference, a meet-and-greet, an autograph session, photos on the field with contest winners, an instructional clinic, and a series of phone interviews. Mantle cursed out loud before realizing that the note was just a prank staged by the PR team. A crowd of 21,000 cheered enthusiastically when he made his official debut in the coach's box. It was a great day all around as Roy White's fifth-inning grand slam lifted New York to a 5–2 win over the Twins.

The Yankees furnished Mantle with a suite at the Hotel St. Moritz. A double door with panes of glass separated the sitting area from the bedroom. One day, Mantle had difficulty getting the door open and ended up smashing his hand through the glass, opening a wound that required stitches.

It didn't take Mickey long to realize that his hiring had been a publicity stunt. "It wasn't for me," he said. "To sign autographs at golf tournaments or show up at father-and-son banquets to give a talk and shake a few hands, that's fine. But to put on a uniform and pretend I was still in baseball, no thanks. As a coach, I felt more like a sideshow attraction at the circus."

Despite his obvious disenchantment, Mantle was able to have a bit of fun on the job. After drawing a leadoff walk one afternoon, Bobby Murcer called for time and asked what Mickey's signs were. The retired slugger jokingly informed Murcer that he was a Libra. Mantle also developed a lighthearted relationship with Munson, offering the rookie catcher ridiculous bits of advice that included detailed instructions on how to put on his uniform. Playing along, Munson got in the habit of facetiously asking Mickey if he had swung properly after every base hit.

At one point during Mantle's return to New York, he was asked to conduct a Q & A session with a group of young fans. Standing on top of the auxiliary scoreboard in left field, he answered their queries and offered assorted nuggets of wisdom. When a teenage girl asked him if she could have his cap, he traded it for the replica she was wearing.

The Yankees played fairly well in 1970, compiling a 93-69 record. Upon clinching second place, they held a party—a highly unusual practice for a team that had won 20 World Series titles. MacPhail's experiment proved to be a failure as the Mets more than doubled Yankee attendance figures in spite of Mantle's presence. Mickey felt bad about displacing Howard and declined an invitation to return as coach in 1971. He held onto his job as a spring training instructor.

INTO THE HALLOWED HALL

In later years, Mantle cited the two biggest moments of his life as the retiring of his uniform number and his induction into the National Baseball Hall of Fame. The latter honor arrived on August 12, 1974. As had so often been the case, it was bittersweet. Just four days earlier, President Nixon had officially resigned from office in the wake of a major political scandal. "I have never been a quitter," he told the American public in a nationally televised speech. "To leave office before my term is completed is abhorrent to every instinct in my body. But as President, I must put the interest of America first."

As millions of Americans worried about the nation's future, Mantle and his family assembled at Cooperstown to celebrate his lifetime achievements on the diamond. The ceremony took place on the back porch of the museum and was attended by a crowd of more than 2,500 fans (a record at the time). Fittingly, the induction class that year included one of his closest friends—Whitey Ford. Negro League great Cool Papa Bell and National League umpire Jocko Conlan were also honored.

The Hall of Fame had only recently begun recognizing Negro League stars, and Bell expressed deep gratitude. "There were a lot of great ones in the Negro Leagues," he told the crowd. "We—Satchel [Paige], [Monte] Irvin, [Roy Campanella], [Buck] Leonard and myself—were the lucky ones. I'm thanking God for letting me smell the roses while I'm still living."

Ford's speech was a bit less serious. "I want to thank my teammates—like Mantle, Roger Maris, and Yogi Berra—for scoring all those runs," he said, "even though Mickey says that if I hadn't thrown so many long fly balls in center field, he could have played 10 years more." The playful remark provoked a burst of laughter from the audience.

When it was Mantle's turn to speak, he mentioned how his father had named him after Mickey Cochrane and joked that he was glad he hadn't received Cochrane's actual birth name of Gordon. He reminisced about growing up poor and chasing baseballs in a pasture with his brothers. He

MICKEY CHARLES MANTLE
NEW YORK A.L. 1951-1968
HIT 536 HOME RUNS.WON LEAGUE HOMER TITLE
AND SLUGGING CROWN FOUR TIMES. MADE
2415 HITS. BATTED .300 OR OVER IN EACH
OF TEN YEARS WITH TOP OF .365 IN 1957.
TOPPED A.L. IN WALKS FIVE YEARS AND
IN RUNS SCORED SIX SEASONS. VOTED
MOST VALUABLE PLAYER 1956-57-62. NAMED
ON 20 A.L. ALL-STAR TEAMS. SET WORLD
SERIES RECORDS FOR HOMERS, 18; RUNS, 42;
RUNS BATTED IN, 40; TOTAL BASES, 123;
AND BASES ON BALLS, 43.

Mantle's Hall of Fame Plaque. He was inducted to Cooperstown on August 12, 1974—just four days after President Richard Nixon officially announced his resignation on national television. Fittingly, Mantle's teammate and longtime friend, Whitey Ford, was enshrined the same year. (Courtesy of Isles Punk Fan on Visual Hunt) acknowledged his mother's efforts in hand-crafting his early uniforms. He also gave credit to scout Tom Greenwade for discovering him. Instead of talking about his 536 home runs and other impressive stats, he pointed out that he had struck out more often than Babe Ruth. He referred to his lifetime strikeout total as a record that would stand forever—an assumption that proved to be incorrect. As of 2022, his career mark of 1,710 whiffs had been surpassed by more than 30 players, including fellow Hall of Famers Willie Stargell, Mike Schmidt, and Reggie Jackson.

Interestingly, Mantle had drafted an alternate speech that was full of salty remarks. One of the milder comments included a shout-out to Hank Bauer for teaching him how to handle hard liquor. He kept the alternate speech folded in his pocket while he delivered the more polished version. He later said that his decision to behave himself that day came out of respect for Ford and members of the Hall itself.

To most baseball insiders, Mantle's first-year selection was a no-brainer. "To us, Mickey Mantle *was* the Yankees," Tony Kubek commented. "You had to see Mickey day after day, year after year, and watch him play on days when his knees hurt so bad that he could barely walk to fully appreciate his greatness as a player."

OUTSIDE LOOKING IN

In 1979, Willie Mays was inducted into the Hall of Fame. At the time, he was working for the Mets as a hitting instructor. Looking to make some money on the side, he signed a contract to become a "goodwill ambassador" for Bally's Park Place Hotel and Casino in Atlantic City. The part-time position required him to do meet-and-greets at various special events. He registered with the gambling commission and was prohibited from wagering as a casino employee. But baseball commissioner Bowie Kuhn decided to make an example of him anyway. Citing MLB's strict policies against gambling, Kuhn forced Mays to leave his position with the Mets and prohibited him from working in baseball.

Mantle found himself in an identical situation in 1983, when he signed a $100,000 contract to do public relations work for the Claridge Hotel and Casino in Atlantic City. Former Yankee GM Lee MacPhail (who had ascended to the AL presidency) tried to warn Mantle about the potential consequences of the deal, but his advice fell on deaf ears. As predicted, Kuhn prohibited the popular Yankee idol from holding any jobs in baseball, including his position as a spring training advisor.

For the next two years, Mantle faithfully carried out his duties at the Claridge. Justifying his decision to keep the job, he said, "People have this picture of me standing outside the casino yelling, 'come on in and gamble,' but in my job I do things for the March of Dimes and the Special Olympics. You know, what I do is not really bad."

Kuhn's days as a commissioner were numbered. Though he had successfully defended the Braves in a lawsuit filed by the city of Milwaukee during his time as a corporate lawyer, he mishandled multiple labor disputes while holding baseball's highest office. In particular, the 1981 baseball strike resulted in the cancellation of more than 700 games while costing team owners an estimated $72 million in revenue. At the end of the 1983 campaign, proprietors from both leagues decided not to renew Kuhn's contract. Peter Ueberroth—who had served as director of the 1984 US Olympic Organizing Committee—was hired as a replacement. One of the first significant moves he made in his new position was to lift the ban on Mays and Mantle. Though he publicly stated that the two Hall of Famers deserved to return to baseball-related activities, he promised that the game would remain "free from any connection between it and gambling."

Informed of the commissioner's decision, Mays told reporters, "This is a happy occasion for Mickey and me to have the ban lifted. I don't think I did anything wrong to leave baseball." Yogi Berra, who had returned to New York as Yankee manager, was in agreement. "It was unfair to begin with," he said. "Owners own race horses. Of course, in the old days, the suspensions would have been justified, but not today."

Interestingly, Kuhn had turned a blind eye to a 1983 Bally's television commercial that included appearances by former Orioles third baseman Brooks Robinson and 1977 Cy Young Award winner Sparky Lyle. They weren't the only high-profile athletes to endorse the popular casino. Hockey great Phil Esposito, basketball icon Walt Frazier, and three-time NFL champion Johnny Unitas had also appeared in the ad.

OFF THE RAILS

In 1981, a New York City–born record producer named Terry Cashman released a song called "Talkin' Baseball," which paid homage to a number of stars from the game's golden era. Cashman's folky tune repeatedly mentioned Mantle, Mays, and Duke Snider in the chorus. Originally released during the 1981 players strike, the popular melody inspired a wave of nostalgia among disillusioned fans who longed for the sport's simpler past. In the years that followed, the baseball trading card industry became a multi-million dollar enterprise. Cashing in on the phenomenon, Mantle began traveling to memorabilia shows all over the country, sometimes receiving tens of thousands of dollars for his appearances. He would later sign a lucrative deal with the Upper Deck Company (a leading sports card manufacturer).

Since people were interested in his story, the former Yankee slugger authored multiple autobiographies with an assortment of cowriters. In 1977, *New York Times* editor Joe Durso collaborated with Mantle and Whitey Ford on a project called *Whitey and Mickey*. In 1985, sportswriter Herb Gluck helped Mantle pen a set of memoirs entitled *The Mick*. Other books followed in subsequent years, including *My Favorite Summer* (with Phil Pepe) and *All My Octobers* (with Mickey Herskowitz).

As it turned out, Mantle was his own greatest asset. But as his postplaying career took off, his personal life began to fall apart. In addition to blackout drinking, he engaged in an ongoing series of extramarital affairs. Evaluating the underlying cause, Tony Castro—author of three Mantle biographies—offered the following insight: "Mantle made no secret of how much he missed baseball and his life in baseball. In Mickey's mind, the women and the drinking were parts of his baseball life he could take with him into retirement. As his body broke down, the ego still needed the sense of conquest that came from being with adoring women."

Naturally, Merlyn suspected for a long time that her husband was sleeping around. But Mickey kept the truth hidden for many years. When irrefutable evidence of his infidelities eventually surfaced, the marriage disintegrated. The couple's separation in 1988 caused Mickey a great deal of anguish. Still, he refused to seek treatment for his chronic alcohol abuse.

Mantle's daily routine included what he jokingly referred to as a "breakfast of champions," which was a beverage composed of Kahlua, brandy, and cream. It wasn't until his twilight years that he admitted how bad the problem had become. "I always took pride in my dependability when I was doing public relations work," he explained. "It was when I had no commitments, nothing to do or nowhere to be that I lapsed into those long drinking sessions. It was the loneliness and emptiness. I found 'friends' at bars and I filled my emptiness with alcohol. In those instances, I was almost totally out of it by early evening. I could hardly talk."

The frequent bouts of heavy drinking led to other problems. On a flight home to Dallas one day, Mantle suffered a highly publicized bout of anxiety. Believing he might be having a heart attack, a flight attendant alertly placed an oxygen mask over his face and instructed the pilot to radio ahead for paramedics. Downplaying the incident, Mantle later joked that a fan had asked him to sign a baseball in the middle of the harrowing episode.

On Christmas Day in 1989, Billy Martin was killed when his truck slid off an icy road into a deep culvert near his farm in Fenton, New York (which is close to Binghamton). Though it was initially assumed that Martin's friend, Bill Reedy, was driving, doubt later surfaced as to whether or not Billy had actually been behind the wheel. The fact that the two men had been drinking was a firmly established fact. Mantle served as a pallbearer at Martin's funeral and, though he was deeply affected by the loss, he minimized the role alcohol had played in his friend's death. "I would like to say something in defense of Bill Reedy," he told a reporter from *Newsday*. "He could drink that whole pickup truck full of beer and not get drunk. I think it wasn't drink but just slick roads." In the same article, Mantle was quoted as saying: "As far as I was concerned, [Martin] was misunderstood terribly. He was like that little cartoon character that walked around with a black cloud over his head. At Billy's roast, I did say that he was the only man alive who could hear someone give him the finger."

Though it was clear in 1989 that Mantle was not yet ready to acknowledge the extent of his drinking problem, he would come to the realization eventually. By then, it was a case of too little, too late.

SOBER AT LAST

By his own admission, Mantle never had a normal father-son relationship with any of his children. He was rarely around during his playing days and continued to travel extensively after his retirement. As his sons grew older, he became a "drinking buddy" to them. Danny—the youngest—frequently accompanied Mantle on business trips. In September 1993, the pair flew to Los Angeles for a series of autograph sessions sponsored by Upper Deck. At some point during the engagement, Danny went AWOL, checking himself into the Betty Ford Center in Rancho Mirage. Angry and unsupportive, Mickey refused to visit him there. "When I found out, my feelings were really jumbled," he later explained. "I was angry and felt betrayed. I told people I thought he shouldn't have spent his money on a problem that wasn't that bad."

Mantle's heavy drinking continued in the months that followed, drawing concern from Upper Deck representatives, who observed the retired slugger slurring his words on multiple occasions. Later that year, Mickey caused a major scene at a charity golf tournament in Georgia. Completely intoxicated, he offended the event's organizers with a series of crude and insensitive remarks. When his handlers told him what he had said, he was deeply ashamed. Upon returning to Dallas, he spoke to his son, Danny, about a possible visit to the Betty Ford Center.

In December 1993, Mantle underwent a full physical exam. The results were unsettling. His red blood cell count was dangerously low, indicating that his liver was likely damaged. An MRI scan confirmed the fact. His doctor informed him that he would eventually need a transplant, and that his next drink could be his last.

Realizing the gravity of the situation, Mantle checked himself into the Betty Ford Center shortly after Christmas. He later claimed that his biggest breakthrough came in grief therapy groups. At one point, he was asked to write a letter to his father. "You talk about sad," he said. "It only took me ten minutes to write the letter and I cried the whole time. . . . I said I missed him and I wished he could have lived to see that I did a lot better after my rookie season with the Yankees. I told him I had four boys . . . and I told him I loved him. I wish I could have told him that when he was still alive."

Mantle lost 10 pounds and began to feel better than he had in a very long time. Clean and sober for the first time in years, he returned to his home in Dallas. But in an all-too familiar pattern, his moment of personal triumph was followed by devastating news. In 1977, Mickey's son Billy had been diagnosed with Hodgkin's disease. A series of invasive procedures (including the removal of his spleen) had kept the disease under control for many years. But an addiction to prescription drugs and alcohol took a major toll on his heart. Just weeks after Mantle's discharge from rehab, Billy died of a heart attack. "I wish it had been me," Mickey wrote in his journal. "I wish I could have taken the cancer from him. I could not help but think, and still think, that if I had stopped drinking earlier, if I had cleaned up my act, I might have been able to help Billy."

Several positive things came in the wake of Billy's death. United in their grief and committed to maintaining their sobriety, Mickey and Merlyn put aside their marital differences, growing close again. Inspired by Billy's cautionary tale, David—the second-oldest of the Mantle sons—successfully completed rehab. Mickey Jr. would follow not long afterward.

MAKING AMENDS

Feeling regretful about the way he had neglected his family over the years, Mantle offered apologies all around and tried to make himself more accessible to loved ones. He also sought to improve his public image, speaking candidly about his addiction on TV with sportscaster Bob Costas. Asked if he had ever played baseball drunk, he recounted a story about a night out on the town with Detroit Lions quarterback Bobby Layne. Mantle was in rough shape the following afternoon, skipping pregame practice at Tiger Stadium. "I could have hurt the team that day," he admitted, "but the first time up, I took the first pitch right down the middle and I yelled at the umpire. . . . I just made him kick me out of the game because I had no business being in that game."

There were other revelations.

Mantle shared a recurring dream he had experienced for several years after his retirement. In it, he was standing outside Yankee Stadium trying to gain access to the field. "I could hear Casey and the team out there playing and all the gates were locked and I had to try to sneak through a hole in the fence to get into the ballpark," he recalled. "And then if I did get in, I'd hit a ball that should have been a hit and I couldn't run. The outfielder would throw me out. Weird things were going on in my mind all the time."

The interview got very emotional when Mantle began to talk about his sons. He expressed deep remorse over the fact that he hadn't been there for them like his own father had been for him. He stated his intention of spending more time with them and opened up about his difficulty forming close personal relationships during his lifetime. In one of the most moving segments of the interview, he said wistfully, "Maybe I do in the back of my mind feel like I've let everybody down some way or another. I know there is something in there that's not fulfilled, but I don't know what it is. I can't explain it."

The Costas interview was followed by a revealing article for *Sports Illustrated*, which Mantle wrote himself. In it, he came across as a negligent father and a sloppy drunk. Despite his promise to be a better person moving forward, Upper Deck began to limit his personal appearances. In November 1994, Mickey filed a lawsuit claiming that the popular trading card manufacturer had discriminated against him on account of his illness. In a prepared statement, Mantle's Dallas-based lawyer, Roy True, asserted, "Mickey is hurt and disappointed that Upper Deck would attempt to stoop to this level in order to deprive him of the money guaranteed to him." In turn, the company tried to absolve itself of the blame. "The discussions regarding restructuring Mr. Mantle's contract were the product of his disability and other performance related concerns. In short, Mr. Mantle has failed to live up to his commitment as an executive spokesperson for the company."

In the end, Mantle received a settlement totaling close to $5 million. Unfortunately, the case was not decided until 1998, and he wasn't around to enjoy it. Upper Deck really missed the boat in severing ties with Mantle. Though the Yankee icon never understood his enduring popularity, his cards and autographs have continued to be the most sought after pieces of memorabilia in the industry.

FINAL SWINGS

In the spring of 1995, Mantle began experiencing severe stomach pains. He ended up at Baylor University Medical Center, where tests revealed a host of serious ailments. Not only was he afflicted with hepatitis C, but he had cirrhosis and cancer of the liver. A tumor was blocking his bile duct, causing his stomach to fill with bacteria. Doctors told him that he would die without a transplant.

Surgery was performed on June 8—just a couple of days after Mantle was placed on the transplant list. Because the waiting period was typically longer, there were those who complained that he had unfairly received special treatment on account of his celebrity status. Squelching some of the ongoing controversy, Goran Klintmalm—head of the Baylor Transplant Institute—explained that Mantle was the only critically ill patient in North Texas whose blood type matched the liver that became available.

Though the transplant procedure was initially believed to be a success, complications soon arose as new cancer cells spread beyond the affected bile duct. Mantle was given medications to prevent his body from rejecting the new liver and also placed on a regimen of chemotherapy. He lost an alarming amount of weight, appearing emaciated and frail.

In subsequent interviews, Mickey warned children not to follow his example and stated bluntly that he was not a good role model. He also talked about starting up an organ donation program to help people in situations similar to his own. "I think God had a purpose for letting me have this extra time," he said. "Let's get a team of people together and see what we can do." The idea came to fruition with the establishment of the Mickey Mantle Foundation—a nonprofit organization dedicated to raising awareness of the dire need for organ donors across the country. Posters placed in New

York hospitals carried the slogan, "Leave Your Own Legacy. Be a Hero. Be a Donor."

Just as Mantle's life seemed to be taking a positive turn, he suffered another setback. X-rays revealed that the cancer had spread to his lungs, necessitating a return to Baylor Medical Center. He was forced to cancel a scheduled appearance on *Good Morning, America*. In a taped video segment that aired on the program, he told fans he was fighting for his life and encouraged them to register as donors.

Over the next two weeks, Mantle's friends and former teammates flocked to the hospital to say their good-byes. Hank Bauer, Moose Skowron, and Johnny Blanchard surprised him by showing up together. Other former Yankees to make appearances included Whitey Ford, Yogi Berra, and Bobby Richardson.

Mantle passed away in the early hours of August 13, 1995. His wife and son David were by his side. As the news spread, major-league stadiums all over the country staged memorials and tributes. In the Bronx, flags flew at half-staff and Yankee players wore black armbands. There was a moment of silence followed by a rousing ovation.

The funeral was held on August 15 at the Lovers Lane United Methodist Church in Dallas. Bob Costas delivered a stirring eulogy to about 1,500 people, provoking laughter and tears. "It occurs to me as we're all sitting here thinking of Mickey, he's probably somewhere getting an earful from Casey Stengel and no doubt quite confused by now," Costas quipped. On a more serious note, he added, "In his last year, [Mickey] finally came to accept and appreciate what he meant to people. He got something more than celebrity worship. He got love.... I just hope God has a place for Mickey where he can run again, play practical jokes and smile that boyish smile. God knows no one is perfect. God also knows there's something special about a hero. So long, Mick. Thanks."

Mantle joked repeatedly that, upon his death, he would be met at the pearly gates by St. Peter, who would promptly inform him, "Mick, we checked the record. We know some of what went on. Sorry, we can't let you in. But before you go, God wants to know if you could sign these six dozen baseballs." On the morning of Mantle's funeral, a cartoon appeared in the *Dallas Morning News*. In it, St. Peter was pictured with his arm around Mantle in heaven. The dialogue bubble read, "Kid, that was the most courageous 9th inning I've ever seen."

REFLECTIONS

"As a ballplayer, Mickey inspired generations of fans with his power and grit. As a man, he faced up to his responsibilities and alerted generations to come to the dangers of alcohol abuse. He will be remembered for excellence on the baseball field and the honor and redemption he brought to the end of his life."

—President Bill Clinton

"This was one of the greatest baseball players ever, one of the greatest symbols of baseball, and one of the great New Yorkers. He's someone that all New Yorkers probably loved in one way or another, and now mourn his passing."

—New York City mayor Rudy Giuliani

"Just as Jesse Owens was to track and field and Michael Jordan is to basketball, Mickey Mantle is to baseball. Great athletes like Mickey Mantle and Joe DiMaggio transcend the game. They are heroes to every fan."

—Yankee owner George Steinbrenner

"I always worried more about what Mickey thought about me being compared to him. We had a lot of laughs about that. I think the reason people loved him so much was that he portrayed the innocence of what we all want to be. I don't think that to this day that Mickey realized how people felt about him, how he touched their lives, so many fans. . . . But everybody knew Mickey Mantle and loved Mickey Mantle."

—Yankee outfielder Bobby Murcer

"It's almost like a part of your childhood has been taken away. I don't care if you're from the South, the North, the East, or the West—kids grew up wanting to be a switch-hitting outfielder for the New York Yankees. I know I did."

—Yankee manager Buck Showalter

"His career was storybook stuff, hewing more to our ideals of myth than any player since Ruth. Spotted playing shortstop on the Barber Springs Whiz Kids, [Mantle] was delivered from a rural obscurity into America's distilled essence of glamour. . . . A lesson reaffirmed: Anything can happen to anybody in this country so long as they're daring in their defeats and outsized in victory. Failure is forgiven in big swingers, in whom even foolishness is flamboyant. . . . The world will always belong to those who swing from their heels."

—*Sports Illustrated* writer **Richard Hoffer**

"More than the numbers and accolades, Mickey Mantle humanized the maturation of American Power. A country kid who spoke with a twang, Mantle oozed charisma and embodied hedonism. He was everything to everyone, a handsome charmer who drank to excess and used vulgar language redolent of The Bambino himself. A notoriously prolific womanizer, Mantle somehow got away with it all, and he somehow kept his persona in check. Mothers and fathers loved The Mick. Grandparents too. To dislike Mickey Mantle was to disparage the United States. There was no denying his oxymoronic purity."

—**Author Ryan Ferguson**

"In the 1950s, as sport itself took on the role in our culture that religion had often played in the past, Mickey Mantle, as the contemporary cultural hero, contributed to American society's necessary business of reproducing itself and its values. Amid the threat of Russian satellites and the unsettling dawn of the computer age, Mantle helped affirm our belief in the power of mankind over technology's invasion of our world. Mickey Mantle gave America hope for such things as life beyond the nuclear threat, reprieve from the Cold War, and a sense that order ruled our lives."

—**Author Tony Castro**

"The drama of Mickey Mantle batting was like a Shakespearean play. We never knew what would happen, but it was usually dramatic. Would this be the at-bat that produced the first ball ever hit out of Yankee Stadium? Would this at-bat result in a crippling injury that would seriously threaten Mickey's career? We had seen him hit balls off facades and over monuments 500 feet away, and we had seen Mickey in agony, his body betrayed by another injury."

—**Author Tom Molito**

"If Mickey Mantle hadn't lived, he would have been invented."

—**Broadcaster Red Barber**

In 1998, a statue of Mickey Mantle was installed outside the Chickasaw Brick-
town Ballpark—home of the Dodgers' Triple-A affiliate in Oklahoma City. The
bronze statue measures 7-foot-6 and sits in the third base pavilion, which is
known as "Mickey Mantle Plaza." (Courtesy of es chipul on Visual Hunt)

PART II:
ASSORTED ANECDOTES

DOGGY PADDLER

Baseball wasn't the only sport Mantle was interested in while growing up. He played basketball, football, and just about any other game that allowed him to demonstrate his marvelous athletic skills. Despite his natural abilities, he was a very poor swimmer.

During the sweltering Oklahoma summers, which typically produce more than two months of 90-degree weather every year, Mantle would join his friends on the banks of the Neosho River. A part of the Mississippi River drainage basin, the Neosho is a 463-mile waterway that winds its way through Kansas and Oklahoma. The portion of the canal that Mantle and his pals frequented was sheltered from the road, and the boys most often swam naked. Since he was barely able to keep his head above water, Mickey relied on his friends to tow him around and keep an eye out for him.

One day, a woman appeared on the shore, causing panic among the frolicking youngsters, who suddenly felt vulnerable and exposed. One by one, they dove off in various directions, leaving the hapless Mantle to fend for himself. Flailing and kicking, Mickey swallowed a mouthful of water and nearly drowned. Fortunately, one of his buddies recognized the seriousness of his predicament and dragged him to the riverbank. The near death experience failed to keep him away from aquatic activities.

Years later, when Mantle was playing for the Yankees, he pulled a fast one over on teammate Roger Maris. During an off day in Baltimore, the team assembled at pitcher Bob Turley's house for a cookout. Mantle told the gullible Maris that he had been a champion swimmer during his high school years and challenged him to a race in Turley's pool. After Maris accepted, Mantle secretly instructed Whitey Ford to grab a pool skimmer and pull him across the water with it once the race was underway.

After the outfielders dove in, Ford fulfilled his duty, dragging Mantle to the other end of the pool well ahead of Maris. Upon completing the route, Maris was surprised to see his teammate already out of the water and drying off. The other players, who had been following the prank closely, burst into laughter when Maris asked how Mantle had finished so quickly.

FAMILY CURSE

Though Mantle lived a charmed life in many respects, he was forced to deal with an ongoing series of tragedies. In 1944, his grandfather, Charlie, was diagnosed with Hodgkin's disease. "Grandpa suddenly became old and feeble almost overnight," the slugger recalled sadly. "My father would help him out of bed and support his wobbly legs that used to stride down Quincy Street with so much vigor." Charlie's battle against the ailment was mercifully brief. He passed away at the age of 60.

Three years later, when Mantle was in high school, his uncle Tunney was hospitalized with a suspected case of appendicitis. When doctors opened him up, they found that his stomach was riddled with cancer. He lost over a hundred pounds in a month and a half, succumbing to the affliction at the age of 34.

After the death of his father to Hodgkin's disease in 1952, Mantle suffered yet another personal blow when his Uncle Emmett contracted cancer and died. His passing profoundly affected Mickey, who spent his entire adult life believing he would die young like most of his predecessors. "Mickey was always a sensitive person," his cousin Max said. "He was that way his whole life. He was always the first one of us [who] would cry."

Misery followed Mantle into his later years as he and every member of his immediate family struggled with addiction. This included his wife and all four of his sons. "I was partying and doing the same thing as Mick," Merlyn admitted in later years. "That was our life and I was part of it. I can't deny that. It ruins families." Danny—the youngest of Mantle's boys—remarked: "I was scared of [my dad] when I was a kid. I didn't really get to know him until we started drinking together. For him, drinking with us was a way to relive his days with Billy [Martin] and Whitey [Ford]."

In 1994, Mantle's life took another unfortunate turn when his second-youngest son, Billy, died of a heart attack at the age of 36. He scarcely had time to recover from the loss before receiving his own cancer diagnosis. Prior to his death in August 1995, he commented wistfully, "If I'd known I was going to live this long, I would have taken better care of myself." Completing the tragic Mantle saga, Mickey Jr. died of non-Hodgkin's lymphoma and Merlyn contracted Alzheimer's disease. Ray and Roy—Mantle's twin brothers—both succumbed to cancer.

How Enos Slaughter Saved Mantle's Career

In 1946 Mantle spent several months battling a serious case of osteomyelitis. Demonstrating the resilience that would come to characterize him in later years, he recovered his health, leaving the hospital on crutches shortly before the 1946 World Series.

In the wake of a second-place finish in 1945, the St. Louis Cardinals—led by future Hall of Famers Stan Musial and Enos Slaughter—won a tight pennant race over the Brooklyn Dodgers. In an attempt to boost his son's spirits, Mutt Mantle surprised Mickey with tickets to the first two games at Sportsman's Park in St. Louis.

The 300-mile trip was the farthest Mickey had ever been from home. He eagerly took in all of the sights and sounds. The opening game ended in a 3–2 loss, but the Cardinals bounced back in the second meeting, winning, 3–0, behind the brilliant pitching of Harry "The Cat" Brecheen. Mickey's passion for baseball was magnified tenfold and, over the next several days, he avidly followed the games on the radio.

The series went the full distance. The Cards jumped out to a 3–1 lead over the Red Sox in Game 7, but couldn't hold it as Dominic DiMaggio (Joe's little brother) delivered a clutch two-run double in the top of the eighth inning. In the bottom of the frame, Slaughter led off with a single. With two outs, he scored all the way from first on a shallow hit by Harry Walker to left-center field. Though coach Mike Gonzalez signaled for Slaughter to stop at third, the aggressive-minded outfielder sensed that the BoSox defense would be caught off guard if he kept running. The play became forever known as "Slaughter's Mad Dash." The Cardinals held on for a 4–3 series-clinching win.

The 15-year-old Mantle was deeply inspired by Slaughter's gutsy play. Though his recent medical ordeal had left him with an uncertain future as an athlete, he adamantly told his parents, "Burn the crutches, I'm going to play ball." The words were music to their ears.

THE SPOOK LIGHT

For more than a century, residents of the Tri-State Missouri, Oklahoma, and Kansas area have talked about a paranormal phenomenon known as the "Spook Light." The light has been described by witnesses as an orb of fire about the size of a baseball or basketball. It flickers, dances, and spins—typically in an east-to-west pattern—while hovering above the treetops. When observers attempt to walk or drive toward it, it disappears.

According to popular legend, the Spook Light was first observed by Native Americans along the infamous Trail of Tears in 1836. Since then, a number of ghostly stories have circulated regarding its origin. One of the oldest tales centers around a Quapaw Indian maiden and her lover, who leaped to their deaths after the girl's father forbade them from marrying. Another oft-told yarn involves the spirit of an Osage tribal chief who lost his head in battle and continues to search for it by lanternlight.

The Spook Light is commonly seen along a desolate stretch of road near the town of Quapaw, which is located just six miles from Mantle's hometown of Commerce. The Yankee slugger grew up with these campfire tales and, like many teenagers of the era, enjoyed the associated benefits. By the time he was in high school, the deserted route known as Spook Light Road (or "The Devil's Promenade" to some) had become a popular make-out spot. In his 1985 autobiography, Mantle remarked, "If you happened to be waiting at the Spook Light and you happened to have a girl with you, it was a pretty good place for necking." Mantle's first social outing with his future wife, Merlyn, was a triple date to Spook Light Road. The youngsters piled into Mantle's 1947 Fleetline Chevy, which he had purchased with his Yankee signing bonus. Though Mantle was paired with another girl that night, he ended up asking Merlyn out on a date after he "struck out" with her friend.

The Spook Light continues to be an enduring legend despite scientific research conducted during Mantle's teen years. In 1945, it was proposed that the phenomenon was caused by the refraction of vehicle headlights over a range of western hills. The following year, an Army major named Thomas Sheard stationed a vehicle in the region he believed the so-called Spook Light was emanating from. He instructed the driver to flash the vehicle's headlights at a designated time after dark. Observers in the vicinity of Spook Light Road were able to see the flashes. In 1965, *Popular Mechanics* magazine recruited professors from the University of Arkansas to investigate even further. They confirmed that distant headlights on Route 66 were being distorted by waves of heat, producing the phenomenon.

Those who still cling to paranormal explanations maintain that the Spook Light was seen long before the invention of automobiles and is, therefore, an unrelated phenomenon. The first verified written account of the eerie spectacle didn't appear until 1935. Multiple sources have claimed that a booklet on the topic was released in the 1880s, but concrete evidence of it has not been uncovered. Detailed information about the ethereal orb—complete with driving directions to Spook Light Road—appear on the Joplin, Missouri, official website.

MICKEY AND MERLYN: A PORTRAIT OF THE EARLY YEARS

As the spouse of a world-famous baseball star and cultural icon, Merlyn Mantle grew accustomed to being invisible. Though she ultimately chose to play the role of a housewife, she could have pursued a career in music. The future Mrs. Mickey Mantle began taking singing lessons at the age of 12. She performed at various public functions and was talented enough to win a local contest. In her senior year of high school, she was awarded a scholarship to Miami Junior College, which had a respectable music program. She hoped to at least become a teacher if a singing career didn't pan out. But all that changed when she met Mickey.

Merlyn came from a religious background. Her father was a deacon in a Baptist church. He worked in the mines until a head injury left him with a seizure disorder. Unable to handle the physical demands of the job, he accepted a clerical position in his father's lumber business. The family was financially stable, but not overtly wealthy. Even after he separated from Merlyn, Mickey sent annual Christmas checks to his mother-in-law to help supplement her income.

Merlyn already had a boyfriend when she first met Mickey. She admitted that her interest in the other boy was based primarily on the fact that he drove a motorcycle. One day, she scheduled an early date with the biker boyfriend and an evening date with Mickey. On the ride home from a movie matinee, she spotted Mickey changing a tire on the side of the road. He had his head down and didn't notice her speeding by on the back of the motorcycle. Merlyn said that the encounter made her so nervous, she decided that she would never again attempt to juggle two boys at once.

A typical date for Merlyn and Mickey involved a movie and a visit to a local drive-in restaurant. In her memoirs, she claimed that she had already fallen in love with him by their third date. Not only did she find him physically attractive, but she was charmed by his shyness and gentlemanly behavior.

Since Mickey was a year older, Merlyn was still in high school when his professional career began. He wrote her often while he was away, frequently expressing his romantic feelings for her. She kept the letters as mementos and published the following excerpts in her 1996 autobiography:

"You say you will probably not be lucky enough to have me for always. Well, honey, I'll let you in on a little secret. I'm yours for as long as you want me...."

"Everyone down here seems to be married, but only a few bring their wives. If you and I ever get married, you are going everywhere this boy goes. I wish you were here now...."

Merlyn longed to experience life outside of rural Oklahoma. Mickey represented a means of escape, and when it became evident that he would be playing for the New York Yankees, she abandoned her musical aspirations. She never regretted the decision. After high school, she took a job in a local bank. When Mickey's father became gravely ill with Hodgkin's disease, he convinced the couple to get married as a kind of dying wish.

Merlyn was well aware of the problems that might lie ahead. "I knew that we loved each other," she professed. "I also knew that marriage was not a real high priority for Mick—he was 20 years-old and just starting to live his dream.... He was married, but in a very small geographic area of his mind. He treated marriage as he did most things, a sort of party with added attractions."

The union of Mickey and Merlyn was very troubled at times, but they managed to stay together for nearly 40 years. They remained close after their 1989 separation, continuing to celebrate their annual wedding anniversary. In later years, Mickey said that he had always loved Merlyn and could never bring himself to divorce her. When he offered her the option, she refused.

ROOKIE JITTERS

Though Mantle and Whitey Ford became the best of friends, they hardly spoke to one another when they first met during the fall of 1950. Ford had joined the Yankees in July and was establishing himself as a reliable member of the starting rotation. Mantle reported to the club in September as a non-roster invitee. "I met the team in St. Louis and I worked out with them," the slugger recalled, "but there was a pretty big crowd there and I was scared to even go out and take infield practice or anything. Jerry Coleman and Bobby Brown talked me into coming out and taking the field for awhile." Ford claimed that, over the next two weeks, Mantle was so uncomfortable he could only grunt in reply whenever a greeting was offered to him. While his fielding abilities at shortstop left something to be desired, his hitting skills caught the attention of the team's most celebrated player.

From St. Louis, the Yankees traveled to Chicago, where Moose Skowron joined the club for a workout. In those days, there was a pecking order during batting practice. Since the established stars weren't enthusiastic about sharing their time with rookies, the low men on the totem pole were lucky to get a handful of swings in. When Skowron and Mantle began hammering balls into the outfield seats during BP in Chicago, the veterans immediately took notice. Joe DiMaggio, who was never known for his charitable treatment of freshmen, told them both to stay in the cage a little longer so that he could study their mechanics.

Though The Yankee Clipper was duly impressed with Mantle's power from both sides of the plate, Mickey was utterly starstruck. Crippled by anxiety, all he could do was stare at DiMaggio and fumble out an occasional "hello." Billy Martin—another up-and-coming Yankee—was an entirely different story.

Mantle's earliest recollection of Martin dates back to spring training in 1951. Frank Crosetti, who had spent 17 seasons with the Yankees before moving on to a distinguished career as a coach, was showing some of the younger players how to turn a double play. According to Mantle, Martin started running his mouth during the demonstration, telling Crosetti that he was doing it wrong. Martin had absolutely no inhibitions around coaches or teammates—DiMaggio included. A habitual prankster, he asked Joltin' Joe for an autograph one day, then squirted him with disappearing ink from a novelty pen he sometimes carried with him. Martin repeatedly encouraged Mantle to establish a relationship with DiMaggio, but Mickey's angst and self-doubt prevented it from happening.

According to Ford, Mantle was constantly homesick and would often fly back to Oklahoma. During spring training in 1951, he got so nervous, he broke out in hives. A doctor advised him to stay out of the sun for a couple of days, and Casey Stengel granted him a brief leave of absence. By the time his flight from St. Petersburg landed, the hives were gone. Determined to make the most of his days off, he went fishing and ended up being spotted by locals. The information ended up on the newswire, prompting a phone call from Stengel, who ordered Mickey to return to camp immediately.

Mantle played his first regular-season game at Yankee Stadium in front of more than 44,000 fans—the largest crowd he had ever seen to that point.

"I was scared out of my mind," he later admitted. Stationed in right field, the first ball hit to him was a towering fly off the bat of Red Sox first baseman Walt Dropo. Mantle grew so anxious waiting for it to settle into his glove that he actually leaped into the air to grab it—a gesture that was awkward and completely unnecessary.

TEMPER, TEMPER!

During his early days with the Yankees, Mantle became notorious for throwing epic temper tantrums. He struck out often in his rookie year, averaging one whiff per every 4.6 at-bats. This served to infuriate him at times. In a story he told to a biographer, there was a season-ticket holder named Mrs. Blackburn who had a box seat next to the Yankee dugout. A kindly woman with a maternal presence, she got in the habit of giving Mantle gum or candy on his way to the on-deck circle. During a particularly frustrating day at the plate, Mickey launched into a vulgar tirade, prompting Mrs. Blackburn to bark at him: "Stop that talk!" In his blind fury, the Yankee slugger shouted back at her, "Shut your goddamn mouth!" He instantly regretted it. The treats stopped coming after that, and he was certain that she would never speak to him again. He was wrong. A couple of days later, she scolded, "Any more outbursts like that and I'm going to make a personal protest to Mr. Topping [Yankee co-owner]."

According to Casey Stengel, most of Mantle's tantrums followed the same pattern. After a particularly vexing strikeout, he would slam his hand on the dugout railing, then stalk to the far end of the bench, where he would lean against the wall brooding. After a brief sulk, he would curse loudly at the pitcher while searching for something to kick.

Though Mantle was accommodating to journalists a great deal of the time, he could be extremely prickly after poor performances. He made it evident what kind of mood he was in on any given day. Beat writer George Vecsey, who covered the Yankees in the 1950s, recalled, "Too often, [Mantle] was unapproachable or worse. Reporters would walk toward his locker and you'd see him sort of cock his head to the side, roll his eyes upwards and say 'FUUUCCCK'—and then burp."

Under manager Ralph Houk, Mantle began to see himself as a team leader. He made a concerted effort to keep his emotions in check. But he was still known to throw bats and helmets from time to time.

Mantle appears poised to throw his bat in disgust. He staged some epic tantrums over the years after strikeouts. Yankee manager Casey Stengel grew so tired of it, he handed Mickey a bat from the rack one day and sarcastically instructed him to club himself over the head with it. (Courtesy of The National Baseball Hall of Fame)

SWITCHING NUMBERS

No major-league team has retired more uniform numbers than the New York Yankees. As of 2022, the club had taken a total of 22 numbers out of circulation to honor the players who wore them. The tradition began when Babe Ruth's number 3 and Lou Gehrig's number 4 were officially made unavailable to future generations. Although Mantle has come to be associated with the number 7, he didn't start out with the digit.

Describing the hype surrounding him during his first spring training, Mantle remarked, "When I came up, Casey [Stengel] told the writers that I was going to be the next Babe Ruth, Lou Gehrig, and Joe DiMaggio all rolled up in one." As word of his tremendous speed and power began to circulate, sportswriters saddled him with a host of nicknames, including "Wonder Boy" and "the Colossal Kid" (neither of which actually stuck).

Yankee PR man Red Patterson was among several executives who believed that Mantle was the legitimate heir to DiMaggio. He wanted this to be reflected in the number Mantle wore. Since DiMaggio was still in possession of the number 5, it seemed logical that Mantle should be the next in line. Pete Sheehy, who served as Yankee clubhouse man for over 50 years, was in charge of assigning lockers and numbers to new arrivals. At Patterson's request, he gave Mantle the number 6 and stationed his locker next to DiMaggio's.

Prior to Mantle, the number 6 had been worn by Hall of Famers Tony Lazzeri and Joe Gordon. In subsequent years, Clete Boyer, Roy White, and Joe Torre would all carry it on their uniforms. It was retired in honor of Torre during the 2014 campaign.

Mantle had his share of ups and downs during his rookie season. Shortly after the All-Star break, he was sent back down to the minors to work on his swing. In his absence, the number 6 was reassigned to third baseman Bobby Brown. Mantle eventually ironed out his problems and rejoined the Yankees. Upon returning to the Bronx in late August, he found a number 7 jersey hanging in his locker. The number is considered lucky by many due to its symmetrical qualities (seven days in the week, seven colors in a rainbow, seven ages of man, etc.). It certainly brought good fortune to Mantle as he smashed more than 500 homers while wearing it.

Mantle's iconic number was retired by the Yankees in 1969. To this day, he is sometimes referred to by fans and historians simply as "Number 7." Several photos were taken of him with the number 6, and he autographed quite

This picture was taken early in Mantle's career. Since he was considered the heir to Joe DiMaggio, he was given the number 6 to wear upon his arrival in New York (DiMaggio wore number 5). Mantle's back is facing away from the camera in the photo and the number is not visible. He eventually ended up with the number 7—which was retired by the Yankees after his playing days were over. (Courtesy of The National Baseball Hall of Fame)

a few copies during his lifetime. Today, a signed picture with the number 6 is worth close to $2,500.

JINXED

Descending from Creek Indian heritage, Allie Reynolds grew up in a devoutly religious household. He was not allowed to play organized baseball during his high school years. He was also forbidden to attend movies or school dances. It wasn't until he enrolled at Oklahoma Agricultural and Mechanical College that he began to excel at sports.

Reynolds got his professional start in the Cleveland farm system. Shortly before the 1947 campaign, he was traded to New York for Hall of Famer Joe Gordon. During the Yankees' five-year run of World Series dominance (1949–1953), he was one of the most successful pitchers on the staff, winning

83 regular-season games while posting a 6-2 postseason record. His commanding presence on the mound and Native American roots earned him the nickname of "Super Chief."

Though Reynolds was a valuable asset to the Yankees, he harbored deep regret in later years for "jinxing" Mickey Mantle during his rookie year. From May 12 through May 18, Mantle went off on a tear at the plate, going 13-for-29 with a pair of homers and nine RBIs. This raised his cumulative batting average considerably. Reynolds had taken a liking to Mantle, offering periodic support and advice. When Mickey mentioned to the hurler that he was among the AL leaders in multiple statistical categories, Reynolds responded jokingly, "Did you ever stop to think what that can mean to you economically?"

For a variety of unrelated reasons, Mantle fell into a slump after the exchange took place. By the end of the month, his batting average had dropped from .316 to .279. During a disastrous doubleheader performance against the Red Sox, he struck out five times and broke down crying in the dugout. "Put someone in there who can hit," he said to Casey Stengel. "I can't." When the slump continued into mid-July, he was temporarily reassigned to the minor leagues.

Years later, Reynolds confided to a writer that he felt responsible for Mantle's hitting woes, believing that his comment had placed unnecessary pressure on the 19-year-old outfielder to perform. While Mantle struggled to turn his season around, Reynolds enjoyed one of the finest campaigns of his career. At season's end, the National Sportswriters and Sportscasters Association designated him Professional Athlete of the Year and awarded him the prestigious Hickok Belt. The belt was made of alligator skin and had a diamond-encrusted buckle. Reynolds reportedly kept it in a bank vault for years since it was too valuable to insure.

MANTLE AND DIMAGGIO: MUCH ADO ABOUT NOTHING

A lot has been written about the contentious relationship between Mantle and Joe DiMaggio. The two have been widely portrayed as mortal enemies who loathed one another's company. At the root of this belief is DiMaggio's presumed cold treatment of Mantle during his rookie season and the gruesome injury Mantle sustained in the 1951 World Series, which some have unfairly blamed on DiMaggio. Adding fuel to the fire, there was a perceived Old-Timers' Day slight that allegedly prompted The Yankee Clipper to hold a grudge against his former teammate. Though details of the alleged feud make for interesting reading, the entire story is based on hearsay and supposition.

In multiple Mantle biographies, DiMaggio is described as an elitist snob who snubbed The Mick in his rookie season. Given his reputation as one of the greatest players of all time, there's no denying the fact that DiMaggio had a sense of entitlement. Beneath the surface, however, he was shy and extremely quiet—even around people he considered his friends. It has been said many times that DiMaggio was jealous of all the hype surrounding Mantle during his big-league debut. But if Joltin' Joe was harboring any bitterness, he kept it to himself during interviews. Asked by a reporter in the spring of 1951 if he resented the rookie slugger, DiMaggio responded demurely, "Hell, no. Why should I resent him? If he's good enough to take my job in center, I can always move to right or left. I haven't helped him much—Henrich takes care of that—but if there is anything I can do to help him, I'm only too willing." Though no such help was forthcoming, this likely had more to do with Mantle than DiMaggio. Mantle admitted a number of times that he was starstruck and tongue-tied around his iconic outfield mate.

In April 1951, as the Yankees were boarding a train to Washington, both players were pulled aside for a radio interview. Their unrehearsed dialogue portrayed them as copacetic teammates. When Mantle admitted to being nervous about playing in his first game, the veteran outfielder reassured him by admitting that he too had been ill at ease during his first big-league appearance.

DIMAGGIO: When I did play my first game, I swung at the first pitch and was very fortunate to get a base hit and that took all the tension out. Now, are you going to do the same thing for us?

MANTLE: Well, I don't know. I'll probably swing at the first pitch no matter what, but I don't know if I'll get a hit.

DIMAGGIO: Well, I hope it's a hit, Mickey, because from there on in, you'll go from there.

In regard to Mantle's unfortunate injury in the 1951 postseason, many of DiMaggio's detractors have faulted him for not making a louder call on a shallow flyball hit by Willie Mays. Mantle was forced to go from an all-out sprint to an abrupt stop when he saw Joltin' Joe about to make the catch. He ended up blowing his knee out in the process. The fact remains that DiMaggio did call for the ball. Mantle made that very clear in retellings of the story. Most everyone who played beside DiMaggio knew that he had a soft voice that didn't carry well. Mantle never blamed him for the mishap.

The two Yankee icons were reunited many times over the years at various functions. A proud, sensitive man, DiMaggio was known for brooding over trivial gestures he perceived as slights. In order to ensure his attendance at Old-Timers' Day games, the Yankees honored his request to be the last player introduced. This more or less guaranteed that he would receive the loudest ovation. When the order was reversed during Mantle's first Old-Timers' Day appearance, DiMaggio was enormously displeased. Though Mantle took some satisfaction in receiving a more resounding welcome that day, he felt compelled to make things right. According to former Yankee shortstop Tony Kubek, "Mantle saw that Joe, a remote guy, a loner, was really offended. Joe told Bob Fishel—the Yankee PR guy—that he wouldn't be back. Fishel, at Mickey's prompting, introduced Joe last at all future Old Timers' Days."

There's another story about an awkward elevator ride in which neither Mantle nor DiMaggio wanted to be the first to say "hello," but in the end it signifies nothing aside from the fact that the two men were not entirely comfortable around one another. By no means was their relationship warm. They were never friends. But for all intents and purposes, they were friendly. Mantle tried to lay the subject to rest in his World Series memoirs, commenting, "There was never any real tension or jealousy between us—we weren't that close. But it's hard to explain how much the players on the team liked to analyze him. I never tired of hearing the stories."

ELUDING THE EYES

Originally built as apartments in 1915, the Hotel Kenmore was later converted to a 400-room guest lodge that hosted each of the major-league teams outside of Boston at various points in time. During the early 1950s, it was still known as the city's primary "baseball hotel." One day, when the Yankees were in town for a series at Fenway Park, Mantle went out for a late dinner with his frequent partner in crime, Billy Martin. Several drinks later, they realized they had violated curfew and needed to get back to the Kenmore.

Upon arriving at the hotel, the guilty pair spotted Casey Stengel in the lobby with about a dozen writers. The garrulous Yankee manager kept a close watch over the comings and goings of players and loved to chat with members of the press. Looking to avoid a confrontation with Stengel, Mantle and Martin went around back.

The rear entrance of the hotel was locked, but a window above the door was open. Martin suggested he climb onto Mantle's shoulders to reach the window. He promised to unlock the door once he got inside.

Mantle was wearing a brand-new sharkskin suit that he was quite fond of. But realizing the gravity of the situation, he grudgingly allowed Martin to climb on top of him. In order to boost Martin high enough, he had to stand on top of a garbage can.

As soon as Martin was inside, Mantle heard him trying to open the door. The infielder's frantic efforts were followed by abrupt silence. After a minute or so, he reappeared at the window with bad news. "Hey, Mick, listen that door's got a chain and lock on it. I can't get it open. I'll see you tomorrow."

Left alone in the alley, Mantle began stacking trash cans up to get into the window. He fell at least four or five times in the process. "That sharkskin suit had lettuce and all kinds of garbage all over it," he later said. He made it safely inside and hustled to his room, where he found Martin pretending to be fast asleep.

"Look at this crap all over me," Mickey growled. "You could have reached down and got me, you son of a bitch!" Billy just laughed and rolled over, closing his eyes again.

Casey and Mickey: A Complex Relationship

Among the most colorful managers in baseball history, Casey Stengel made a name for himself with his erratic behavior. Early in his managerial career, he was known to stage mock fainting spells during arguments with umpires. He got more than he bargained for one day when arbiter Beans Reardon lay down on the ground next to him. "When I peeked out one eye and saw Reardon on the ground, too, I knew I was licked," Stengel later said.

Though Mantle repeatedly told biographers that Casey was like a father to him, the Yankee skipper was not always terribly supportive. The two had similar personality traits. Both had grown up in the Midwest and both were mischievous types prone to periodic displays of anger. The primary difference was that Casey was an avid student of the game while Mickey was not. "I don't think [Mickey] knew what the definition of constructive criticism might be, because I don't think he'd ever listen to it," said Mantle's brother, Larry.

Describing the muddled relationship between Mantle and Stengel, pitcher Ryne Duren remarked, "Casey should have been the father image rather than what he was and [Mickey] resented him for it. *'Why can't you treat me decently instead of being such an old bastard?'* Casey didn't see the little boy in [Mickey] that needed a father."

Though Mantle never openly defied Stengel's instructions, he had a tendency to ignore them. Casey showed his disapproval on multiple occasions by yelling at Mantle in front of teammates. He also developed a habit of venting his frustrations to members of the press, referring to Mantle repeatedly as a disappointment. In 1958, when Stengel named the best players he had worked with during his tenure, he deliberately left Mickey's name off the list.

Mantle's frequent injuries were another point of contention between the two. During training camp one year, Stengel complained, "If he did what he

Mantle posing with Yankee manager Casey Stengel. Though Mickey said that Casey served as a father figure to him, the two had a somewhat contentious relationship. Stengel often criticized Mantle openly in front of teammates. And in a 1958 interview, Casey left Mickey's name off a list of the top players he had managed. (Courtesy of The Leslie Jones Collection: Boston Public Library)

was told after the first operation, he would be able to play now. This kid—you can't ever teach him nothing in the spring because he's always hurt. . . . You want to do something for him and he don't let you. What's the good of telling him what to do? No matter what you tell him, he'll do what he wants."

Stengel's insensitive handling of Mantle was not limited to verbal jabs. Billy Martin once saw Casey grab Mickey by the back of the neck and shake him vigorously while cursing him out. A master manipulator, Stengel learned how to coax Mantle into playing when he was hurt. All he had to do was appeal to Mantle's fierce sense of pride. If Stengel approached the slugger and told him he wouldn't be playing on a given day, it invariably prompted a request from Mantle to be penciled into the lineup.

BIRTH OF THE "TAPE-MEASURE HOMER"
Some sports legends evolve organically while others are artificially manufactured. Mantle's fame can be attributed to a combination of the two scenarios. In 1946, the Yankees hired Arthur "Red" Patterson as their first publicity director. A former reporter for the *New York Herald-Tribune*, he knew how to pique the interest of fans. During his long career in baseball, Patterson introduced Old-Timers' games, concessions stand souvenirs, yearbooks, and promotional events such as Cap Day. In 1953, he helped make Mantle a household name.

"It was my job to make Mickey look good," Patterson said in later years. "I saw that the Yankees were not just competing against the Giants and Dodgers. They were competing against every leisure-time activity that you have in summer. If you decided to go to Jones Beach, you didn't go to Yankee Stadium. . . . I was trying to make the Yankees more interesting than the Giants and Jones Beach as well."

Mission accomplished.

Though attendance figures for Jones Beach are not readily available, the Yankees nearly doubled the Giants' paid admissions in 1953. They outdrew the Dodgers by more than 374,000. A lot of that had to do with a tall tale cooked up by Patterson.

On April 17, the Yankees were facing the Senators at Griffith Stadium in Washington. With the Bombers nursing a 2–1 lead in the fifth inning, Mantle came to bat against left-hander Chuck Stobbs. With two outs and Yogi Berra on first, Stobbs made the mistake of delivering a high fastball over the heart of the plate. Hitting right-handed, Mantle pulverized it. The ball cleared 32 rows of bleachers and nicked the edge of the National Bohemian

Beer sign located 460 feet from home plate and nearly 60 feet above the field. It sailed out of the stadium and ended up in the backyard of a nearby apartment building.

Patterson knew a good story in the making when he saw one. Describing what happened next, a reporter from the *Christian Science Monitor* hyperbolically wrote, "Patterson, his sense of theater twanging like the strings of an electric guitar, set off on foot in the gloaming to find where the ball had landed. Never had anyone pursued anything with so much vigor since Stanley sought Livingstone." Patterson allegedly found the ball in the possession of a neighborhood kid named Donald Dunaway, who claimed to have retrieved it from the yard of a tenement on Oakdale Street. Patterson returned to the stadium with the youngster in tow and instructed Senators radio announcer Bob Wolff to officially report Mantle's homer as a new major-league record.

Grilled by reporters, Patterson claimed he had measured 105 feet (in paces) from the edge of the stadium to the spot where the ball had landed. Including the distance from home plate, he arrived at a figure of 565 feet. He omitted the obvious fact that existing impediments such as houses and perimeter fences had prevented him from walking in a straight line. But his efforts gave birth to the phrase, "tape-measure homer," which has found a permanent place in baseball vernacular.

Mantle's star burned brighter than ever before in the wake of Patterson's publicity stunt. And Stobbs, who compiled a sub-.500 record with a lifetime 4.29 ERA, managed to avoid being completely forgotten. Patterson's career path landed him in Brooklyn for the 1954 slate. He remained with the Dodgers as VP of public relations until 1975, when he was hired by Angels owner Gene Autry as club president. "He loved his work, always looked on the bright side and always had an anecdote," said Dodger president Peter O'Malley. In 1992, Patterson posthumously received a lifetime achievement award from the Los Angeles–Anaheim chapter of the Baseball Writers' Association of America.

THE PRICE OF FAME

Anyone who has lived in the public spotlight for an extended length of time would agree that there is a dark side to being famous. For Mantle, it was darker than most. In early September 1953, the Yankees received an anonymous threat in a letter postmarked from Boston. It stated that if Mantle played at Fenway Park over Labor Day weekend, he would be shot.

Taking no chances, the Yankees contacted the authorities and the FBI became involved. With agents keeping a close watch over him, Mantle appeared in both games of the scheduled holiday doubleheader against the BoSox. In the opener, he blasted a two-run homer off of Mel Parnell. He later joked that he had never rounded the bases so quickly after a home run.

The 1953 incident was not the only one of its kind. In July 1960, Mantle was opening mail in the visitor's locker room at Cleveland Stadium when he stumbled upon an envelope postmarked from Tonawanda, New York, which is located just north of Buffalo. It contained a handwritten letter that read precisely as follows: "I had a son that was drafted with a bad leg and bad eyes he got killed but a rotten draft dodger that could run like you gets turned down. I have a gun with micrscopic [sic] lenses and I'm going to get you thru both your knees and its [sic] going to happen soon." Again, the FBI became involved and nothing came of the ominous note.

Mantle dealt with other unpleasantries over the course of his career. A female stalker once threatened to kidnap his wife and one of his sons if he didn't buy her a diamond ring. And in 1958, he was attacked twice. One of his assailants was a 13-year-old girl who slapped him in the face and pulled his hair as he was exiting a cab at the players' entrance to Yankee Stadium. Earlier that season, he was poked in the eye and punched in the jaw by an unruly group of fans, one of whom stole the cap right off his head.

THE BUBBLE GUM INCIDENT

On September 10, 1953, the Yankees were closing out their season series against the White Sox in New York. With a nine-game lead in the standings and 15 games left to play, another pennant seemed to be a foregone conclusion. Lefty junkballer Eddie Lopat was in command for the Yankees that day, allowing just four hits. In the late innings of the game—which was played on a Thursday afternoon in front of a relatively small crowd—Mantle began blowing bubbles from a clump of gum that was bulging from his cheek. An Associated Press photographer captured the moment on film, creating a major stir.

Despite his remarkable skills, Mantle had still not emerged as the eminent power threat he was made out to be. Though many of his home runs traveled considerable distances, he went deep just 21 times in 127 games while finishing second in the American League in strikeouts. A handful of sportswriters questioned his commitment to the team and accused him of not playing hard enough. The bubble gum photo, which was printed in local newspapers across the country, made Mantle appear as if he was slacking off.

Casey Stengel was livid. An article published in the *Sporting News* described the subsequent confrontation between the two men as such: "[Stengel] hauled Mantle on the carpet and asked him what he thought he was doing out there. Casey uttered about fifty dozen choice words, and Bubbles, of course, had nothing to say except, 'It will never happen again.'"

After admonishing Mantle for his actions, Stengel vented his frustration to an army of reporters, using phrases such as "juvenile silliness" and "kid stuff." Mantle pouted a bit, but kept quiet about the incident, which ended on a positive note. During the early 1950s, the Bazooka and Bowman companies supplied major-league dugouts with free gum hoping to win the loyalty of players and gain exclusive rights. Frank Scott—the agent handling Mantle's commercial affairs—called up Bowman and cut an endorsement deal. Ironically, it was Bazooka gum that Mantle had been chewing in the controversial photo.

NIGHTMARE AT 20,000 FEET

In the game's early days, players traveled primarily by bus or train. With the growing sophistication of commercial aircraft in the 1950s, flying became the standard mode of transportation for major leaguers. Not all players took to it well. Whitey Ford admitted to being uncomfortable on planes, and outfielder Jackie Jensen developed a crippling phobia that ultimately shortened his career.

A highly touted prospect in college, Jensen was the first man to appear in the Rose Bowl, the MLB All-Star Game, and the World Series. After joining the Yankees in 1950, he was slow in developing, prompting a trade to Washington two seasons later. He blossomed into a reliable run producer while playing for the Senators. After the Yankees beat the Dodgers in the 1953 World Series, pitcher Eddie Lopat assembled a squad of all-stars for a barnstorming tour of Hawaii and Japan. In spite of his extreme fear of flying, Jensen agreed to join the team. Other members of the roster included Yogi Berra and Billy Martin. Though Mantle was unable to attend, he enjoyed telling the story of what happened during the trip overseas.

Before the flight was underway, Jensen grabbed a seat in the front of the passenger compartment and worked himself into a deep state of meditation. A few hours into the flight, the plane encountered severe turbulence. Martin, who was seated in the back, decided to play a cruel joke on Jensen. Donning a Mae West vest and oxygen mask, the Yankee infielder rushed down the aisle shouting, "Jackie—Get Up!! We're going down!!" Jensen abruptly awoke from his trance-like state in a panic, fumbling for his vest and mask. When he realized that no one else was doing the same, he chased Martin all over the plane. Other players had to literally restrain him.

The Jensen incident wasn't the only misadventure involving Yankee players at high altitudes. During another flight (Mantle couldn't recall the specific year), members of the club were celebrating a playoff berth. Drinks began to flow copiously and a number of revelers became extremely intoxicated, including utility man Johnny Blanchard and relief specialist Ryne Duren. Accompanying the team that day was reporter Joe King, whose writing career spanned nearly four decades. As Blanchard began roaming the aisles socializing with teammates, he stumbled upon King, who had somehow fallen asleep amidst all the hoopla. For no discernible reason, Blanchard grabbed King's moustache and yanked out a fistful of hair. King cried out in pain and alarm. Furious with Blanchard for accosting him, he stomped off to notify manager Ralph Houk.

While Blanchard was rudely grooming King, Duren stumbled to the back of the plane and drunkenly announced that he was going to open the emergency hatch. This prompted everyone in the immediate vicinity to abruptly vacate their seats. By the time Houk arrived on the scene, the passenger compartment was in a state of utter chaos. According to Mantle, it was the last time that players were allowed to order drinks on a flight.

PERSONS OF INTEREST

Mantle became so famous as his career progressed that he captured the attention of FBI director J. Edgar Hoover. A controversial figure with questionable methods of gathering information, Hoover kept tabs on millions of Americans. Although Mantle was never actually the subject of a formal investigation, his name was brought up in connection with other cases on multiple occasions. This prompted Hoover to maintain a running file on the Yankee slugger. In 1969, the file was accessed by White House advisor John Ehrlichman, who requested a background check on several ballplayers. Ehrlichman learned that Mantle had been blackmailed by a woman in 1956 after reportedly being caught in a "compromising situation" with her. Mantle was also linked to a well-known gambler and bookmaker in Washington, DC, who had allegedly arranged for several Yankee players to be "entertained" by prostitutes in an upscale brothel.

Hoover was not the only one keeping tabs on the Bronx idol. Always on the hunt for information to use against his players, Yankee GM George Weiss hired private detectives to follow Mantle on several occasions. He also encouraged Red Patterson—the team's traveling secretary—to report back to him on Mantle's activities. Whitey Ford and Billy Martin were on Weiss's watch list along with a few others.

One night, the so-called Dead End Kids (Mantle, Ford, and Martin) were at a club in St. Louis watching comedian Ben Blue perform. In the middle of the show, Martin got into an argument with the bartender and Ralph Houk (who was still a player then) got involved. As the dispute came to a head, the club owner reportedly pulled a revolver on Houk. When Houk boldly proclaimed that he wasn't intimidated at all by the gun, the owner stood down and cooler heads prevailed.

Concerned that Weiss might find out about the incident, Mantle and Ford devised a plan to determine if there was an information leak. From St. Louis, the team traveled to Chicago. After a matinee against the White Sox at Comiskey Park, the Yankee duo returned to their hotel. They were well behaved that evening, watching a golf tournament on TV, ordering room service, and turning in early (11:00 by Ford's report). On the bus to the stadium the following day, they deliberately spoke loudly so they would be overheard. Their conversation contained the following dialogue:

FORD: How are you going to play today after getting in at six in the morning?

MANTLE: How the hell are you going to pitch—you were with me?

As it turned out, someone was listening. The leak was confirmed when the Yankees returned to New York. Weiss summoned the two conspirators to his office and imposed a $250 fine for breaking curfew in Chicago. After Whitey and Mickey explained that they had been at the hotel all evening and invented the story as a ruse, Weiss let them off with a stern warning not to misbehave in the future. "I guess we were damned if we did and damned if we didn't," Ford told biographer Joe Durso years later.

THE FORGOTTEN TWINS

Though it is often overlooked in retellings of Mantle's life story, he had twin brothers who both played professional baseball. Ray and Roy were born in February of 1936—five years after the arrival of their famous sibling. Both were multi-sport stars at Commerce High School, excelling at baseball and football. During his junior year, Ray scored 16 touchdowns as a left-side half-back—one of them on a 95-yard run. Roy scored eight TDs from the right-side halfback position that season. Their combined efforts helped the team to a district championship. Mickey followed both of their high school careers closely, attending games when he was able. In a 1953 newspaper article, he commented that he would like to see his brothers enroll at the University of Oklahoma and play football.

In 1954, Yankee scout Tom Greenwade signed Ray and Roy to minor-league contracts. Interestingly, their cousin, Max, was also acquired by the Yankees and released shortly before their arrival. One can only imagine the sensation it would have created had the Mantles patrolled the New York outfield together.

But it was not to be.

Ray, who swung from the right side of the plate, spent one season in the Class D Sooner State League and another in the Class C Cotton States League. He hit .231 in 97 games before enlisting in the Army. He never returned to baseball, spending his later years in the Las Vegas casino trade.

Roy—a lefty-swinger—played three seasons in four minor-league cir-cuits, making it as high as the B-level. He had his best year in 1955, when he was named to the Cotton States League all-star team. In 218 games, he hit .273 with 51 extra-base hits and 79 RBIs. He might have continued playing had a leg injury not forced him into premature retirement. Like his brother, he settled in Las Vegas, where he worked in the casino business.

In 1963, the Alou brothers—Felipe, Matty, and Jesus—became the first sibling trio to form an outfield tandem, appearing together for the San Francisco Giants. By then, Ray and Roy Mantle had faded from the public consciousness.

A VISIT TO THE FAR EAST

After the Yankees were beaten in the 1955 Fall Classic, they received an invi-tation to travel to Japan for a series of exhibition games (a tradition that had begun in the days of Babe Ruth). By October 1955, US involvement in the Korean conflict was winding down and Japan was still in post–World War II recovery. The tour was seen as a way to bridge the cultural gap between the two nations. Mantle was less than enthusiastic about it, commenting, "It was sort of a pain in the ass after playing all year long from back in February in Florida and all. But most of the guys had never been anywhere near Japan, so it was kind of exciting too."

Before arriving in the Far East, the team stopped off in Honolulu to play a pair of warmup games. From there, they continued on to Tokyo, where thousands of fans packed the streets to extend a hero's welcome. The Yankee entourage included owner Del Webb and baseball commissioner Ford Frick. The visitors received loud ovations and were treated like royalty. During the games, geisha girls appeared at home plate to hand out gifts after every Yankee home run.

The Bombers rattled off a long string of victories before locking horns with Japanese pitching great Masaichi Kaneda. A left-hander with a fastball that was rumored to travel around 110 mph, Kaneda was the only Japanese hurler to win 400 games. Even more impressive, he gathered most of those victories with one of Japan's worst teams—the Kokutetsu Swallows. The Yankees sent Whitey Ford to the mound against Kaneda. After walking the leadoff batter in the first inning, Ford delivered a pair of wild pickoff throws. The latter attempt hit the second base umpire squarely in the forehead and bounced all the way to the right field line, allowing a run to score. "He didn't flinch or even blink as far as I could see," Ford said of the umpire's reaction. "It was like nothing happened. He just turned around and watched Billy [Martin] chasing the ball down the right field line." Ford combined with Don Larsen for a no-hitter that day, but the Yankees managed just one run off of Kaneda as the game ended in a tie.

Mantle enjoyed the early part of the trip but soon began to feel homesick. Looking for a way out, he contacted his business partner—construction magnate Harold Youngman—with instructions to send a telegram stating that his wife was close to delivering their second child and required his presence. (Merlyn was entering her third trimester at the time.) Youngman did as instructed, and when Mantle presented the telegram to Casey Stengel, the Yankee skipper gave him permission to catch a flight home immediately. The Yankees completed the tour without him, compiling a 15-0-1 record. Merlyn didn't give birth until the day after Christmas. When word spread that the telegram was a sham, Mickey was reportedly fined $1,000 by commissioner Ford Frick.

MANTLE VERSUS THE SHIFT

Baseball in the modern era has become a game of analytics. Instead of playing hunches and trusting their instincts, managers use statistical data to guide them in their decisions. This is especially true in the case of defensive alignments. During the 2015 season, major-league managers collectively used more than 24,000 defensive shifts. That number was even higher the following year. It has become quite common for hitters to find opposing players clustered together on the left or right side of the field with gaping holes on the opposite side. The strategy is not a new one. In fact, it began long before Mickey Mantle wore a major-league uniform.

One of the earliest examples of a defensive shift can be linked to a player named Cy Williams. A left-handed hitter, Williams regularly finished among the top 10 in home runs during the Dead Ball Era, when rules against the use of spitballs were not enforced and umpires kept balls in play until they were soft and misshapen. Williams's 45 homers between 1915 and 1919 are not impressive by today's standards, but they were off the charts at a time when balls rarely left the park on the fly. After Indians shortstop Ray Chapman was struck and killed by a pitch in 1920, umpires were instructed to introduce new balls into play more often while cracking down on pitchers who were defacing them. The result was an unparalleled offensive explosion. Benefiting tremendously from the cozy dimensions of Philadelphia's Baker Bowl, Williams won three National League home-run crowns during the 1920s. Though he peaked at 41 homers in 1923, he had one glaring weakness as a player. "I couldn't hit a ball to left if my life depended on it," he admitted. Opposing managers began moving players to the right side whenever he came to the plate. It worked to an extent as his batting average dropped from a personal-high of .345 in 1926 to .274 the following year. Interestingly, he was not the only player named Williams to encounter defensive shifts in the game's early days.

In July 1941, White Sox manager Jimmy Dykes employed a shift against Boston slugger Ted Williams, shading all of his players to the right side of the infield. According to newspaper accounts, Williams was thrown out after hitting a hard grounder into right field. But he also blasted a double to the unoccupied left field corner, ultimately prompting Dykes to abandon the tactic.

Williams was forced to deal with the shift again in July 1946. This time, it was Hall of Famer Lou Boudreau who invoked the strategy. After driving in eight runs against the Indians in the opening game of a doubleheader,

Williams doubled and scored in his first at-bat of the nightcap. Looking to put an end to the onslaught, Boudreau employed a variation of the old shift, leaving the corner outfielders in their usual positions while moving everyone else to the right side. The alignment produced mixed results as Williams walked twice and grounded out. "If teams start doing that against me, I'll start hitting right-handed," he joked after the game. He ended up with a .342 cumulative batting average that year with a .385 mark against Cleveland.

Boudreau shelved the strategy for quite some time but revived it during Mantle's Triple Crown season of 1956. Entering a June 5 game against the A's, Mantle was hitting over .400 with 50 RBIs. He was on pace to break Babe Ruth's long-standing single-season record of 60 homers. Boudreau, who had accepted the managerial post in Kansas City the previous year, decided to use the shift on Mantle during the slugger's first at-bat. This time, it worked. Mickey had never seen the alignment before and was initially flustered, gazing into the dugout for assistance from Casey Stengel. Stengel flashed the bunt sign twice, but both of Mantle's attempts went foul and he ended up striking out. After going hitless in his next two at-bats, the Bronx idol caught a break. Hank Bauer reached on a single and Boudreau was forced to employ a standard defensive setup. In the absence of the shift, Mantle swatted a two-run homer. He hit .450 against the A's that year.

Though a handful of other players (Willie McCovey and Boog Powell among them) faced shifts in the decades that followed, the practice did not become standard procedure until the 21st century. Along with a variety of other factors, defensive shifts have contributed to declining batting averages in the majors. The aggregate big-league mark peaked at .270 in the year 2000. By 2021, it had fallen to .244. In the spring of 2022, the Major League Baseball Players Association agreed to multiple changes for the 2023 campaign, including a pitch clock, larger bases, and the termination of defensive shifts.

MANTLE VERSUS "TERRIBLE TED"

During Mantle's career, there were a number of ongoing debates about where he ranked in comparison to other star players. Fans in New York were known to come to blows when discussing who was the most talented center fielder in the Big Apple—Mantle, Mays, or Duke Snider. Loyal Red Sox followers argued that Ted Williams was the greatest natural hitter of the modern era. But in 1956, Mantle challenged the latter assertion.

At the age of 23, Williams became the last player to hit .400 in a season. He went on to claim a pair of Triple Crowns in 1942 and 1947. There is no telling how incredible his lifetime numbers could have been had he not sacrificed the better part of five seasons to military duty. During the 1950s, when the Red Sox finished no higher than third place, Williams was the primary gate attraction in Boston. To this day, he is considered by many to be the greatest player in franchise history.

Williams and Mantle were polar opposites. While Williams maintained a strict exercise regimen and prided himself on staying in shape, Mantle abused his body with alcohol. To Williams, there was a precise science to hitting, and he sought to be the game's undisputed master. In contrast, Mantle was less familiar with the technical aspects of hitting, relying instead upon raw power—a kind of "grip it and rip it" philosophy. Multiple batting crowns had given Williams an exaggerated sense of self-importance. Mantle, on the other hand, was plagued by self-doubt throughout his playing days.

Mantle got off to a torrid start in 1956, maintaining a .400 batting average through early June. After going 3-for-4 in his season debut, Williams injured his foot in the shower and was limited to pinch-hitting duty for the next several weeks. Upon returning to full-time action, he worked his batting average up to .363. Despite his commendable efforts, Boston writers began speculating that Mantle had replaced him as the premier hitter in the American League. Williams dedicated the rest of the season to proving them wrong.

Mantle led Williams by 26 points in the batting race entering the month of July. But an 8-for-14 performance in the first three games of the month helped Williams gain some ground. New York fans issued a collective groan on July 4 when Mantle came up limping after making a throw from the outfield in a game against the Red Sox. Later that evening, the Yankee icon received bad news from doctors at Lenox Hill Hospital. He had sprained his medial collateral ligament and would be forced to wear a heavy brace until it healed.

The All-Star break arrived in the nick of time, giving Mantle a bit of a rest. He was the only player on the ballot to receive more than 200,000 votes. To the delight of American League fans, Williams and Mantle crushed back-to-back homers against Warren Spahn in the sixth inning of the All-Star Game. Mickey performed well in the second half despite his knee injury, capturing the batting title by eight points over his rival in Boston.

For Williams, the low-point of the season came on August 7 in a game against the Yankees at Fenway Park. After he dropped a wind-blown popup hit by Mantle in the 11th inning, fans booed Williams mercilessly.

"The Splendid Splinter" followed with a spectacular game-saving catch on a hard smash hit by Yogi Berra, drawing cheers from the fickle Boston crowd. Recapping the incident in his 1969 memoirs, Williams groused, "I hate front-runners—people who are with you when you're up and against you when you're down. Well, if I'd had a knife, I probably would have stuck it in somebody." In the absence of a weapon, the fiery Red Sox slugger vented his frustration by spitting in the direction of fans. He received a $5,000 fine, which was the largest ever imposed upon a player for misconduct (equivalent to the penalty imposed on Babe Ruth by Miller Huggins in 1925). Williams later apologized to Boston executives and was permitted to keep the money.

Mantle and Williams battled for the crown again in 1957. Although Mantle assembled a career-high .365 batting average, it was Williams who came out on top, posting a lofty .388 mark. In later years, Mantle said that Williams was the best hitter he had ever seen. Williams, who could be gruff and critical to the point of virtual cruelty, was not quite as flattering in his assessment of Mantle. "I used to think Al Kaline could hit .400 or Mantle," he said. "But Mantle missed the ball too much. Too many strikeouts. He was forever going for the long ball, even with two strikes. Not quite enough finesse." There is truth in that statement. Mantle averaged one strikeout per every 4.73 at-bats during his career. In comparison, Williams averaged one whiff per every 10.86 at-bats.

THOSE WHO CAME BEFORE

Though Mantle had established himself as a bona fide star by the end of the 1955 campaign, he had yet to reach his full potential as a slugger. His Triple Crown performance in 1956 placed him in elite company. Only five AL players before him had led the league in home runs, RBIs, and batting average in the same season. While he was duly honored for the accomplishment, another major milestone went largely unnoticed that year.

In 1870, Bob ("Death to Flying Things") Ferguson became the game's first switch-hitter. Many players replicated the strategy in the years that followed, but it was Mantle who carried it to another level. Prior to 1956, the all-time mark for most homers by a switch-hitter was held by a little-known infielder named Ripper Collins. Only the most knowledgeable trivia buff could have associated him with the record in Mantle's era.

A fun-loving first baseman known more for his impish behavior off the field, Collins helped the St. Louis Cardinals to a pair of World Series titles in 1931 and 1934. He put forth his finest offensive effort in the latter campaign, leading the National League with 35 homers and 369 total bases. The arrival of Hall of Famer Johnny Mize in 1936 made Collins expendable. He was traded to Chicago, where his career took an unfortunate turn.

The Cubs had built a six-game lead over the second-place Giants by early August 1937. During a team visit to the Cook County Jail, Collins thought it would be amusing to sit in the facility's famous electric chair, which carried the nickname "Old Sparky." Several teammates advised Collins against it, believing that it would bring him bad luck, but he did it anyway. The next day, Collins broke his ankle sliding into home plate. In his absence, the Cubs dropped to second place, where they remained for the rest of the season. Collins never had another great slugging season. He was out of the majors by 1942, retiring with 135 lifetime homers.

Before Mantle, only a handful of players challenged Collins's record. The man who came the closest was Roy Cullenbine—a journeyman outfielder who played for six teams between 1938 and 1947. He might have claimed the all-time mark for himself had his career not ended prematurely.

Prior to the 1947 slate, a correspondent from the *Sporting News* reported that Tigers slugger Hank Greenberg was hoping to close out his career with the Yankees. Greenberg had said nothing of the sort, but the article provoked the ire of Detroit owner Walter Briggs, who promptly shipped the slugger off to Pittsburgh. With an opening in the Tiger lineup, Cullenbine was installed at first base. Appearing in 142 games, he slugged 24 homers and set a franchise record with 137 walks. On the downside, he compiled a feeble .224 batting average while committing 15 errors—fourth most among players at his position.

When the Phillies went shopping for a power hitter before the 1948 campaign, Tigers GM Billy Evans offered up Cullenbine's services. Having completed the most successful season of his career, Cullenbine showed up to the Phillies' training camp out of shape and overconfident. Twenty-one-year-old outfielder Richie Ashburn had a spectacular spring, and Cullenbine was released to make room for him on the Opening Day roster. Ashburn went on to a Hall of Fame career while Cullenbine disappeared from the majors with 110 switch-hit homers—second to Collins on the all-time list.

Collins's obscure record held up until May 18, 1956. In the opening game of a doubleheader at Comiskey Park in Chicago, Mantle went deep twice. The first homer—a two-run blast off of White Sox staff ace Billy Pierce—tied the game at three runs apiece. It also tied Mantle with Collins. In the top of the ninth, the Yankee center fielder struck again, launching a solo shot into the bleachers in right field. Though he had broken a major-league record, he got more attention for sending the game into extra innings. The Yankees ended up winning that day, 8–7. It was Mantle's third multi-homer effort of the season. He would turn the trick four more times that year.

As time marched on, Mantle significantly padded his lifetime totals. As of 2022, only five switch-hitters had reached the 400-homer plateau. Among those five, only Mantle and Eddie Murray exceeded the 500-mark.

THE WRATH OF NEWCOMBE

An intimidating presence at 6-foot-4, 220-plus pounds, pitcher Don New-combe enjoyed his finest season on the mound in 1956. In addition to winning 27 games, he finished among the league leaders in strikeouts, shutouts, and earned run average. His numbers were good enough to capture the first-ever Cy Young Award along with MVP honors.

Newcombe relied heavily on his fastball, but he also had an elusive curve that behaved like a slider. He reached the 20-win threshold three times between 1951 and 1956, sacrificing two full seasons in his prime to military service. In spite of all his success, the ornery right-hander's volcanic temper landed him in hot water throughout his career.

Prior to the 1956 World Series, Newcombe had lost all of his postseason outings to the Yankees. Selected to pitch in Game 2, he was hoping to shake the stigma of failure. But 36 starts and 268 innings of work had taken a heavy toll on his arm. Though he was in a considerable amount of pain, he was too proud to tell manager Walter Alston about it.

It was fairly obvious early on that Newcombe was ailing. After tagging him for a run in the first inning, the Yankees nearly batted around in the second. Yogi Berra's grand slam, which sailed out of Ebbets Field and bounced across a nearby gas station parking lot, put the Bombers up 6–0. Having seen enough at that point, Alston removed Newcombe from the game and replaced him with reliever Ed Roebuck.

In a fit of anger and frustration, Newcombe headed straight for the clubhouse, changed out of his uniform, and left the ballpark. On his way out, a parking attendant made some disparaging remarks, bringing him to the boiling point. In their biography, *A Season in the Sun: The Rise of Mickey Mantle*, authors Randy Roberts and Johnny Smith explained, "[Newcombe's] fury was shaped by the racism he experienced as a black man off the field and the epithets hurled at him in stadiums across the country." The Dodger moundsman went ballistic, punching his tormentor in the stomach. An on-duty patrolman separated the two men and transported them both to the police station. The lot attendant later refused to press any charges.

Had Newcombe kept his cool and returned to the Brooklyn dugout, he would have seen his teammates immediately climb out of the hole he had put them in. The Dodgers sent nine men to the plate in the bottom of the second. Roy Campanella and Pee Wee Reese each drove in a run and Duke Snider hit a grand slam that tied the score at 6 apiece. The rest of the afternoon went very poorly for the Yankees as their crosstown rivals tacked on seven more runs, winning the game handily, 13–8. One New York newspaper ran the headline, "Murder at Ebbets Field."

Mantle had a mediocre day at the plate, going 1-for-4 with a walk and a run scored. He said afterward that the entire team was embarrassed. Throughout the Series, a ghostwritten column bearing his name appeared in the *New York World-Telegram and Sun*. After the Game 2 defeat, Mickey and his ghostwriter thanked Brooklyn fans for not booing the Yankees off the field.

Alston gave Newcombe another chance to shake his postseason curse in Game 7. It was an utter disaster as Yogi Berra tagged him for a pair of home runs. After yielding a leadoff blast to Elston Howard in the fourth, he was replaced with Don Bessent. He finished his undistinguished World Series career at 0-4 with an unwieldy ERA of 8.59.

UNRULY GUESTS

Mantle's ability to stir up trouble in hotels was legendary. One day, after missing the team bus from Baltimore to Washington, DC, he and Whitey Ford paid a cab driver to make the 40-mile trip between the two cities. While traveling along US Route 1, Mickey spotted a roadside vendor selling fireworks and asked the cabbie to stop. After purchasing a generous supply of Roman candles, the Yankee duo set off again toward the Shoreham Hotel, where the team was staying. Like a couple of mischievous kids, they ignited one of the fireworks in the backseat of the taxi, scaring the driver half to death. Their impromptu pyrotechnic display continued in Mantle's room at the hotel as he and Ford fired off all of the remaining Roman candles, filling the hallway with smoke and alarming guests, who had no idea where the noise and acrid stench was coming from.

According to pitcher Jim Bouton, the fireworks incident was not the only mischief Mantle engaged in at the Shoreham Hotel. In his tell-all book, *Ball Four*, Bouton referred to the Shoreham as "the beaver shooting capital of the world." The term "beaver shooting" is a euphemism for the act of spying on women in various states of undress. According to Bouton, the L-shaped hallways of the Shoreham Hotel made the bedroom windows easily visible from particular vantage points on the roof. He claimed that Yankee players would head out onto the roof in large groups, sometimes led by Mantle himself, in an attempt to get a glimpse of some nudity. "One of the biggest thrills I had with the Yankees was joining about half the club on the roof of the Shoreham at 2:30 in the morning," Bouton confessed. "I remember saying to myself, 'so, this is the big leagues.'"

Mantle's voyeurism was not limited to the Shoreham Hotel. One night, while the team was staying in Detroit, Mickey and Billy Martin climbed out of their hotel window onto the ledge to see what was going on inside the rooms of their teammates. It didn't take them long to realize that it was the middle of the night and just about everyone was fast asleep. The ledge was too narrow for them to turn around, so they had to literally retrace their steps. It was a challenging process considering the fact that they had consumed quite a few drinks and the ledge was located several stories off the ground. Fortunately, they made it back to their room without becoming a cautionary tale.

STUFFING THE BALLOT BOX

Though civic pride is an admirable trait, it can also be carried to an extreme. Such was the case in 1957 when fans in Cincinnati conspired to send a team composed entirely of local players to the All-Star Game. They almost got away with it.

The movement began when the Kroger supermarket chain sponsored a daily ballot in the *Cincinnati Times-Star*. Names of hometown players at each position were prominently displayed along with the slogan, "Vote Often— Vote Early!" (Interestingly, executives in Cincinnati had officially changed the team name to Redlegs in 1954 to avoid being associated with communism.) Bolstering the campaign, Ruth Lyons—host of the popular morning TV show *The 50/50 Club*—began urging her viewers to vote. Ballots were also supplied to local bars by the Burger Brewing Company—an official team sponsor. One tavern known as "The Z-Bar" was responsible for submitting 10,000 completed ballots.

As the results of fan voting began to filter into the office of the commissioner, Ford Frick realized that something needed to be done. To avoid an all-Reds starting lineup, Frick inserted Willie Mays into center field in place of Gus Bell. Right fielder Wally Post was swapped out for Hank Aaron. And

Stan Musial was installed at first base instead of George Crowe. Frick justi-fied his actions with the following statement: "I took this step in an effort to be entirely fair to all fans and with no reflection on the honesty or sincerity of the Cincinnati poll. . . . [We] felt that the overbalance of Cincinnati bal-lots has resulted in the selection of a team which would not be typical of the league."

Shortly after Frick's decision was announced, Reds GM Gabe Paul sent a message to Frick chastising him for ignoring the votes of fans and request-ing that Crowe, Bell, and Post all be included on the NL roster as reserves. One fan even went so far as to hire a local attorney to sue the Commissioner's Office. The lawsuit was dropped when Frick added Bell to the team. Crowe and Post were ultimately excluded. The starting lineup included five Cincin-nati players.

There was far less drama in the American League as fans voted for an evenly balanced roster. Six of the eight AL teams were represented in the starting lineup. The reserves included players from both of the remaining clubs—the A's and Senators. Mantle was the top vote-getter at his position for the fifth year in a row.

The game was played at Busch Stadium in St. Louis. More than 30,000 fans saw Mantle single and score in the top of the second as the AL jumped out to a 2–0 lead. Yogi Berra—the other Yankee starter—padded the AL lead in the sixth with an RBI single. Trailing 6–2 in the bottom of the ninth, the NL broke through for three runs off of pitchers Billy Pierce and Don Mossi. With two outs and the tying run on base, Yankee closer Bob Grim retired the dangerous Gil Hodges on a flyball to left field.

In the wake of the 6–5 AL victory, Frick told a writer from the *Sporting News*, "I strongly object to our league making a burlesque out of the All-Star Game. I never want to see such an exhibition again." To prevent similar incidents from occurring in the future, he stripped fans of the right to vote. Players, coaches, and managers chose the rosters until 1970, when commis-sioner Bowie Kuhn turned things back over to the fans. Mantle was named to 14 more All-Star teams before he retired.

A LITTLE HELP FROM HIS FRIENDS
Humble about his own abilities, Mantle once told a writer, "I was never known for being a smart baseball player. . . . I could run and throw and hit. But I didn't know the game." Pitcher Bob Turley was among several team-mates Mantle turned to for help over the years.

A Cy Young Award winner and World Series MVP in 1958, Turley was adept at stealing signs from opposing teams. He acquired the skill while pitching for the lowly St. Louis Browns during the early 1950s. "That's always been a part of the game and it will be part of the game forever," said Hall of Famer Whitey Ford. "[Turley] was the best at it on our team. Some guys liked to know what was coming. Mickey did, especially batting left-handed."

Utilizing his sharp observational skills, Turley was able to reliably predict the arrival of curves and fastballs. Though players like Yogi Berra and Moose Skowron preferred not to know what pitches were on the way, Mantle (a dead fastball hitter) used Turley's advance notifications to a distinct advantage. If Mantle heard Turley whistle, he knew a heater was coming. If the Yankee hurler remained quiet, it meant that a breaking pitch would follow.

In addition to stealing signs directly from catchers, Turley learned to interpret the idiosyncrasies of pitchers. Some were more obvious than others. For instance, Connie Johnson of the Orioles had a habit of moving his right foot to the left side of the mound when he delivered his signature screwball. Early Wynn positioned his hands at different levels depending on what he was going to throw, and Jim Bunning had slight variations in his windup. "All pitchers are trying to be perfect and if you observe them, you can pick it all up," Turley told a writer from the *Daily News*.

Mantle estimated that Turley's predictions were accurate about 70 percent of the time. He gave the hurler credit for a quarter of his home runs between 1955 and 1962. "Mickey exaggerated a little bit," Turley joked. "It was good for my ego."

EXTRACURRICULAR ACTIVITIES

Though Mantle genuinely loved his wife, he had numerous trysts over the years. From his earliest days as a major leaguer, he chased after women in almost every city he visited. One of his first conquests was an actress named Holly Brooke, who released details of the fling in a 1957 issue of *Confidential* magazine. In a full-length article she wrote herself, she claimed to have struck a deal with Mantle's personal agent entitling her to 25 percent of the slugger's publicity earnings.

Around the same time that he was sneaking around with Brooke, Mantle allegedly slept with a Vegas showgirl nicknamed "Peaches," who was a close personal friend of notorious mob boss Joe Bonanno. Bonanno considered putting a hit out on Mantle, but ultimately decided against it. The slugger's escapades continued throughout his career and beyond. According to gossip columnist Ben Widdicombe, Mantle once went out on a "date" with actress Angie Dickinson. He was so drunk by the time he got her in bed, he vomited while performing a sexual act on her. On another occasion, he handed sports reporter Diane Shah a card that read: "Wanna Fuck?"

A number of Mantle's late-night hookups were with call girls—a habit that greatly concerned Casey Stengel. "You can't tell me he [isn't] getting some of them all the time," the veteran skipper said in confidence to a writer. "He's got enough ailments, so he [doesn't] need to get the clap too. His taste [in] broads isn't great, except for that one he's married to and hasn't been together with in a million years. . . ."

During 1960s road trips, Mantle would stay at the home of Kansas City businessman Dan Tanner, whom he had met through friends at a country club. Tanner revealed that Mantle had an extensive collection of women's undergarments, which he kept as trophies. Though Merlyn was vaguely aware of some of her husband's affairs, she ignored the behavior for years. As the slugger grew less and less discreet about his infidelity over time, her patience was tested to the limit. During a dinner with friends one night, she blurted out, "I'm just trying to figure out how many of the women at this table my husband has slept with." Mantle angrily told her to shut up and go back to Oklahoma. On another occasion, after Mickey had asked a waitress for her phone number at a fantasy camp dinner, Merlyn threw a chair at him, breaking a glass coffee table in the hotel suite they were staying in. Guests in neighboring rooms overheard the ruckus and called the police. Though officers placed the two in separate quarters, Mickey called Merlyn later and convinced her to spend the night with him.

Around the 50th anniversary of Yankee Stadium, team officials handed out questionnaires to the most prominent players asking them to share their fondest memories. Demonstrating the crude side of his personality, Mantle listed his most outstanding experience as having oral sex performed on him by a woman under the right field bleachers near the Yankee bullpen. He provided explicit details of the encounter and signed the questionnaire, "Mickey Mantle—The All-American Boy."

In 1983, reporter Jane Leavy was dispatched by the *Washington Post* to do a feature on Mantle after he was hired as a greeter by the Claridge Hotel and Casino in Atlantic City. Over the course of three days, he frequently embarrassed her with his vulgar behavior. Not only did he make an unwelcome sexual advance, but he shared a number of inappropriate stories, including an anecdote detailing how he and Billy Martin used to shoot water up the skirts of women waiting in line for tickets at Yankee Stadium through a clubhouse window. As a sad reminder of the cringe-worthy three-day encounter, Leavy received a signed picture from Mantle that read, "To Jane: Sorry I farted. Your friend, Mick."

While working at the Claridge Casino, Mantle began seeing a woman named Linda Fetters, whom he introduced to Merlyn as his secretary. When that relationship cooled off, he took up with a former Georgia schoolteacher named Greer Johnson. According to Leavy, "[Johnson] arrived at a precipitous moment in the development of the memorabilia trade. She would become [Mantle's] companion, his drinking buddy, his lover, and employee, playing an indispensible role in the rebranding and marketing of The Mick."

Merlyn found out about Johnson on their 35th wedding anniversary. The truth came out after Mickey had a one-night stand with the wife of a well-known country singer at a celebrity golf tournament. There was a horrible argument between Mickey and Merlyn, during which the identities of Mickey's lovers were revealed. In the wake of the argument, Merlyn suffered a mild stroke, which was said to be stress induced. Johnson claimed that Merlyn called her afterward and told her, "I will never divorce Mickey. I like being Mrs. Mickey Mantle."

Acting as Mantle's business manager, Johnson earned 20 percent of all the bookings she arranged for him. As it turned out, he was in great demand, and the two of them made out quite well. In 1988, Mantle finally decided to leave Merlyn, referring to it as "one of the hardest and dumbest things [he] ever did." They remained separated but never got a divorce. In the wake of the split, Mantle shared a condo in Greensboro, Georgia, with Johnson.

After a rehab stint at the Betty Ford Center in 1994, Mantle began making amends. He accepted blame for the destruction of his marriage and expressed deep regret for the anguish his actions had caused family members. Before his passing, he reconciled with Merlyn and his surviving children. As he grew increasingly ill, Merlyn began to reassert her presence in Mickey's life. Looking to avoid a confrontation, Mickey cut Johnson out of the picture to a great extent. They did continue to speak on the phone until he lay on his deathbed. Johnson attended the funeral with Mantle's good friend Pat Summerall. Summerall was invited to sit in front of the church with the family but chose to remain in the back with Johnson.

In 1997, Johnson auctioned off hundreds of Mantle's personal belongings, including his birth certificate and some empty prescription bottles. Upon contacting the Mantle family beforehand, she was was hit with a lawsuit

Mantle's boyish good looks attracted scores of female admirers. He had numerous trysts over the years, and this ultimately led to a divorce from his wife, Merlyn. (Courtesy of The National Baseball Hall of Fame)

prohibiting her from selling a number of items. In the end, she made more than $500,000, which she put in trust to be donated to charity upon her death. A bag of Mantle's hair, which had been assembled by a barber, sold for over $6,000.

THE ALL-STAR BET

In 1959, Major League Baseball began raising money for the players' pension funds by holding two All-Star Games. The experiment continued until 1962, when attendance and television ratings started to decline. The first game of the 1961 Midsummer Classic was held at Candlestick Park in San Francisco. Named for the birds that still inhabit the area, the stadium was built on the western shore of San Francisco Bay. Strong winds frequently gusted into the ballpark, making it one of the dampest, chilliest venues in the majors. During the game in question, blustery conditions directly affected the events on the field.

With the National League nursing a 3–2 lead in the ninth, manager Danny Murtaugh called upon Giants closer Stu Miller to get the last two outs. While facing Tigers slugger Rocky Colavito, Miller faltered in his delivery as a blast of wind pushed him slightly off balance. The umpire called a balk, sending Roger Maris to second base and Al Kaline to third. This led to a game-tying run. The next day, the Associated Press exaggerated the story, reporting that Miller had literally been blown off the mound. "They couldn't have made it any bigger," the hurler later recalled. "They made it out to be like I was pinned against the center field fence." The incident became the defining moment of Miller's career.

While the atmospheric conditions in San Francisco generated headlines that day, another drama was unfolding behind the scenes. During the 1950s and early 1960s, there was an ongoing debate among fans as to who was the best center fielder in the majors. Duke Snider figured prominently into the mix for a while, but as his numbers went into decline, the primary focus shifted to Mantle and Willie Mays. Most fans assumed the rivalry between the two was less than friendly, but they actually had an amicable relationship, sometimes golfing together in the offseason.

Prior to the 1961 All-Star Game, Mantle and Whitey Ford flew out to San Francisco to get in a round of golf and relax. Giants owner Horace Stoneham arranged for the pair to play at the country club he was a member of. Neither had the proper attire, so they visited the pro shop and purchased the necessary items. They also had a few drinks at the bar.

Mantle and teammate Roger Maris (kneeling) posing for a photo with other members of the 1961 American League All-Star team. Pictured from left to right are Harmon Killebrew of the Twins, Jim Gentile of the Orioles, Norm Cash of the Tigers, and Rocky Colavito, also of the Tigers. The game, which was held at Fenway Park in Boston, ended in a 1–1 tie. (Courtesy of The Leslie Jones Collection: Boston Public Library)

Since the club didn't accept cash, they charged it to Stoneham's account. According to Mantle, the bill came to around $400 (equivalent to about $3,600 today).

Later that evening, Mantle and Ford attended a party hosted by Stoneham. When Ford tried to pay the Giants executive back, he refused, offering the following wager instead: If Ford faced Mays in the All-Star Game and got him out, the debt would be erased. If Mays reached safely, Stoneham would be entitled to twice the amount owed. Ford enjoyed a good challenge and promptly agreed. But Mantle—realizing that Mays was among the most successful hitters in All-Star history—scoffed at the idea. Ford eventually talked him into playing along.

The anticipated matchup took place in the bottom of the first inning. Ford retired Maury Wills and Eddie Mathews on groundouts, bringing Mays to the plate. Mantle watched nervously from his outfield post as the Giants slugger struck out on three pitches, freeing him from his obligation to Stoneham. Mantle later claimed that Ford secretly admitted to throwing a spitball during the at-bat.

THE ORIGINAL HOME RUN DERBY

The annual Home Run Derby, which precedes the MLB All-Star Game, has become a popular attraction among fans. Held for the first time in 1985, its format has changed dramatically over the years. Many people don't realize that the event was inspired by a 1960s television show.

The idea of a slugging competition between the game's premier power hitters was first proposed by Lou Breslow—a Hollywood writer, producer, and director who had worked with a number of comedy icons such as The Marx Brothers and The Three Stooges. In 1959, Breslow teamed with Mark Scott to bring the concept to life. Scott—a Pacific Coast League broadcaster and host of a Los Angeles TV program called "Meet the Dodgers"—had no problem convincing some of the game's brightest stars to participate. Though the major networks showed no immediate interest in Breslow's brain child, a company known as Ziv Productions, which provided syndicated TV programs to the three broadcasting giants, green-lighted the project.

The rules of the competition were simple. Two major leaguers squared off in a home-run-hitting contest lasting for nine "innings." Outs were charged for every batted ball that failed to clear the fence in fair territory. Batters could take pitches, but any offering ruled a strike by the home plate umpire also counted as an out. At the end of the ninth inning, the player with the most homers was declared the winner. Scott served as the announcer while Art Passarella, a former American League arbiter, called balls and strikes. There were also umpires stationed along both foul lines.

The show ran on a tight budget and prizes were modest—$2,000 to the winner and $1,000 to the runner-up. An additional $500 was awarded to any player who hit three consecutive homers (a somewhat rare event). Filming took place at Wrigley Field in Los Angeles, which had been built in 1925 by Cubs owner William Wrigley. It served as the home of the Pacific Coast League Angels and Hollywood Stars for three decades. By the time filming for *Home Run Derby* began, neither team was in residence.

Some of the greatest matchups of all time were featured on the show, including Hank Aaron versus Duke Snider, Ernie Banks versus Gil Hodges, and Rocky Colavito versus Harmon Killebrew. To draw the interest of fans from the onset, the series premiere was a showdown between the game's most celebrated center fielders—Mickey Mantle versus Willie Mays. Though Mantle wore a permanent grin throughout the half-hour episode, Mays appeared rather serious. There were a few isolated moments when the Giants slugger chuckled politely at comments made by Scott.

Mantle chose to bat right-handed, remarking that most of his longest homers had come from that side of the plate. He got off to a very slow start, falling behind by a score of 8–2. At the end of the fifth, the following exchange took place between Scott and Mantle:

SCOTT: Mickey, you've now gone through a stretch of 10 straight outs without a homer, but you still have time to get back in the race.

MANTLE: I know. This is getting embarrassing.

SCOTT: Well, I wouldn't call it that. You just don't happen to have your swing with you so far.

After managing a single homer in the bottom of the sixth, Mantle conceded, "This ain't my day." He spoke too soon as Mays failed to pad his lead in four consecutive innings. The Yankee slugger rallied with three homers in the seventh and two more in the eighth. He hammered the winning shot on the first pitch of the ninth, claiming the $2,000 prize.

Mays returned in a later episode, soundly beating Senators outfielder Bob Allison. Mantle was a frequent contestant, making five appearances and winning four times. His only loss came in a tightly contested match against Killebrew.

Sadly, the show ended up being cancelled after Scott died of a heart attack at the age of 45. The first season had just completed its run when he passed away. In 1985, ESPN purchased the rights and re-broadcast all 26 episodes. A DVD of the entire season was released in 2007.

THERE'S ONE BORN EVERY MINUTE

Mantle was never particularly lucky in business. Though the Holiday Inn he owned in Joplin, Missouri, was sold for a profit in the mid-1960s, most of his other ventures were complete flops. In fact, he was fleeced by con-men multiple times during his playing days. In his rookie year, he signed with a slippery agent named Alan Savitt, who milked him for 50 percent of the profits from endorsements. Strapped for cash, Savitt later sold 25 percent of his shares to a showgirl that Mantle was sleeping with. Hank Bauer helped Mantle recover by setting him up with a more reputable agent, Frank Scott, who had worked in the Yankees front office.

Evaluating her husband's business instincts, Merlyn Mantle wrote in her memoirs, "Mickey believed nearly everything he heard and trusted just about anyone he met." Realizing he was an easy mark, salesmen (many of them shysters) regularly showed up at his front door. In 1956, a man referring to himself as C. Roy Williams rolled up in a fancy Cadillac and offered Mantle a chance to invest in a new insurance company. Though Mickey was warned by Merlyn and his business partner, Harold Youngman, not to trust the fast-talking stranger, he forked over a significant portion of his World Series bonus. It turned out that the insurance company didn't even exist. Williams—an ex-con—was eventually apprehended by the FBI for a string of white-collar crimes, but Mantle never got his money back.

In 1959, Mantle and Whitey Ford were contacted by Cleveland pitching ace Bob Feller, who had developed a reputation as a savvy investor. Feller told the pair about a lucrative opportunity in the fallout shelter trade. Intrigued, Mantle and Ford agreed to meet with a Toronto businessman named Ted Boomer—founder of the Canadian Bomb Shelter Survival Corporation. Boomer claimed that his company was on the verge of expanding into the United States and promised to make the Yankee idols rich by offering them a $10,000 stake in the business (equivalent to roughly $95,000 today). Mantle and Ford walked away with 45,000 shares of stock and a seat on the board of directors.

Like most of Mantle's investments, it was too good to be true. Boomer cashed the checks and, after a couple of follow-up consults, disappeared entirely. Mantle and Ford never pursued legal action. They didn't even discuss the matter with Feller until many years later. By then, it had become a private joke between the two. In his 1977 autobiography, Ford commented, "To this day, I still have the 45,000 shares of stock at home. . . . Canadian bomb shelter company, my ass." Mantle continued to make business deals in the years that followed, joking that his involvement in any endeavor might scare off other interested parties.

THE BALLAD OF MICKEY AND GEORGE

Elected to the Hall of Fame in 1971, George Weiss was never noted for his warm relationships with players. A Yale University dropout, he made the jump from minor-league director to Yankee general manager in the late 1940s. During his 13 years on the job, he kept the team well stocked with talented prospects and dynamic veterans. But his tight-fisted business practices curried no favor with any of them. "Weiss cared nothing about the players as people," said infielder Jerry Lumpe. "We were meat, and our only reason for existing was what we could do for George Weiss and the franchise."

Though he received due credit for the seven World Series titles won by the Yankees on his watch, Weiss's poor treatment of Mantle was highly unjustified. Not only did he hire private detectives to monitor the slugger's late-night activities, but he traded Billy Martin—Mantle's closest friend—to the A's for questionable reasons (a topic covered in a previous section of this book). Between 1953 and 1956, when Mantle was establishing himself as the greatest center fielder in the American League (and perhaps all of baseball), Weiss offered only modest salary increases.

Even after being shown up by superiors, the incorrigible Weiss continued to drive a hard bargain with Mantle and other players. Pitcher Bob Turley remarked, "When you talked salary with George Weiss, it was like pulling teeth." Relief specialist Ryne Duren was in complete agreement. "Players just despised Weiss," said Duren. "He was cheap and aloof. We all felt exploited and frustrated."

In spite of ongoing shoulder and knee miseries, Mantle finished among the AL leaders in runs scored, total bases, and home runs during the 1959 slate. Even so, his numbers weren't on par with previous seasons, prompting Weiss to propose a massive $17,000 pay cut. Feeling cheated and under-appreciated, the Yankee slugger held out for two weeks. His decision drew criticism from a number of New York sportswriters. Joe Trimble of the *Daily News* referred to Mickey as a "hillbilly in a velvet suit." Hall of Fame scribe Dick Young labeled him "emotionally immature."

Mantle's public image took another hit when he joined several teammates on a booze-filled harbor cruise. In an unfortunate turn of events, the boat they were on caught fire and sank in St. Petersburg Bay. Players (some of them naked) were pulled from the water by the harbor patrol. Though Casey

Stengel was somewhat amused, Weiss and other Yankee executives were not. It marked the end of Mantle's holdout. He ultimately agreed to a $10,000 salary cut.

Weiss left the Yankee front office in 1961, but Mantle held a long-standing grudge. At a 1984 awards dinner sponsored by the Baseball Writers' Association of America, Mickey launched into an alcohol-fueled tirade against the former executive (who was more than 10 years in his grave by then). Mantle's profanity-laden rant stunned the crowd, which included a number of children.

BOX OFFICE BONANZA

During the celebrated home-run race of 1961, Mantle and Roger Maris became the most sought-after personalities in baseball. Not only did they land starring roles in the family friendly comedy *Safe at Home!*, but they made cameo appearances (along with Yogi Berra) in the Universal Pictures romantic comedy *That Touch of Mink*. Both films were released in June 1962. Although *Safe at Home!* was a commercial and critical flop, *That Touch of Mink* was a box office smash, becoming the fourth highest-grossing film of the year. Starring Hollywood icons Cary Grant and Doris Day, the movie inspired a subsequent novelization.

In the early part of the 1950s, a majority of comedies were prudish in their portrayal of male/female relationships. Even married couples slept in separate beds on television. But in the late 1950s and early 1960s, Day appeared in a series of films that were a bit more risqué. In *That Touch of Mink*, the virgin Cathy Timberlake (played by Day) is pressured by Grant's character (Philip Shayne) to engage in an intimate relationship out of wedlock. The movie's popularity signified a shift in American paradigms regarding casual sex. One of the film's most amusing scenes is set at Yankee Stadium, where Shayne—part owner of the team—arranges for Timberlake to watch a game from the dugout.

The clip opens with a faraway shot of the field as an unidentified player takes a called strike. The camera jumps to the Yankee bench, where Timberlake is sitting with Maris, Mantle, Berra, and Shayne. "Hey, Ump!" Timberlake shouts. "Shake your hands! Your eyeballs are stuck!" Responding to the remark, the umpire—played by former AL arbiter Art Passarella—appears in front of the dugout. The following dialogue unfolds:

PASSARELLA: Little lady, will you let me umpire this game? You've been on my back all night.

TIMBERLAKE: (Turning to Mantle) Mickey, you saw that pitch. It was a ball wasn't it?

MANTLE: . . . Looked like it.

PASSARELLA: (irritably) You're out of the game, Mantle!

TIMBERLAKE: (agitated—turns to Maris) What?! Roger, how'd that pitch look to you?

MARIS: It could have missed the corner.

PASSARELLA: (aggravated) You're out, Maris!

TIMBERLAKE: (outraged—springs from her seat and walks over to Berra) Yogi?

BERRA: (sardonically) It's a perfect strike. The ump was right.

PASSARELLA: I don't like sarcasm, Berra. You're out of the game, too.

TIMBERLAKE: You can't do that!

PASSARELLA: Lady . . . !!

TIMBERLAKE: (to Shayne) Where's the manager?

SHAYNE: I think he's hiding.

To help promote the film, Day and Grant posed for a number of photos with all three Yankee superstars. They also clowned around with members of the Los Angeles Angels. Interestingly, Day was 39 years old at the time the movie was shot but playing a character in her 20s. The popular actress described her handsome co-star as private and immensely closed off. "Our relationship in *That Touch of Mink* was amicable but devoid of give and take," she wrote in her memoirs. "Not that he wasn't friendly and polite—he certainly was. But distant. Very distant."

Grant didn't actually like the finished product, but critics did. A *New York Times* writer praised the film for its "lively, lilting script," its "glittering verbal wit," and "briskly propulsive pace." In comparison, *Safe at Home!* was not as well received, getting mostly negative reviews. It failed to appear among the top 20 films of 1962 in terms of box office earnings.

KEEPING IT UNDER WRAPS

In the early days of New York baseball, Babe Ruth frequently engaged in scandalous behavior. Because he was a beloved figure to fans and sportswriters, a number of unsavory episodes were kept out of the newspapers. Mantle enjoyed the same privilege at the height of his career.

One night, Mickey and his wife were having dinner at a restaurant with Yogi and Carmen Berra. While other members of the party drank in moderation, Mickey admitted to being intoxicated by the end of the evening. As the two couples were leaving in separate cars, Yogi spotted Merlyn climbing into the passenger seat and strongly advised her to take the wheel. A spirited debate over who should be operating the vehicle ended with Mickey tearing stubbornly out of the parking lot.

When it became obvious that Mickey's driving was impaired, Merlyn implored him to let her take over. He ignored her objections, continuing up the road. Angry and frustrated, Merlyn began swatting him with her purse. As Mickey tried to grab it from her, he swerved off the road and collided with a telephone pole. Miraculously, neither of them was seriously hurt, though Merlyn needed stitches for a deep cut on her head.

The officer who arrived on the scene was the couple's next-door neighbor. He called in the accident and drove them to the hospital. A police report was filed and Mickey was fined for damage to the pole, but no DUI charges were ever pressed. "The cop covered for me," the slugger recalled in his memoirs. "But I realized right then and there that I might have a problem. So, while I'm proud of everything I accomplished in my career, if I had to do it over again, I would definitely have cut down on the booze."

After writing those words, Mantle waited nearly a decade to enter rehab. The car accident story, which appeared in a book he coauthored in 1985 with

Herb Gluck, was followed by the haunting remark: "I'll say this—in the past few years my drinking has been confined to social occasions. Merlyn has been successful in reminding me if I forget. As a matter of fact, if it wasn't for her, I probably would have wound up an alcoholic like so many other ballplayers who did come to a tragic end that way." He had no idea that his statement would serve as foreshadowing of his own sad demise.

PITCHERS WHO OWNED THE MICK

There was no shame in giving up a home run to Mickey Mantle. He hit 536 of them during his career. And he made a point of running with his head down so as not to embarrass opposing pitchers. This is not to say that he was above engaging in a bit of friendly trash-talk from time to time.

On May 4, 1961, the Yankees held a 3–2 sixth-inning lead over the Twins at Metropolitan Stadium. With stiff winds blowing toward home plate and Mantle at bat, Minnesota pitcher Ted Sadowski allegedly shouted, "I bet you can't hit one out against this gale. I bet you a case of beer you won't do it." As the story goes, Mantle replied "I'll take a Budweiser" before pounding the next pitch into the right field bleachers.

Even some of the greatest pitchers of all time looked bad against Mantle. The Yankee icon compiled a .474 batting average against Hall of Famer Hal Newhouser and a .500 on-base percentage against Jim "Catfish" Hunter. Oddly enough, there were less talented hurlers Mantle couldn't buy a hit off of. Some of his no-name nemeses are listed below.

Joe Sparma

A right-hander, Sparma won 16 games for the Tigers in 1967 while posting a mediocre 3.76 ERA. His lifetime mark was even higher. Nevertheless, Mantle had his share of difficulties against the little-known curveballer, managing an anemic .162 batting average in 40 plate appearances.

Saul Rogovin

In the early part of his career, Rogovin captured an ERA title while relying heavily upon his fastball. He later added a changeup and slow curve to his repertoire. Though opponents tagged him for a cumulative .262 batting average, Mantle was far less successful, managing just six hits in 48 plate appearances for a .125 mark.

Dick Radatz
Radatz had three very good seasons with the Red Sox in the early 1960s, and then lost his effectiveness after slugger Ted Williams convinced him to broaden his pitch selection with the addition of a sinker. The big right-hander compiled a 4.54 ERA from 1965 through 1969—pretty awful for a reliever. Even so, Mantle struggled against him, going 3-for-16 in 19 plate appearances with 12 strikeouts.

Dave Boswell
A slender right-hander, Boswell peaked in 1969 with the Twins, winning 20 games. Injuries destroyed his career after that. Had every batter in the AL fared as poorly as Mantle did against him, he might have hung around the majors a lot longer. The Yankee slugger went 3-for-26 against Boswell while striking out 11 times.

For the record, there were plenty of middling hurlers who were punished by Mantle over the years. The Bronx masher compiled a collective .442 batting average with 13 homers and 45 RBIs against journeymen Hal Brown, Hank Aguirre, and Bill Wight. Jack Harshman of the White Sox once griped, "They ought to create a new league for that guy!"

BATTING UNDER THE INFLUENCE
In 1963, Mantle spent a significant amount of time on the disabled list. On the night before a weekend matinee against the Orioles, Mantle and Whitey Ford had dinner with some friends who had just purchased a farm outside of Baltimore. Since Ford had pitched that day and Mantle was on the DL, they overindulged before and after dinner, failing to make it back to the team's hotel. They woke up on the front porch of the farmhouse in time to get to the ballpark before warmups.

Mantle was in rough shape, and after a shower and a soak in the whirlpool, he fell asleep on the trainer's table. During batting practice, it was obvious he was still feeling the after-effects of the previous night's activities. Before the opening pitch, he and Ford positioned themselves on the bench as far away from manager Ralph Houk as possible. Mantle was wearing sunglasses to keep the light from exacerbating his pounding headache. As the late innings arrived, the Yankees were trailing and Houk began looking for a pinch-hitter. When Ford saw him headed their way, he elbowed Mantle in the ribs, jolting him awake.

"Can you hit?" the Yankee skipper asked Mantle.

"I'm not eligible," the slugger replied. "I'm on the disabled list."

"No, you're not. You were activated today," Houk informed him.

Mantle found himself in a tight spot. He was in no condition to hit, but didn't want to risk a suspension or fine by admitting he was hungover. To avoid an unpleasant scene, he put his cap on and ambled to the bat rack. Ford advised him to make contact with the first pitch.

When Mantle was announced as a pinch-hitter, former teammate Hank Bauer—by then a coach for the Orioles—went out to the mound to talk with his pitcher. Having seen the slugger's ineffectual swings during BP, he figured that Mantle would be an easy out.

Mantle took the first pitch for a called strike and then tomahawked the next offering into the bleachers for a home run. Pitcher Stan Williams said that there were tears streaming down the slugger's face as he crossed home plate. Upon returning to the dugout, Mickey sat down next to Ford and allegedly said, "Hitting the ball was easy. Running around the bases was the tough part." According to Ford, Bauer was on the steps of the Orioles' dugout swearing at Mantle as he completed the route. (NOTE: This story, which was featured in Whitey Ford's book *Few and Chosen: Defining Yankee Greatness Across the Eras*, is likely a combination of separate incidents. Ford claimed that the game took place early in the season at Baltimore. He stipulated that the pitcher was Mike McCormick. Mantle did slam a pinch-hit homer off of McCormick at Memorial Stadium that year, but it was on September 1. He blasted an earlier pinch-hit homer against the Orioles on August 4—his first appearance after coming off the DL—but that one was at Yankee Stadium against pitcher George Brunet. The anecdote has been retold a number of times over the years, and like so many aspects of Mantle's life and career, it appears to be part fact, part fable.)

THE KING OF SWING

Not only did Mantle hit home runs in bunches, but he hit them farther than any player in history (excluding Babe Ruth). The longest homer of his career came on May 22, 1963, at New York. The Yankees had squandered an early 7–0 lead over the A's, and the game had meandered into extra innings. Batting left-handed against pitcher Bill Fischer in the bottom of the 11th, Mantle hammered a fastball that traveled in a straight line toward the façade in right field. It struck the decorative facing just inches from the top and bounced back onto the infield. A's manager Jimmy Dykes said it was "the hardest ball any man ever hit." Mantle agreed that it was the hardest one he ever personally hit, adding, "I thought it would go out. I really did."

In more than eight decades of play at the old Stadium, no one ever hit a ball out of the park in fair territory (though legend has it that both Mantle and Ruth turned the trick during batting practice). Using a geometric formula, it was estimated that Mantle's 1963 blast might have traveled up to 734 feet had it not struck the façade. Since today's Doppler technology was not available, exit velocity and spin rate were not figured into the equation. Direction and speed of the wind were not considered as factors either.

Mantle hit the façade at Yankee Stadium on two other occasions—both in May 1956. He smashed at least five other homers that were said to be in excess of 600 feet. The longest ones are listed below.

March 26, 1951: Bovard Field, USC Campus
In an exhibition game against the USC college team, Mantle (just 19 years old and appearing in his first spring training) slammed a pitch from Tom Lovrich over the right-center field wall. It carried across an adjacent football field and sailed over a fence on the perimeter—an estimated 656 feet from home plate. It wasn't Mantle's only titanic blast of the game. He also drove a ball over the left field wall onto the roof of a residential home.

June 11, 1953: Briggs Stadium, Detroit
Facing right-hander Art Houtteman, Mantle hit a seventh-inning homer that reached the roof in right field and bounced off a light tower. Had the ball continued unimpeded, it would have touched down about 650 feet from its point of origin. The home run marked a 16-game hitting streak for Mantle—a season high.

September 10, 1960: Briggs Stadium, Detroit
With two outs and two men on in the seventh, Mantle worked the count to 2-0 against pitcher Paul Foytack. When the right-hander tried to slip a fastball past him, Mantle drove the pitch over the roof onto Trumbull Avenue. It landed in a lumberyard neighboring the ballpark, traveling a total of 643 feet. It was a rough year for Foytack, who posted a 2-11 record and 6.14 ERA. Mantle's homer was among the lowlights.

September 12, 1953: Yankee Stadium

With two men on and a 3-2 count in the seventh inning, Mantle launched a Billy Hoeft pitch into the upper deck in left field. It smashed a seat and

Mantle is being congratulated by teammate Tony Kubek after a homer. Mantle retired with 536 lifetime blasts—an all-time record for switch-hitters that still stands today. As of 2022, only one other switch-hitter had reached the 500-homer threshold: fellow Hall of Famer Eddie Murray. (Courtesy of The National Baseball Hall of Fame)

bounced back onto the field. The broken seat was located 425 feet from home plate and 80 feet above field level. Mathematical estimates placed the shot at around 630 feet. The Yankees pulverized the Tigers that afternoon, 13–4.

ACTS OF GENEROSITY

Though the pages of Mantle's biographies are littered with stories of his drinking, womanizing, and coldness toward reporters, there was a charitable side to The Mick that has been less extensively documented. Mantle frequently treated teammates to fancy dinners and nights out on the town. He was fiercely loyal to friends and family. He bought a house for his parents and actually had one built for his son Danny. As Mantle got older, he began to recognize how important he was to fans and made a concerted effort to connect with them—especially after he began making a comfortable living in the memorabilia trade.

Mantle was far from perfect, but beneath the obvious flaws, there was a fundamental decency about him. Some of his kindest gestures were extended to complete strangers. Mantle's oldest son, Mickey Jr., remembered one particular Christmas Eve when the two were running errands together. They stopped for gas and, while filling up, noticed an old car in poor condition with a flat tire near the pumps. There were Christmas presents piled up in the backseat. As Mantle and his son went inside to pay, they encountered a middle-aged Black man standing near the counter and looking distraught. When Mantle asked him if he needed help, the man explained that he didn't have a spare tire and that the gas station attendant had refused to acknowledge him. He was worried he might not be able to get the presents home to his children.

After hearing the man's story, Mantle was angry. He called the attendant over gruffly and set $300 on the counter. "Put two new tires on this man's car," he growled. "Do it right now, dammit, so he can get home and give his kids their Christmas presents!" Responding to his firm request, the attendant quickly sprang into action. Mickey Jr. wasn't sure if the man with the flat tire even knew who his father was. But his gratitude was obvious. "It wasn't just the season, or the spot the man was in that moved him," Mickey Jr. later wrote. "He didn't like seeing someone's pride get trampled. Some people give millions and have buildings named after them. His were small acts of charity, but he did them all the time." Mantle frequently gave out money to panhandlers on the streets of Texas and was on a first-name basis with some of them. For the record, not all of his acts of charity were particularly small.

After Mantle received a liver transplant in 1995, he used his celebrity status to help establish the Mickey Mantle Foundation—a nonprofit business dedicated to recruiting organ donors. "Thousands will live because Mickey Mantle died," his wife Merlyn remarked. "This is the truth of what happened in August 1995. The future will leave no doubt. The organ donor networks used to count their responses by the tens. Now they count them by the thousands. It does not stretch the facts to say that this increase in the public's awareness was due to Mick's transplant, even though in the end it could not save him."

MARIS UNDER SIEGE

Roger Maris's struggles during the celebrated 1961 home-run duel with Mickey Mantle have been extensively documented over the years. Explaining the root cause of Maris's thorny relationship with reporters and fans, author Glenn Stout wrote, "In 1927, the performance had been delivered by the game's greatest star, Babe Ruth, and recorded by perhaps the best group of working journalists who ever covered a major league team. . . . But in 1961, the performance was delivered by the wrong man—a player who was merely very good, not great, and recorded by a group of journalists who spanned the full spectrum from the best to the most pedestrian. . . . It took place at a time when America was beginning to question its heroes."

A shy, unassuming man who was extremely uncomfortable in the spotlight, Maris gradually lost his composure as the media coverage grew more intense. One day, when Joe Trimble of the *Daily News* asked him if he would break the record, Maris bluntly responded, "How the fuck should I know?" From that point forward, Maris's attitude became as much of a story as his quest for 61 home runs. "He was a quiet guy and he didn't know how to respond," said teammate Bobby Richardson. "Finally, he got upset and they tagged him as arrogant. He was not that way at all."

Fortunately for Maris, he wasn't alone. Mantle, who was in the heat of the race until late September, helped take some of the pressure off. Both players were detained after every game, sometimes facing dozens of reporters at once. Since Maris's dry remarks provided little fodder for their columns, members of the press began relying on Mantle for printable quotes. Mickey kept things light with humorous, self-deprecating quips.

Behind the scenes, Mantle helped relieve Maris's tension by poking fun at the situation. The two shared an apartment in Queens with outfielder Bob Cerv, who fondly remembered the two sluggers engaging in mock arguments about who was better. "We laughed like heck about that," Cerv reminisced. "Every day, one of them would say, 'I'm going to hit one today' and the other would say, 'Well, I'm going to hit two.'" Mantle, who had experienced his own troubles with sportswriters in the past, sympathized with Maris and validated his feelings.

In spite of their close relationship, journalists inaccurately reported that the M & M Boys were embroiled in an ongoing feud. It became a source of amusement to both players. Mantle recalled being regularly awoken by Maris, who would swat him with the morning paper and announce, "Wake up, roomie—we had another fight!"

When Mantle went on the disabled list in late September, the pressure on Maris became almost unbearable. "It was a nightmare," said Maris's good friend Julius Isaacson. "It was worse than the papers printed. It's true he did lose clumps of hair from pressure and nerves. A lot of the time, he wouldn't eat." Though a majority of Maris's teammates had secretly been rooting for Mantle to break the record, they rallied behind Maris in the end, providing encouragement and support. Reporters were a different story. Some of them held long-term grudges—especially syndicated reporter Jimmy Cannon, who referred to Maris as a "whiner" in the spring of 1962 and condemned him for "treacherous smallness."

With unimaginable expectations heaped upon him, Maris was never able to duplicate the success of his record-setting 1961 campaign. The Yankees eventually gave up, trading him to the Cardinals in 1966. "Every day I went to the ballpark in Yankee Stadium as well as on the road, people were on my back," Maris said acidly after his retirement. "The last six years in the American League were a mental hell for me. I was drained of my desire to play baseball."

THE QUALITY OF BLUNTNESS

In 1956, Massachusetts senator John F. Kennedy released a book entitled *Profiles in Courage*, which chronicled acts of bravery and integrity in the careers of eight US senators. Not only did it become a national best seller, but it earned JFK a Pulitzer Prize. Attempting to capitalize on the success of Kennedy's work, the Doubleday publishing company hired a ghostwriter to work with Mickey Mantle on a similarly themed baseball book. Robert Creamer, renowned for his work with *Sports Illustrated*, was recruited for the job.

Mantle and Creamer began work on the project (which carried the title, *The Quality of Courage*) in 1963. When the book was released the following year, Creamer received no official credit as coauthor. In fact, his name didn't appear in connection with the work until it was re-released many years later. Over the course of 23 relatively brief chapters, Mantle recounted the stories of people he most admired for their courage on and off the field. Creamer was careful not to overly polish the prose, allowing Mantle's voice to actually come through. While some would argue that this is one of the book's primary assets, it also creates a bit of a problem at times. Mantle, who grew up in rural Oklahoma, was never known as a gifted orator or a master of the English language. Consequently, some of his observations are unintentionally insulting. Several examples appear below.

(On Billy Martin:)
When he broke into professional ball . . . he had a hard time because he was so scrawny looking. . . . And the thing was, he didn't have a lot of natural ability. He had to use brains and hustle and sharp observations to make his skills valuable to a team.

(On Nellie Fox:)
Nellie is a girl's name, right? If names matter, shouldn't a man with a girl's nickname get upset by it? But if you ever saw Mr. J. Nelson Fox, second baseman and .300 hitter, stick a chaw of tobacco in his cheek before going up to poke a base hit or two off the best pitchers in the league, you know how much that name bothers him.

(On Yogi Berra:)
Yogi isn't the handsomest man in the world, and neither is he the best educated. When he broke into baseball, a short, stocky man with a powerful build and a short neck, a fairly homely face, a deep guttural voice, and a way of speaking that didn't sound much like Harvard, the deep thinkers really got on him, the ones that couldn't carry his glove, let alone his bat.

(On Roger Maris:)
Roger is honest and blunt and he says what he thinks. If a reporter asks him what he thinks of a man the reporter knows Maris doesn't like, Roger will say "I don't like him" and think nothing more about it.

But when outspoken comments like that got printed in 1961—when everything Maris did made news—it made Roger sound like a loud-mouth and a pop-off, which he isn't.

The 1999 edition of the book contains an introduction by Creamer. In keeping with Mantle's frank narrative, Creamer was open about the problems he encountered working with the slugger. "When I went to Yankee Stadium and introduced myself to Mickey as the writer assigned to do the book with him, he was not very cooperative," the veteran scribe recalled. "He was polite enough, but withdrawn and at first not very friendly. He avoided getting started. He put off meetings. He was obviously reluctant to sit down and talk."

THE EIGHTH WONDER

In response to the perceived threat of a proposed third major league, the AL added multiple expansion franchises in 1961. Following the junior circuit's lead, the Mets and Colt .45s made their NL debuts the following year. While the Mets were warmly received in New York, the fledgling Houston squad had a tougher time attracting fans. Described by one source "as a barn-like thing," Colt Stadium's open-air setting subjected visitors to the miserable Texas heat and the hordes of mosquitoes that came with it. Players had to tread carefully as rattlesnakes could sometimes be found slithering in the outfield grass.

Hoping to provide a more pleasant experience, Houston executives financed the construction of the Astrodome—a colossal 18-story covered stadium. The first of its kind, it was billed as "The Eighth Wonder of the World" when it opened in 1965. The team name was changed to keep up with the space-age theme.

The original Astrodome had shoeshine stations behind home plate and cushioned seats like the ones found in movie theaters. The 474-foot scoreboard, which featured an animated fireworks display, was the largest in sports. Massive air-conditioning units pumped cool air into the stadium, providing a welcome escape from the sweltering temperatures outside. Though the original playing surface was natural grass, the lack of sunlight made it impossible to maintain, inspiring the invention of Astroturf the following year. The semitransparent panels in the roof had to be altered as well because they created a poor backdrop for outfielders.

To celebrate the opening of the Astrodome, a three-game exhibition series was scheduled against the Yankees—baseball's most storied franchise. Marveling at the new ballpark's architectural features, Mantle commented, "It reminds me of what I imagine my first ride would be like in a flying saucer." Houston outfielder Rusty Staub was equally impressed, later remarking, "The opening night against the Yankees was one of the most electrifying nights I've spent in baseball. . . . It was hard not to look up and be just as awed as any fan."

The inaugural game was attended by a number of luminaries, among them US president Lyndon B. Johnson and Governor John Connally, who threw out the ceremonial first pitch. Yankee manager Johnny Keane—also a Texas native—penciled Mantle into the lineup despite an injury that had kept him out of action for several days. Keane left his best players in the game longer than he normally would in an exhibition.

Though he didn't receive official credit for it, Mantle set a number of precedents. Batting in the leadoff spot and playing left field, he slapped an offering from Turk Farrell past future Hall of Famer Joe Morgan at second base, recording the first hit in the stadium's history. Two innings later, Mantle launched a solo homer into the first row of seats in center field. It was the first homer, the first RBI, and the first run ever scored in the Astrodome. In the end, the Astros came out on top, tying the game in the sixth and winning it in the 12th on an RBI single by Nellie Fox.

On the 10th anniversary of the stadium's inaugural game, Mantle was invited to participate in an old-timers' exhibition. Proving he could still hit with power at the age of 43, he crushed three homers. When the 20th anniversary celebration rolled around, Mickey was in physical decline. He was limited to a handful of obligatory swings at the plate.

TOLERATING THE PAIN

Because of his extraordinary slugging ability, Mantle was often asked to play through injuries. When Johnny Keane took over the Yankee managerial post in 1965, he got in a habit of asking Mantle before every game how he was feeling. Regardless of what Mantle reported (acute leg discomfort, back pain, etc.), Keane would offer him a day off followed by the statement, "We need you out there." It came to be a running joke between Mantle and starting pitcher Jim Bouton.

In his celebrated book *Ball Four*, Bouton recalled a humorous conversation he allegedly had with Mantle during batting practice one day.

BOUTON: Mick, how does your leg feel?

MANTLE: Well, it's severed at the knee.

BOUTON: Yes, but does it hurt?

MANTLE: No, I Scotch-taped it back into place.

BOUTON: And how's your back?

MANTLE: My back is broken in several places.

BOUTON: Can you swing the bat?

MANTLE: Yeah, I can swing . . . if I can find some more Scotch tape.

BOUTON: Great. Well, get in there, then. We need you.

HALF-BAKED

From a statistical standpoint, Mantle's 1965 season was among the worst of his career. Not only did his batting average drop to an uncharacteristic .255, but his 19 homers and 46 RBIs were new personal lows. Hampered by the cumulative effects of multiple injuries, he sat out 40 games. The Yankees slid to sixth place without his daily services.

On June 20, the Bombers hosted Bat Day at Yankee Stadium. In front of more than 70,000 fans, Mantle went 1-for-5 and struck out twice. After one of those whiffs, a journalist snapped a picture of him throwing his batting helmet in frustration. It became one of the most famous photos of Mickey in the latter stages of his career.

On July 30, *Life* magazine ran an article detailing the slugger's struggles. It was aptly entitled, "Mantle's Misery." In it, the popular Yankee idol admitted, "It isn't any fun when things are like this. I'm 33, but I feel like 40." Describing the physical condition of his legs at that time, writer John R. McDermott wrote, "There was no longer enough cartilage in his knees to absorb the shock of running—and the pain would be almost unbearable if he had to change direction."

Despite the woeful state of the Yankees and of his physical health, Mantle still found time to party with teammates. Joe Pepitone—a hotshot first baseman and outfielder who became more famous for his vanity than his on-field performances—claimed to have smoked marijuana with Mantle. The story appeared in Pepitone's 1975 autobiography, *Joe, You Coulda Made Us Proud.* According to Pepitone, Mantle got high with him before a spring training game and struck out four times. After the game, Mickey allegedly remarked, "I don't know what that shit is, but keep it away from me."

Mantle denied that the story was true, but Pepitone went on record insisting that he had gotten his facts straight. In an interview with a correspondent from *Rolling Stone,* Pepitone claimed that he had talked both Mantle and Whitey Ford into trying marijuana for the first time. "They each took a hit," he asserted, "[and] next thing I know, they're talking to me about all kinds of shit, and they're laughing at anything I said. I could have had them jumping up and down on the bed if I'd wanted to." Pepitone said that the use of marijuana was not common among Yankee players during the mid-1960s. "I think I was probably the only one that was doing shit. I wish some other guys on the team were doing it because maybe I could have gotten the shit for nothing. Maybe they'd give me some. But when you'd come into the clubhouse with glassy eyes, they all thought you'd been out drinking because most of the guys on the club drank pretty good, you know?"

Pepitone's story about Mantle and Ford's behavior seems at least slightly suspect given the fact that a vast majority of first-time marijuana users do not feel the psychoactive effects of the drug. In one survey taken during the 1960s, nearly 60 percent of subjects polled did not report feeling high after their first marijuana experience—a well-known phenomenon known as "reverse tolerance." One theory of "reverse tolerance" alleges that CB1 receptors in the brain, which bind to THC and create a feeling of euphoria, completely shut down when they are unprepared for a sudden rush of cannabinoids. The receptors eventually grow accustomed to the presence of the naturally occurring chemicals and begin to perform their job properly. In certain individuals, it can take up to three or four sessions before the full effects of THC are experienced.

DRAMA AT MICKEY MANTLE DAY

Mantle was honored with several Mickey Mantle Days, one of which was held posthumously in 1997. The first celebration took place in September of 1965 to mark the occasion of his 2,000th career game. More than 50,000 fans were on hand to see the beloved Yankee slugger receive a treasure trove of gifts that included a Winchester rifle and a 6-foot, 100-pound salami. Red Barber served as the master of ceremonies, and Joe DiMaggio was recruited to introduce Mantle to the crowd. There were a few interesting developments behind the scenes.

DiMaggio received a warm reception as he walked onto the field. When he saw Mantle's mother standing by herself off to the side, he escorted her to where assorted players and dignitaries were stationed along the infield grass. The gesture was completely unrehearsed. Before he addressed the crowd, The Yankee Clipper noticed Senator Robert F. Kennedy pacing the dugout waiting for his own introduction. According to multiple observers, his face twisted into a scowl. Kennedy's affair with Marilyn Monroe was well known and DiMaggio (who had been married to the glamorous starlet for nine months) hated him for it. Despite his obvious displeasure, Joltin' Joe performed his duties commendably. "I am proud and honored to introduce the man who succeeded me in 1951 out in center field," he began. "He certainly has lived up to his expectations and there's no doubt in my mind when he calls it a career he will be in the Hall of Fame."

Mantle was treated to a standing ovation that lasted for several minutes. After posing for some photos (including a few with Senator Kennedy), he delivered a short speech. He made sure to acknowledge DiMaggio, who was very sensitive about being slighted. "I think just to have the greatest baseball player I ever saw introduce me is tribute enough for me in one day," Mantle said diplomatically.

After Kennedy had been introduced by Barber, he began shaking hands with the assembly of guests. When DiMaggio spotted the New York senator working his way down the line, he backed away in a casual snub that went unnoticed by virtually everyone (including Kennedy himself). But esteemed journalist Gay Talese witnessed the gesture and later wrote about it.

Mantle was floundering that year along with the Yankees. Earlier in the season, former teammate Norm Siebern had commented bluntly, "I don't see how the heck he keeps going." A *Sports Illustrated* writer maintained the same opinion, remarking, "Mantle, the one-man orthopedic ward, is even more a symbol of the Yankees in crisis than he was in their predominance." Before Mantle's first at-bat of the afternoon, Tigers pitcher Joe Sparma walked to home plate and shook hands with the Yankee icon. "You know, I've never had a chance to meet you in person," he said, "and I've always admired you."

Once the game was underway, Sparma was all business, retiring Mantle on a flyball, a groundout, and a strikeout. After the whiff, Mickey grumbled half-jokingly to Detroit catcher, Bill Freehan, "They have a day for me and your manager's got to put some hard-throwing kid out there. Couldn't he have put some soft-tossing left-hander for me to hit off of, so I could look like a hero in front of all those people?" Mantle finished the day at 0-for-3 with a walk.

GAME SHOW CELEBRITY

Though Mantle landed some lucrative endorsements during the early part of his career, his star burned brightest during the 1961 home-run race with Roger Maris. Over the course of that storied season, the M & M Boys lent their names and likenesses to a number of commercial products, earning more than $100,000 apiece (equal to about $900,000 today). In addition to a backyard game, a line of men's clothing, and various other deals, the two sluggers landed roles in two major motion pictures (one of which was rated among the 10 worst baseball films of all time).

Though Maris's popularity quickly faded, Mantle remained an American icon throughout his lifetime. Even as his baseball skills went into decline, his services as a pitchman were in great demand. In 1967, he became the first sports figure selected as a spokesman for Maypo cereal. In a famous TV ad, he was asked to cry on demand and tearfully declare, "I want my Maypo!!" Other athletes were later recruited to peddle the popular oatmeal product (Willie Mays, Johnny Unitas, and Wilt Chamberlain to name a few), but Mantle's performance is the one that is best remembered.

Mantle's engaging public persona made him an ideal fit for talk shows. He was a guest of Johnny Carson, Merv Griffin, and Mike Douglas during the 1970s. In the mid-1960s, he became a regular on the popular TV game show, *The Match Game*. Hosted by Gene Rayburn, the star-studded half-hour quiz program debuted on NBC's daytime lineup in 1962 and ran for more than 1,700 episodes. It has been rebooted several times since then, most recently in 2016.

The original *Match Game* pitted two celebrity teams composed of three contestants against one another. Ordinary questions such as "Name a breed of dog" were paired with humorous fill-in the blank queries such as, "Mary likes to pour gravy all over John's___." A team scored 25 points if two team members gave the same response and 50 points if all three were in agreement. The first team to score 100 points advanced to a money-earning bonus round.

During the show's earliest incarnation, celebrity guests included Lauren Bacall, Rod Serling, and Betty White. On September 10, 1965, the celebrity panels were composed almost entirely of Yankee players. Mantle, Whitey Ford, and Joe Pepitone squared off against Roger Maris, Tom Tresh, and former Cardinals catcher turned TV broadcaster, Joe Garagiola.

There were a few amusing exchanges between Yankee teammates. In response to the question, "Name the easiest position on a baseball team," first baseman Joe Pepitone answered "outfield." When Mantle's response was revealed as "first base," the TV audience broke into laughter.

In the money-earning round, contestants were required to match the answers from a studio audience poll. Mantle, Ford, and Pepitone were asked which major-league team had been named as the audience's favorite. The Yankees finished in sixth place that season several games below .500. Figuring the New York audience would favor their crosstown rivals, all three Yankee players answered "Mets." Again, the audience laughed when the answer was revealed as "Yankees."

Mantle participated in 25 episodes of *The Match Game*. He also appeared on *What's My Line?*—a guessing game in which celebrity panelists tried to determine the occupation of guests by asking only yes or no questions. Near the end of each episode, the panelists put on blindfolds and a famous "mystery guest" was brought out. Mantle's 1953 "mystery guest" appearance was brief as Bennett Cerf—founder of Random House publishing—recognized Mickey's voice and determined his identity very quickly. "Are you able to manipulate the spheroid from either side of the plate—I mean, are you a switch-hitter?" Cerf asked the slugger. When Mantle answered in the affirmative, he followed up with, "Did you ever hit a ball 565 feet?"

"PEPI" AND THE MILLION-DOLLAR BAT

On Mother's Day in 1967, a Yankee Stadium crowd of around 19,000 witnessed a historic moment. With two outs in the bottom of the seventh and the Yankees clinging to a 5–4 lead, Mantle stepped in to face Stu Miller of the Baltimore Orioles. Batting lefty against the right-handed-throwing Miller, The Mick sent a 3-2 pitch into the lower right field stands, making him the sixth player in history to reach the 500-homer mark. He commented afterward: "It felt like when you win a World Series—a big load off your back. I wasn't really tense about hitting it, but about everybody writing about it. We weren't doing well and everywhere you'd see 'When is Mantle going to hit 500?' instead of about the team winning or losing. Now maybe we can get back to getting straightened out." The Yankees never did get back on track, finishing in ninth place with a 72-90 record. Several decades later, Mantle's landmark homer generated unexpected controversy.

The bat Mantle used to secure a place in the record books was borrowed from teammate Joe Pepitone. Mantle returned the lumber to its rightful owner, but it turned up missing. Upon inquiring about it, Pepitone learned that the bat—a Louisville Slugger model with his name emblazoned on the barrel—had been taken from his locker and donated to the National Baseball Hall of Fame by team executives. For many years, it remained on display at Cooperstown. Pepitone allegedly came to an agreement with William Guilfoile—the museum's PR director—that the bat would be returned to him upon request. But things got complicated after Guilfoile passed away. When Pepitone asked for the bat back in September 2020, his request was denied.

Had this been an ordinary piece of memorabilia, Pepitone might have let it go. But according to multiple appraisers, Mantle's 500th home run bat is worth more than $500,000. In July 2021, Pepitone filed a lawsuit in a US Federal Court located in Ithaca, New York. The associated legal document asserted, "The museum has unreasonably and unlawfully refused Pepitone's demand to return the bat and continues to possess the bat without legal cause or justification over Pepitone's objection." Cooperstown representatives countered with the statement, "The Hall of Fame has preserved it and proudly put it on display for millions of fans to see. The bat is where it belongs."

In October, Pepitone voluntarily withdrew the lawsuit, which could potentially have earned him $1 million in compensatory damages. Officials from the Hall of Fame stated that they were confident the case would have been decided in their favor had it been fully litigated.

A NEUROMUSCULAR GENIUS

Few players in baseball history have demonstrated as much raw power as Mantle. Multiple sources agree that he hit at least 10 homers that traveled in excess of 500 feet. But the sport took a tremendous toll on his body. In the spring of 1968, Yankee trainer Joe Soares commented, "Mickey has a greater capacity to withstand pain than any man I've ever seen. Some doctors have seen X-rays of his legs and won't believe they are the legs of an athlete still active."

Mantle's troubles began in the 1951 World Series, when his spikes got caught in an irrigation outlet at Yankee Stadium, sending him crashing to the turf with a severe knee injury. Though doctors were able to partially repair Mantle's right knee, there was no MRI technology available in those days to determine the full extent of the damage. Modern experts believe that Mantle likely tore his anterior cruciate ligament in the mishap. The ligament—commonly abbreviated as "ACL"—is a band of tissue that connects the femur (thigh bone) to the tibia (shinbone). Injuries to the ACL are usually sustained during sudden stops or changes in direction. The knee typically swells, becoming unstable and incapable of bearing weight. Since the ACL can't be stitched back together, reconstructive surgery is often required—a procedure that was rarely performed in Mantle's day.

During the 17 seasons that followed Mantle's World Series injury, he sat out hundreds of games and endured an unimaginable amount of physical discomfort. His knee had a grotesque flexibility that astounded (and repulsed) many observers. One of Mickey's minor-league teammates recalled him showing off the deformity as a sort of party trick. He demonstrated it to his children as well. "It was like [the knee] would come apart," his youngest son, Danny, said.

After analyzing archival footage of Mantle's swing, Preston Peavy—an Atlanta-based hitting instructor—concluded, "This was pure blue-collar, farm-boy aggressiveness.... If you wanted to build a baseball player from scratch, Mickey Mantle was it." Yankee trainer Gus Mauch, who worked with Mantle during the 1950s and early 1960s, likened the slugger's speed and muscle mass to a lightweight boxer. But Soares—Mauch's successor—observed some flaws in Mantle's physical makeup. "[Mickey] had a severe congenital condition. His muscles were so large, but his joints—wrists, knees, ankles—were frail."

The fact that Mantle may have been able to amass more than 500 home runs with a torn ACL is astounding. Dr. Stephen Haas, an orthopedist specializing in sports medicine, referred to Mantle as a "neuromuscular genius" and asserted that he was "one of a select few who are so well wired that they are able to compensate for severe injuries like this and still perform at high levels.... It is a phenomenon comprised of motivation, high pain threshold, strength, reflexes, and luck." Anyone intimately familiar with Mantle's career would say that luck had little to do with it. In addition to his ongoing knee issues, the Yankee idol sustained a broken foot, a fractured finger, a severe shoulder injury, an abscess of the hip, and numerous hamstring pulls (a consequence of his unstable knees). He also underwent a tonsillectomy prior to his Triple Crown season of 1956.

Mantle batting left-handed in an exhibition game. He generated 620 extra-base hits during the regular season as a lefty, 372 of which were home runs. (Courtesy of The National Baseball Hall of Fame)

NOW PITCHING FOR THE YANKEES: ROCKY COLAVITO

In 1968 the Yankees finished in fifth place and never seriously contended for the pennant. Though Mantle's skills were clearly fading, die-hard followers found reasons to keep up with his daily activities as he surpassed Ted Williams on the all-time home-run list in May and tied with Jimmie Foxx in August.

Entering an August 25 doubleheader against the Tigers, Mantle was hitting .230 with 16 home runs on the season—numbers that indicated to many that the end was near. Disappointing a sparse Sunday crowd at Yankee Stadium, he went 0-for-4 in the opener, failing to hit the ball out of the infield until his fourth at-bat. If not for a dramatic rally by the Yankees and a peculiar managerial decision on the part of Ralph Houk, the game would have been entirely forgettable.

New York starter Steve Barber gave up a pair of runs in the first and two more in the third. He got into trouble again an inning later, issuing a walk, a wild pitch, and an RBI-single to outfielder Mickey Stanley. Shortstop Dick Tracewski followed with a single, prompting Houk to make an unusual move. Instead of summoning one of his full-time relievers to take over, Houk sent outfielder Rocky Colavito to the mound.

Colavito had come up through the Cleveland farm system and quickly established himself as one of the premier power hitters in the American League, capturing the 1959 home-run crown. In one of the most unpopular front office moves in franchise history, the Indians traded Colavito to Detroit for Harvey Kuenn in 1960. Kuenn's skills went into rapid decline, while Colavito reached the 30-homer plateau on five more occasions. The transaction prompted rumors of a jinx in Cleveland. Even today, Indians fans still talk about the "Curse of Rocky Colavito"—which is supposedly to blame for the team's extensive World Series drought (which dates back to 1949).

Colavito started the 1968 campaign with the Dodgers, but after hitting .204 in 40 games, he was released. Looking for a veteran bat in the lineup, the Yankees signed him as a free agent. Though he had spent a majority of his career in right field, he was not a complete stranger to pitching. In 1958, he had tossed three scoreless innings against the Tigers. And in 1951, he had made a successful mound appearance for the Daytona Beach Islanders of the Florida State League.

Describing his strategy that day, Colavito remarked, "When I got in the game, I threw mostly fastballs. A few curves and some sliders. My slider worked better in the bullpen than on the mound, but it was there." In spite of his limited pitch selection, Colavito completed 2.2 scoreless innings. Meanwhile, the Yankees rallied to take a 6–5 lead, which held up as the final score. Colavito was credited with the win, becoming the last non-pitcher in the majors to pick up a victory until the 2000 campaign, when Colorado catcher Brent Mayne turned the trick.

In the second game of the doubleheader, Colavito outperformed Mantle again, appearing in right field and smashing a long homer off of Tiger southpaw Mickey Lolich. Mantle was limited to one unsuccessful pinch-hitting appearance. The Yankees won, 5–4, evening their season record at 63-63.

THE GIFT-WRAPPED HOMER

Denny McLain put up some very good numbers during his 10 years in the majors, but was never able to match the level of success he enjoyed in 1968. In the so-called Year of the Pitcher, he became the first hurler since Dizzy Dean to collect 30 wins. His 28 complete games and miserly 1.96 ERA helped him capture Cy Young and MVP honors.

By the time the Tigers hosted the Yankees on September 19, McLain had already compiled a 30-5 record. The Yankees were out of the pennant race and the Tigers were sitting on top by a substantial margin, so there was very little at stake. When Detroit jumped out to a 6–1 lead through seven innings, McLain decided to make things interesting.

With one out in the eighth inning and Mantle coming to the plate, the Tiger ace called for time and consulted with his catcher, Bill Freehan. Mantle overheard McLain saying something about deliberately laying a pitch in there and asked Freehan about it.

"Yeah," the veteran backstop confirmed. "I mean, he's not going to work on you. He's just going to throw you fastballs."

Mantle was a bit skeptical, so he let the first pitch go by. As promised, it was a fastball in the heart of the strike zone. McLain shot Mantle a look as if to say, "What was wrong with that one?" and the slugger knew the fix was on.

The next offering was a cream puff right down the middle, but Mantle got under it, fouling it back to the screen. With the count at 0-2, McLain allegedly shouted at Mantle, "Where the fuck do you want it?" The Yankee slugger pointed to the spot and McLain accommodated him. This time, Mickey got all of it, blasting it into the upper deck in right field. The home run moved Mantle into third place on the all-time list.

Like all good stories, "the gift homer" tale has been embellished over time. In later years, Mantle claimed that Joe Pepitone came to the plate next and asked McLain to groove a pitch to him. McLain allegedly responded by whistling a fastball behind Pepitone's head.

DIRTY LITTLE SECRETS

Pitcher Jim Bouton played on three consecutive pennant-winning Yankee squads from 1962 through 1964. He was known for his lively fastball and wild delivery that usually ended with his cap lying in the dirt. An arm injury in 1965 slowed his fastball, and he spent the next four seasons trying to regain his effectiveness—without much success. Sold to the Seattle Pilots in June 1968, he kept a journal of his activities with the club. His daily observations became the basis for the landmark publication *Ball Four*.

Prior to the release of Bouton's tell-all book in 1970, there was a code of silence among major leaguers equivalent to the modern day mantra of "What happens in Vegas stays in Vegas." Bouton violated the unspoken rule by unveiling a host of clubhouse secrets. Dirty jokes, shameless philandering, and alcohol abuse were just a few of the many taboo topics covered by Bouton in the controversial work. Needless to say, it was not well received by members of the baseball establishment. Commissioner Bowie Kuhn condemned it as a work of fiction and attempted to have it removed from bookstores and libraries. Sportswriter Dick Young condescendingly referred to Bouton and his *Ball Four* collaborator, Leonard Schechter, as "social lepers." Baseball's all-time hits leader, Pete Rose, took to shouting, "Fuck you, Shakespeare!" every time Bouton pitched against the Reds.

Though rampant alcohol consumption among players was not a shocking revelation, Bouton exposed a little-known aspect of the game's seedy underbelly when he wrote about amphetamine use. Originally given to members of the US military during World War II to help them carry out their duties, the pills became popular among ballplayers in the 1940s. Ralph Kiner—a seven-time National League home-run king—later confessed, "All the trainers in the ballparks had them. You needed to perform your best and you were going to use everything that was legal to help you do it. You worked to get that job and you wanted to stay in the lineup."

Amphetamines, known to players as "greenies," were available over the counter until 1970, when they became a controlled substance. Positive effects included increased energy and alertness along with quicker reaction times. On the downside, "greenies" were addictive and carried the risk of strokes, seizures, and kidney damage. Long-term use could induce paranoia and hallucinations.

In *Ball Four*, Bouton basically outed everyone in the majors for amphetamine use, including Mantle. Adding insult to injury, he provided scattered details about Mantle's habitual drinking—a topic that had been largely kept out of the press until then. His musings on the Yankee slugger were not entirely negative. In one of the book's early passages, he proclaimed, "I've always felt that there are three kinds of athletes. First, there's the guy who does everything instinctively and does it right in the first place. I think Willie Mays is that kind of guy, and so was Mantle." But several pages later, Bouton denigrated the Yankee icon with the following statement: "On one hand, I really liked his sense of humor and boyishness. . . . On the other hand, there were all those times when he'd push little kids aside when they wanted his autograph, and the times when he was snotty to reporters, just about making them crawl and beg for a minute of his time."

Like many of the personalities whose flaws were exposed in Bouton's work, Mantle wasn't entirely pleased. He spent the next several years avoiding the retired hurler's periodic attempts at reconciliation. The Yankees snubbed Bouton too, imposing an Old Timers' Day ban that remained in place until 1998. Mantle and Bouton patched up their differences following the death of Mantle's son Billy in 1994. Mantle assured Bouton that he wasn't angry about *Ball Four* and that he had nothing to do with the Old Timers' Day ban as some sportswriters had suggested.

WHERE HAVE YOU GONE, MICKEY MANTLE?

Born in Newark, New Jersey, and raised in Queens, New York, singer-songwriter Paul Simon forged an illustrious career that spanned six decades. A winner of multiple Grammy awards, he is perhaps best known for his collaboration with Art Garfunkel on the song, "Mrs. Robinson," which was featured in the 1967 film *The Graduate*. Simon had no idea when he wrote the lyrics that he would offend two of the greatest Yankee players of all time.

Simon grew up attending Yankee games and was a self-proclaimed fan of Mickey Mantle. "Mantle was my guy," he told a reporter from the *New York Daily News*. "Mantle was about the promise of youth." In spite of those sentiments, Simon paid homage to Joe DiMaggio when he penned his famous song asking where Joe DiMaggio had gone.

Mantle never understood why he was never mentioned in the song and, during a 1970 appearance on the *Dick Cavett Show*, he decided to ask Simon about it in-person. Simon assured the former slugger that there was no intentional slight. "It's about the syllables, Mick," he explained. "It's about how many beats there are." Mantle seemed satisfied with Simon's response, and there were no hard feelings. But it was not the first time Simon was forced to explain himself.

As the song began climbing the pop charts in 1968, rumors swirled that DiMaggio believed he was being ridiculed and was considering a legal suit against Simon. A chance encounter between the two at an Italian restaurant in Central Park South helped smooth things over. Simon approached DiMaggio at his table and introduced himself. Well aware of who the singer was, The Yankee Clipper invited him to sit down. Simon explained that there was no insult intended in the lyrics and that DiMaggio was actually being hailed as a hero. The Yankee icon was relieved to hear it.

Proving that Mantle was still "his guy," Simon recruited The Mick to appear in a video for the song, "Me and Julio Down by the Schoolyard." Originally released in 1972, the song reappeared on Simon's 1988 greatest hits album, *Negotiations and Love Songs*. The opening sequence of the video, which was shot at Mathews-Palmer Park in Hell's Kitchen, features appearances by Warner Brothers recording artists Big Daddy Kane and Biz Markie. NBA point guard Spud Webb is pictured playing basketball with neighborhood kids in another scene. Mantle turns up a bit later in a stickball segment. Batting left-handed, he swings through one of Simon's pitches and then launches another one clear out of the schoolyard. The video ends with former NFL coach John Madden attempting to offer advice to some kids engaged in a pickup football game. "They don't listen to coaches the way they used to," Madden grouses as the players ignore his instructions. Simon's *Negotiations and Love Songs* attained certified platinum status, selling over a million copies.

SHOOTING SPREE

Underrated during his playing days, Billy Martin gained far more acclaim as a manager, guiding four different clubs to playoff appearances. In 1974, he transformed the Rangers from 100-game losers to divisional contenders. He did such a fine job that team executives gave him a hunting rifle as a gift.

Martin and Mantle kept in touch over the years, spending time together during the offseason. Excited about the new rifle, Martin asked his old teammate if he would like to go deer hunting. Mantle was receptive to the idea, suggesting that they drive down to San Antonio, where a friend of his owned an expansive ranch. Although it was four hours away, Martin agreed.

The ranch owner—a wealthy doctor—allowed Mantle and Martin to use his property under one condition: There was a sickly mule that needed to be put out of its misery.

"I just don't have the heart for it," the ranch owner told Mantle, as Martin waited in the car out of earshot. "He's old and suffering. . . . You'd really be doing me a big favor."

Mantle agreed to shoot the mule, but on his way back to the car, he decided to pull a devious prank, tricking Billy into believing he was angry with the ranch owner. He ran to the vehicle and yanked open the door, ordering Martin to hand him his rifle.

"What's the matter?" Martin said.

"We drove four hours to get down here to go deer hunting and now this guy won't let us. I'm going to shoot his mule."

Martin pleaded with Mantle not to do it and the two wrestled for possession of the weapon. After a brief struggle, Mantle ran down to the barn where the mule was stabled and shot it. As it fell to the ground, he heard three more shots ring out behind him. He turned around to see Martin standing there holding his new rifle. He had killed three of the rancher's cows.

AN EASY TARGET

Among the most popular figures in Yankee history, Phil Rizzuto was the starting shortstop on seven World Series–winning squads, including the teams that won five in a row from 1949 through 1953. Nicknamed "The Scooter" for the way he ran the bases, his skills went into decline in the mid-1950s. He called it quits as a player in 1956, then spent 40 years as a radio and TV broadcaster. He became famous for his trademark expression, "Holy cow!" Rizzuto—who stood just 5-foot-6—was a hypochondriac with a number of phobias, including a fear of lightning, snakes, spiders, and assorted insects. This made him a prime target for practical jokes. Good-natured almost to a fault, he never held any grudges and rarely if ever lost his temper.

Though many players in Rizzuto's day left their gloves on the field between innings, Rizzuto started carrying his back to the dugout and guarding it closely when teammates—particularly Johnny Lindell—began stuffing worms inside of it. Whitey Ford once hung a dead mouse over Rizzuto's steering wheel, and Mantle allegedly stuck a firecracker under the hood. Even when Charlie Keller stuffed Scooter in his locker one day and shut the door, the unflappable infielder was able to laugh it off. "That [was] Phil," Mantle said. "A beautiful guy—not a bad bone in his body. Always trusting and so gullible it made him a pushover for all the pranks we used to play on him."

During a 1952 road trip, Mantle sat next to Rizzuto on a train bound for Cleveland and initiated an in-depth discussion about snakes. As Rizzuto literally began to squirm in his seat, Mantle laid it on thick, knowing that his teammate had grown up in New York City and knew very little about country life. "I owned one," he said. "Pulled out his fangs with my fingers and trained him as a house pet. Cute little bugger."

Rizzuto had heard enough at that point. "Please, Mickey," he pleaded. "What are you trying to do, make me blow the pennant?"

Mantle continued to play jokes on Scooter long after his retirement. On July 11, 1992, the Yankees held their 46th annual Old Timers' Day celebration. In addition to Mantle, the event included appearances from Joe DiMaggio, Whitey Ford, Hank Bauer, and Allie Reynolds. Rizzuto, who had retired from his broadcasting job by then, was working as a special correspondent. He was wandering the dugout talking to senior Yankee alumni when Mantle called him over. Rizzuto notified Tom Seaver in the broadcast booth that he was going to engage with his former teammate.

"How you doing, Mick?" Rizzuto said.

"That thing on?" Mantle asked, tapping Scooter's mic.

"Sure is," Rizzuto confirmed.

"Fuck, fuck, cocksucker," Mickey chirped into the microphone. "Cocksucker, shitbag, fuck!"

Rizzuto was flabbergasted. "Mary Mother of God!" he stammered, covering the mic with his hand and beating a hasty retreat. "Holy Cow, Mick!"

Players within earshot burst into fits of laughter.

When Rizzuto was elected to Cooperstown in 1994, he was characteristically humble. "I never thought I deserved to be in the Hall of Fame," he said. "The Hall of Fame is for the big guys, pitchers with 100 mph fastballs and hitters who sock homers and drive in a lot of runs. That's the way it always has been and the way it should be."

SOBER INSIGHTS

Mantle's 1994 stint in rehab triggered a quest to find his own truth, to set the record straight, and to make amends. Some of his sober realizations appeared in the 1996 book *A Hero All His Life*, which is a revealing family portrait written by Mantle's wife and sons. The first chapter—penned by Mickey himself after he regained his sobriety—paints a picture of the beloved baseball icon as a flawed and vulnerable addict riddled by guilt and self-loathing.

"I don't think I was ever really nervous on a baseball field, in any league, in any situation," Mantle confessed. "But I thought I might pass out the first time I stood up in a meeting at the Betty Ford Center and said, 'I'm Mick and I'm an alcoholic.'" Mantle was deeply touched by the fact that, after coming clean about his alcoholism, he received thousands of encouraging letters (which were published in a 1995 book entitled *Letters to Mickey*). He disclosed that he felt unworthy of the admiration he received from family members, friends, and fans.

In tracing the origins of his alcoholism, Mantle contended that it was a sign of the times. He played in baseball's golden era for the game's most storied franchise. His matinee idol looks and unparalleled power at the plate transformed him into a demigod. Everyone wanted to be close to him at the height of his career and temptations abounded. There was a different attitude toward drinking in Mantle's heyday. Intoxication was considered a source of comic relief. And being able to handle liquor was identified as a masculine trait. "It was a macho time," he wrote. "If you could drink all night, get a girl, get up the next day, and hit a home run, you passed the test."

Nearly everyone in Mantle's family had died young, and he anticipated the same fate for himself. He adopted a "live for the moment" philosophy with little consideration for his long-term health. When his career was over, he struggled with the knowledge that he had not lived up to his full potential as a player. He was convinced that his father would have been disappointed in him.

Other candid insights offered in *A Hero All His Life* included Mantle's admission that he had been a negligent husband and father. Though he sincerely loved his wife, she had never been a top priority to him. As a father, he was rarely around when his children needed him most. Together, Mickey and Merlyn negatively influenced their sons with their habitual drinking. "We gave them everything but discipline and sense of purpose," Mantle asserted. In later years, Mickey furthered their descent into alcoholism by playing the role of a drinking partner.

By the late 1980s, Mantle was intoxicated almost every day. The hangovers got worse, and his ability to recover from them diminished. He began to suffer from stomach issues. His deteriorating health became apparent to colleagues, especially members of the country club he regularly golfed at—many of whom were doctors. Unable to handle the responsibilities of marriage, he separated from Merlyn, later developing a deep-rooted fear of falling gravely ill and dying alone. In spite of his ongoing issues, he invested in a New York tavern called Mickey Mantle's Restaurant and Sports Bar. It became his base of operations whenever he was in the city.

Mantle's closest acquaintances began to pass away over time—Casey Stengel in 1975, Roger Maris in 1985, and Billy Martin in 1989. Though Martin's death in a car crash was linked to alcohol, Mantle refused to acknowledge the role it had played. He was in denial of his own problem until December 1993, when a doctor confirmed that his physical health was in serious jeopardy. During his first few days at the Betty Ford Center, he was unable to participate in group sessions without crying. Mantle's contribution to *A Hero All His Life* concludes with the emotional statement: "Our lives have been in shambles for a lot of years, much of it flowing from my drinking. . . . We have drawn closer and we're able to be more open about expressing our feelings. I love my family and they love me. I just have to learn to love myself."

The Controversial Transplant

In late May 1995, Mantle was admitted to Baylor University Medical Center with stomach pains. A battery of tests revealed that he was suffering from hepatitis C in addition to cirrhosis and cancer of the liver. Doctors concluded that only a transplant could save his life. Just two days after being placed on the list, a suitable organ became available.

The transplant procedure took almost seven hours due to various complications. Mantle's surgeon had to cut through many layers of scar tissue created by a gallbladder removal operation performed several years earlier. The bile duct was blocked by an aggressive tumor, and a copious amount of bacteria-laden fluid had to be drained. The liver itself was described as "swollen, lumpy, and hard." Though microscopic cancer cells had spread beyond the surgical site, doctors were not aware of it at the time.

When news of Mantle's procedure went public, there was a backlash from a number of sources who felt he had been given preferential treatment. Dr. Goran Klintmalm—director of the Baylor Transplant Institute—was not surprised by the ensuing controversy. "When I knew we had a donor for Mickey, knowing the questions we would face, I thought 'Oh, no!'"

Standard protocol at Baylor called for several weeks of low-dose chemotherapy before transplantation, but Mantle was considered exempt. "Because [his] liver failure had taken a turn for the worse, his need for a transplant was so urgent that part of the protocol was shelved," Klintmalm explained. He pointed out that Mantle would only have lived two to four weeks without the surgery.

Alison Smith—a coordinator at the Southwest Organ Bank (which serves the Greater Dallas Area)—was in full support of the procedure. "When a patient is admitted to the hospital and is suffering as severely as Mr. Mantle, that candidate is given priority because of their extreme need to be transplanted as soon as possible," she asserted. "This is the standard practice regardless of age, gender, race or social status. I'm sure there will be people who refuse to believe there wasn't some special consideration because of who he is, but that was not the case. He was the sickest person with blood type O in the weight range."

Smith's remarks failed to stifle the ongoing debate. David Cain—founder of the Children's Organ Transplant Association—remarked bitterly, "Maybe Mantle was on his deathbed, maybe he was sicker than everybody else, but I think this makes a lot of people angry. It takes a lot of time to get livers and there are three things that really help to get a liver transplant: money, fame, and getting exposure from the media."

The plot thickened in early August when Mantle's medical team confirmed that the cancer had spread to his lungs. Reacting to the news, a correspondent from the *Washington Post* wrote, "Why waste a potentially life-saving organ on someone who was going to get cancer in another place anyway?" Doctors at Baylor pondered the same question, admitting that they would probably not have proceeded with the transplant had they detected the presence of cancer cells elsewhere during initial testing.

Mantle's surgery was not the only one of its kind performed on a well-known celebrity. In 1994, musical icon David Crosby underwent a liver transplant in spite of many years of alcohol abuse. According to multiple sources, the procedure was at least partially financed by another music industry giant—Phil Collins. Years later, critics of both Crosby and Mantle were still crying foul. Richard Kaplan of the National Cancer Institute mused, "I am not saying that decisions about transplanting celebrities hinge only on their [star power], but if two candidates for a transplant are equally eligible and one of them happens to be famous, there is surely a temptation to tip the balance his way because the transplant community has learned that the media attention high-profile patients attract increases organ donation. That likely will be the way of the transplant world for as long as donor organs are in short supply."

In the end, Mantle's replacement liver did him no good. He was gone within two months of receiving it. Crosby, on the other hand, was still alive (and recording music) nearly three decades later.

THE CARDS THAT NOBODY WANTED

During the 1880s, baseball cards were mass produced and distributed nationally for the first time. The cards were inserted into packs of tobacco or cigarettes as a bonus feature (similar to the toy surprise inside a Cracker Jack box). They continued to be produced through the First World War and included some of the game's most celebrated pioneers, such as Ty Cobb, Napoleon Lajoie, and Christy Mathewson.

In the 1930s, baseball cards became associated with bubble gum. Companies like Fleer, Goudey, and Bowman cornered the market until Topps arrived on the scene in 1951. The first Topps cards were actually components of a board game that never caught on. Looking to make their product more marketable, sales executive Sy Berger and graphic artist Woody Gelman came up with an attractive new design featuring brightly colored player portraits and facsimile autographs. Unfortunately, the 1952 football season was underway by the time the set was released and sales were sluggish. The unsold cards ended up in a Brooklyn warehouse, where they remained until 1960.

Though Berger made numerous attempts to sell the surplus cards over the years, he eventually gave up. Since they were taking up a significant amount of space in the Topps warehouse, he arranged for the cards to be loaded onto a barge and dumped into the Atlantic Ocean. Roughly 500 cases of vintage memorabilia ended up in the watery depths (or so the story goes).

Mantle's 1952 Topps card was not the first one issued with his likeness (Bowman beat Topps to the punch in 1951), but it was destined to become one of the most valuable collectibles of the postwar era. As a massive wave of nostalgia transformed the sports card industry into a multi-million-dollar enterprise, Mantle became the most sought-after personality in the business. The value of his baseball cards began to skyrocket. In 1978, his debut Topps card was valued at around $600. By 1989, it was up to $40,000 (depending on the condition). His 1951 Bowman rookie card sold for $1.4 million in 2013, and in keeping with the old expression, "one man's junk is another man's treasure," Mantle's 1952 Topps card has continued to appreciate. Even in poor condition, it has been known to sell in the $30,000 range. In January 2021, actor and entrepreneur Rob Gough shelled out $5.2 million for a mint copy, officially making it the most valuable card in history. At the time of Gough's purchase, only six mint copies were known to exist. But in 2022, another mint card unexpectedly surfaced, selling at auction for $12.6 million—a new industry record. Although there are a plethora of Mantle autographs still floating around, it can be difficult to find an authentic one. "Mickey's signature is magical," wrote Kelly Eisenhauer of *Sports Collectors Digest*. "In fact, the demand is so great that Mantle's signature is one of the most counterfeited signatures in the world of sports memorabilia collecting. It has been said that 60-80 percent of the Mantle signatures on the internet are fakes."

Mantle was baffled by his own popularity. He told his son Danny multiple times that he wished he had a real job and was ashamed of the fact that peddling autographs was all he knew how to do. "He hated the whole card show deal," Mantle's wife, Merlyn, asserted. "He felt like a whore because they hired him out." Expressing his contempt, Mantle was known to make obscene inscriptions on baseballs from time to time. "Fuck Yogi," "Tough Shit, Asshole," and "Have a Ball, Cocksucker!" are just a few of the charming sentiments he left behind for posterity. On an interesting side note, the balls with vulgar messages actually carry more value than the ones bearing standard autographs.

The Voice of God

Bob Sheppard—known to many as the voice of Yankee Stadium—was raised in Queens, New York, during the early 20th century. Though he was oddly secretive about his age during his lifetime, it is generally believed that he was born in 1910. A gifted athlete, he earned more than half a dozen varsity letters from St. John's University. He went on to attain a master's degree in speech education from Columbia University.

After a stint in the Navy during World War II, Sheppard worked as a public address announcer for St. John's football and basketball games. He also announced professional football games for the Brooklyn Dodgers of the AAFC. In 1948, he delivered a rousing tribute to Babe Ruth at Ebbets Field. The performance earned him a job offer from the Yankees, which he accepted.

Sheppard made his Bronx debut on April 17, 1951. For more than a half-century, he was a vital element of the Yankee Stadium experience. He had the privilege of announcing some of the greatest ballplayers of all time. His distinctive baritone voice prompted Hall of Famer Reggie Jackson to famously remark, "Bob Sheppard's words sound like the voice of God." Similarly, Red Sox great Carl Yastrzemski once said, "You're not in the big leagues until Bob Sheppard announces your name."

Sheppard took pride in getting all the pronunciations correct, but he was not infallible. In Game 2 of the 1995 ALDS, rookie Jorge Posada was inserted as a pinch-runner for Wade Boggs. Posada was a relatively new arrival, and Sheppard was not yet familiar with him. In announcing the substitution, he pronounced Posada's name with an "o" on the end. As the story goes, Derek Jeter was amused by the mistake and frequently called Posada "Sado" from that point forward. Jeter became so attached to Sheppard's voice that he asked the longtime Yankee PA-man to record an introduction to be used after his retirement (which was announced after the 2008 campaign). Sheppard's voice continued to reverberate throughout the stadium before every Jeter at-bat through the Yankee shortstop's final 2014 season.

Of the thousands of players Sheppard introduced over the years, there were particular names he enjoyed more than others. Asked by author Tom Molito to point them out, he was very specific. "Of all the names I have announced, my favorite is Mickey Mantle. My other favorites are Alvaro Espinoza, Jose Valdivielso, Salome Barojas, and Shigetoshi Hasegawa."

Mickey Mantle is the perfect name because the two 'Ms' make it alliterative and the 'L' sounds very good." According to Sheppard, Mantle once told him that he got goosebumps every time he heard Sheppard announce his name. "I felt the same way about announcing him," Sheppard said. In May 2000, the Yankees thanked Sheppard for his many years of service by honoring him with a plaque in Yankee Stadium's Monument Park.

Appendix I

Genealogy

Father's Side

James David Mantle (1841–1930) and Elisa C. Moore (1840–1906) produced Charles Edwin Mantle (1883–1944), who was Mickey's biological grandfather.

Braxton S. Clark (1849–1934) and Sarah E. Elam (1854–1910) produced Mary Mae Clark (1890–1920), who was Mickey's biological grandmother.

Charles Edwin Mantle and Mary Mae Clark produced Elvin Charles ("Mutt") Mantle (1912–1952), who was Mickey's biological father.

Mother's Side

Jesse Monroe Richardson (1837–1911) and Mariah Elizabeth Baldwin (1838–1916) produced Charles Lewis Richardson (1871–1951), who was Mickey's biological grandfather.

John Dennison Thomas (1854–1916) and Malinda Annis Leonard (1859–1932) produced Annie Laurie Thomas (1879–1967), who was Mickey's biological grandmother.

Charles Lewis Richardson and Annie Laurie Thomas produced Lovell Velma Richardson (1904–1995), who was Mickey's biological mother.

SIBLINGS AND CHILDREN

Elvin "Mutt" Mantle and Lovell Richardson had four children in addition to Mickey:

Roy Mantle (1936–2001)

Ray Mantle (1936–2013)

Larry "Butch" Mantle (1941–2020)

Barbara Mantle (b. 1937)

Mickey married Merlyn Louise Johnson (1932–2009) in 1951. The couple produced four sons: Mickey Jr. (1953–2000), David (b. 1955), Billy (1957–1994), and Danny (b. 1960).

Appendix II

Lifetime Batting Statistics and Franchise Rankings (Among Retired Players)

	AB	R	H	2B	3B	HR	RBI	BB	BA
(18 yrs.)	8102	1676	2415	344	72	536	1509	1733	.298

ON-BASE %		SLUGGING %		GAMES	
Babe Ruth	.484	Babe Ruth	.711	Derek Jeter	2747
Lou Gehrig	.447	Lou Gehrig	.632	*Mickey Mantle*	2401
Mickey Mantle	.421	Joe DiMaggio	.579	Lou Gehrig	2164
Charlie Keller	.410	*Mickey Mantle*	.557	Yogi Berra	2116
Jason Giambi	.404	Reggie Jackson	.526	Babe Ruth	2084

RUNS		HITS		TOTAL BASES	
Babe Ruth	1959	Derek Jeter	3465	Babe Ruth	5131
Derek Jeter	1923	Lou Gehrig	2721	Lou Gehrig	5060
Lou Gehrig	1888	Babe Ruth	2518	Derek Jeter	4921
Mickey Mantle	1676	*Mickey Mantle*	2415	*Mickey Mantle*	4511
Joe DiMaggio	1390	Bernie Williams	2336	Joe DiMaggio	3948

HOME RUNS		RBIs		WALKS	
Babe Ruth	659	Lou Gehrig	1995	Babe Ruth	1852
Mickey Mantle	536	Babe Ruth	1978	*Mickey Mantle*	1733
Lou Gehrig	493	Joe DiMaggio	1537	Lou Gehrig	1508
Joe DiMaggio	361	*Mickey Mantle*	1509	Derek Jeter	1082
Yogi Berra	358	Yogi Berra	1430	Bernie Williams	1069

EXTRA-BASE HITS		TIMES ON BASE	
Lou Gehrig	1190	Derek Jeter	4717
Babe Ruth	1189	Babe Ruth	4405
Mickey Mantle	952	Lou Gehrig	4274
Joe DiMaggio	881	*Mickey Mantle*	4161
Derek Jeter	870	Bernie Williams	3444

APPENDIX III

RECORDS HELD

Home runs, switch-hitter, career, 536

Home runs, switch-hitter, season, 54, 1961

Home runs, World Series, career, 18

Runs batted in, World Series, career, 40

Runs scored, World Series, career, 42

Total bases, World Series, career, 123

Bases on balls, World Series, career, 43

MVP awards won by a Yankees player, career, 3 (tied with Joe DiMaggio, Yogi Berra)

On-base percentage, switch-hitter, career, .421

On-base percentage, switch-hitter, season, .512, 1957

Slugging percentage, switch-hitter, career, .557

Slugging percentage, switch-hitter, season, .705, 1956

On-base percentage plus slugging percentage (OPS), switch-hitter, career, .977

On-base percentage plus slugging percentage (OPS), switch-hitter, season, 1.177, 1957

Total bases, switch-hitter, season, 376, 1956

Strikeouts, switch-hitter, career, 1710

Walks, switch-hitter, career, 1733

Walks, switch-hitter, season, 146, 1957

Appendix IV

Products Endorsed

As Mantle gradually became a household name, he made a bundle of cash from the endorsement of commercial products. Many of the goods he came to be associated with are listed below.

Mickey Mantle's Isometric Minute a Day Gym

Fedtro electronics (megaphones, intercoms, indoor-outdoor speakers)

Jell-O

Rawlings fielders' gloves

Westerns blue jeans

Delco-Remy auto parts

Brylcreem

Afrin nasal spray

Ajax combs

Triple Crown pound cake

Maypo cereal

Meadow Sweet milk

A & W soda

Post cereal

Bowman gum

Bazooka gum

Pitch-N-Hit backyard game

Hawthorne catchers' gear

Armour franks

Gem razors

Yoo-Hoo chocolate drink

Kodacolor film

Wonder Bread

Timex watches

Karo syrup

Mickey Mantle's Grand Slam Baseball (board game)

Bantron smoking cessation pills

Viceroy cigarettes

Camel cigarettes

Phillies cigars

Louisville Slugger bats

Budweiser beer

Natural Light beer

MP-27 athlete's foot spray

AT & T phones

Beech-Nut gum

Butternut coffee

El Rancho supermarkets

Weller tools

Appendix V

Annual Salary

1951	$7,500	(Median American Income $2,200)
1952	$10,000	(Median American Income $2,300)
1953	$17,500	(Median American Income $3,200)
1954	$21,000	(Median American Income $4,200)
1955	$32,000	(Median American Income $3,400)
1956	$32,000	(Median American Income $4,800)
1957	$60,000	(Median American Income $5,000)
1958	$65,000	(Median American Income $5,100)
1959	$70,000	(Median American Income $5,400)
1960	$60,000	(Median American Income $5,600)
1961	$70,000	(Median American Income $5,700)
1962	$90,000	(Median American Income $6,000)
1963	$100,000	(Median American Income $6,200)
1964	$100,000	(Median American Income $6,600)
1965	$100,000	(Median American Income $6,900)
1966	$100,000	(Median American Income $7,400)
1967	$100,000	(Median American Income $7,200)
1968	$100,000	(Median American Income $8,600)

Appendix VI

Chronology

- **10/20/1931:** Mantle is born in Spavinaw, Oklahoma.
- **1935:** Mantle moves with his family to Commerce, Oklahoma.
- **1942:** Mantle plays catcher for a Pee Wee League team in Douthat, Oklahoma.
- **1945:** Mantle joins a Ban Johnson League team in Miami, Oklahoma, and begins high school. His grandfather, Charlie, dies of Hodgkin's disease.
- **1946:** Mantle sustains a football injury that leads to a serious case of osteomyelitis.
- **1947:** Mantle plays shortstop for the Baxter Springs Whiz Kids. His Uncle Tunney dies of cancer at the age of 41.
- **5/16/1949:** Mantle signs with Yankees for a $140 per month salary and modest bonus.
- **10/6/1949:** Mantle meets his future wife, Merlyn, at a football game.
- **9/17/1950:** Mantle joins the Yankees as a non-roster invitee.
- **3/26/1951:** In spring training, Mantle hits a home run measuring over 600 feet.
- **5/1/1951:** Mantle hits first official career home run at Comiskey Park in Chicago. It comes off of right-hander Randy Gumpert.
- **August 1951:** Mantle receives 4-F classification from US military, exempting him from duty.
- **10/5/1951:** Mantle injures his right knee in Game 2 of the World Series. His father, Mutt, is diagnosed with Hodgkin's disease.
- **12/23/1951:** Mickey and Merlyn are married.
- **1952:** Mantle loses his father to Hodgkin's disease.

- **4/15/1953:** Merlyn Mantle gives birth to the couple's first son, Mickey Mantle Jr.
- **4/17/1953:** Mantle slams 565-foot homer off Chuck Stobbs of the Senators.
- **1954:** Mantle's Uncle Emmett dies of cancer.
- **5/13/1955:** Mantle hits three homers in one game, going deep from both sides of the plate.
- **12/26/1955:** Merlyn Mantle gives birth to the couple's second son, David.
- **1956:** Mantle captures a Triple Crown and the first of three MVP awards. He moves his family to Dallas, Texas.
- **1957:** Mantle signs a $65,000 contract, hits for the cycle, and wins second straight MVP award. His third son, Billy, is born on 12/5.
- **3/19/1960:** Merlyn Mantle gives birth to the couple's youngest son, Danny.
- **1961:** The celebrated home-run chase with Roger Maris ends for Mantle when he is sidelined with a hip infection.
- **1962:** Mantle captures his third MVP award, and appears in two movies: *Safe at Home!* and *That Touch of Mink*.
- **2/27/1963:** Mantle signs first $100,000 contract.
- **5/22/1963:** Mantle hits home run off the façade at Yankee Stadium.
- **9/18/1965:** Mickey Mantle Day is held at Yankee Stadium.
- **1967:** Mantle begins playing first base.
- **9/20/1968:** Mantle hits last career home run.
- **9/28/1968:** Mantle logs last official at-bat.
- **February 1970:** Mantle accepts coaching position with the Yankees.
- **1974:** Mantle is inducted into the Hall of Fame.
- **9/29/1975:** Casey Stengel dies.
- **1983:** Mantle accepts position with Claridge Hotel and Casino in Atlantic City. He ends up being banned from baseball by commissioner Bowie Kuhn.
- **12/14/1985:** Roger Maris dies of cancer.

- **1985:** Mantle gets reinstated to MLB by commissioner Peter Ueberroth.
- **1988:** Mickey Mantle's Restaurant & Bar opens in New York City.
- **12/25/1989:** Billy Martin dies in a car crash.
- **1994:** Mantle enters the Betty Ford Center for alcoholism.
- **3/12/1994:** Mantle's son, Billy, dies from complications of Hodgkin's disease.
- **3/19/1995:** Lovell Mantle, Mickey's mother, dies.
- **6/8/1995:** Mantle undergoes a liver transplant at Baylor University Medical Center.
- **8/13/1995:** Mantle dies of liver cancer.

Appendix VII

Favorite Home-Run Victims and Ballparks

Victims

PITCHER	HOME RUNS
Early Wynn (HOF)	13
Pedro Ramos	12
Camilo Pascual	11
Frank Lary	9
Gary Bell	8
Dick Donovan	8
Billy Pierce	8
Chuck Stobbs	8

TEAM	HOME RUNS
Athletics	77
Tigers	73
Senators/Twins	72
White Sox	72
Red Sox	69

Ballparks

BALLPARK	HOME RUNS
Yankee Stadium	266
Briggs/Tiger Stadium (Detroit)	42
Fenway Park (Boston)	38
Cleveland Stadium	36
Comiskey Park (Chicago)	30
Griffith Stadium (Washington)	29

Appendix VIII

Movie and TV Credits

Safe at Home! (1962)

Released by Columbia Pictures, this full-length family comedy stars Mantle and Roger Maris. Whitey Ford and Ralph Houk also make appearances. Bryan Russell plays Hutch Lawton, a Florida Little Leaguer who lies to his teammates about being personally acquainted with the M & M Boys and promises to bring them to the team's annual banquet. Lawton goes to great lengths to meet the Yankee duo and learns a valuable life lesson about honesty in the process.

That Touch of Mink (1962)

This Universal Pictures romantic comedy was among the top-grossing films of the year. It stars Doris Day and Cary Grant. Mantle appears in a short scene with Roger Maris and Yogi Berra. All three players end up being kicked out of a Yankee game by umpire Art Passarella following a heated discussion about a called strike.

It's My Turn (1980)

A Columbia Pictures release, this romantic comedy stars Jill Clayburgh and Michael Douglas. Douglas plays a prematurely retired baseball player who starts up a relationship with Clayburgh's character despite their obvious differences. More than two dozen major leaguers (some of whom were still active at the time) have cameos in the film. In addition to Mantle, there are appearances by Elston Howard, Bill White, Bob Feller, Larry Doby, Monte Irvin, and Bobby Thomson.

The White Shadow (1980)

The White Shadow is a TV sports drama starring Ken Howard as Ken Reeves, a retired NBA player who takes a job as a head basketball coach at a primarily

Black and Hispanic inner city high school in Los Angeles. The show ran for three seasons from 1978 to 1981. Mantle appeared in an episode entitled "Reunion: Part 2," in which Reeves spends time with his terminally ill father before returning to Carver High School.

REMINGTON STEELE (1984)
A popular detective drama, Remington Steele ran for five seasons (1982–1987). Pierce Brosnan and Stephanie Zimbalist are cast in lead roles. Mantle played himself in an episode entitled "Second Base Steele," during which a retired baseball player hires the Remington Steele Agency to determine who is responsible for a series of accidents at a sports camp.

MR. BELVEDERE (1989)
This long-running sitcom (1985–1990) stars Christopher Hewett as a butler who takes a job with a family headed by character George Owens (played by former major leaguer turned broadcaster Bob Uecker). In an episode entitled "The Field," Mr. Belvedere arranges for George to play alongside some of the all-time greats as a birthday present. Mantle appears along with Reggie Jackson, Johnny Bench, Willie Mays, Hank Aaron, Ernie Banks, and Harmon Killebrew.

In addition to movies and fictional TV programs, Mantle made dozens of appearances on talk shows, game shows, and variety shows over the years, including *Hee Haw*, *The Ed Sullivan Show*, and *Candid Camera*.

Appendix IX

Honorary Plaques

Mantle's National Baseball Hall of Fame Plaque

MICKEY CHARLES MANTLE

NEW YORK A.L. 1951-1968

HIT 536 HOME RUNS. WON LEAGUE HOMER TITLE AND
SLUGGING CROWN FOUR TIMES. MADE 2415 HITS. BATTED
.300 OR OVER IN EACH OF TEN YEARS WITH TOP OF .365
IN 1957. TOPPED A.L. IN WALKS FIVE YEARS AND IN RUNS
SCORED SIX SEASONS. VOTED MOST VALUABLE PLAYER
1956-57-62. NAMED ON 20 ALL-STAR TEAMS. SET WORLD
SERIES RECORDS FOR HOMERS, 18; RUNS, 42; RUNS BATTED
IN, 40; TOTAL BASES, 123; AND BASES ON BALLS, 43.

Mantle's Original Monument Park Plaque

MICKEY MANTLE
A MAGNIFICENT YANKEE
536 HOME RUNS
THE MOST POPULAR PLAYER OF HIS ERA
IN RECOGNITION OF HIS TRUE GREATNESS
IN THE YANKEE TRADITION AND
FOR HIS UNEQUALED COURAGE
THIS PLAQUE PRESENTED TO MICKEY MANTLE
BY JOE DIMAGGIO IN A CERMONY AT
YANKEE STADIUM ON JUNE 8, 1969

MANTLE'S UPDATED MONUMENT PARK PLAQUE

MICKEY MANTLE
"A GREAT TEAMMATE"
1931–1995
536 HOME RUNS
WINNER OF TRIPLE CROWN 1956
MOST WORLD SERIES HOMERS 18
SELECTED TO ALL-STAR TEAM 20 TIMES
WON MVP AWARD 1956, 1957, 1962
ELECTED TO HALL OF FAME 1974
A MAGNIFICENT YANKEE
WHO LEFT A LEGACY OF
UNEQUALED COURAGE
DEDICATED BY
NEW YORK YANKEES
AUGUST 25, 1996

Appendix X

Honors and Awards

AMERICAN LEAGUE ALL-STAR TEAM

1952, 1953, 1954, 1955, 1956, 1957, 1958, 1959 (Twice), 1960 (Twice), 1961 (Twice), 1962 (Twice), 1963, 1964, 1965, 1967, 1968

ASSOCIATED PRESS ALL-STAR SELECTION

1952, 1957, 1958, 1964

SPORTING NEWS ALL-STAR SELECTION

1952, 1956, 1957, 1961, 1962, 1964

HICKOK BELT

(Given to the top professional athlete of the year)

1956

SPORTING NEWS MAJOR LEAGUE PLAYER OF THE YEAR

1956

AMERICAN LEAGUE MVP

1956, 1957, 1962

HUTCH AWARD
(Given annually to the Major League player who best exemplifies the fighting spirit and competitive desire of former player and manager Fred Hutchinson)

1965

BIBLIOGRAPHY

"61 Home Runs by Roger Maris: Roger Maris Breaks Babe Ruth Record." Baseball
-almanac.com, https://www.baseball-almanac.com/feats/feats12b.shtml.
"500th Home Run." MickeyMantle.com, http://mickeymantle.com/500th-home-run/.
1957 All-Star Game Page, Baseball-Almanac.com, https://www.baseball-almanac.com
/asgbox/yr1957as.shtml.
"1962 Cary Grant Movie Set in Bermuda." Bernews.com (online news site), https://
bernews.com/2012/01/video-cary-grant-bermuda-sex-comedy/, January 1, 2012
(retrieved September 6, 2021).
Adams, Beau. "Swingin' Mick." *This Land* (online magazine), September 7, 2012, https://
thislandpress.com/2012/09/07/swingin-mick-2/ (retrieved August 20, 2021).
Appel, Marty. "National Pastime Museum: Mantle Coaching at First." Appelpr.com,
www.appelpr.com/?page_id=3157 (retrieved August 22, 2021).
Baker, Al, Michael O. Allen, David Lewis, and Jere Hester. "We'll Miss You, Mick's
Fans Cry, City Grieves as Slugger Dies at 63." *New York Daily News*, August 14,
1995.
"Ball Four: The Book That Changed Baseball." npr.org, April 26, 2012 (retrieved July 25,
2021).
Barra, Allan. *Yogi Berra: Eternal Yankee* (New York: W.W. Norton & Co., 2010).
Berra, Yogi, with Tom Horton. *Yogi: It Ain't Over . . .* (New York: McGraw Hill Publishing, 1989).
Bloom, Steve. "Mickey Mantle, the Yankees, and Marijuana." CelebStoner.com
(blog), https://www.celebstoner.com/sports/sporting-highs/2015/07/13/mickey
-mantle,-the-yankees-and-marijuana/, July 13, 2015 (retrieved September 22,
2021).
"A Brief History of Baseball Cards." Cycleback.com, www.cycleback.com/1800s/brief
history.htm.
Buschel, Bruce. "Where Have You Gone, Mickey Mantle?" *Atlantic City Magazine*,
https://thestacksreader.com/where-have-you-gone-mickey-mantle-new-york
-yankees-the-mick/, April 1984.
Calcaterra, Craig. "Today In Baseball History: When Mantle and Mays Were Banned
From Baseball." NBCSports.com, March 18, 2020.
Casey Stengel Quote Page, BrainyQuote.com, https://www.brainyquote.com/quotes
/casey_stengel_139528.
Castro, Tony. *Mickey Mantle: The Best There Ever Was* (Lanham, MD: Rowman and
Littlefield, 2019).
Coffey, Alex. "Mickey Mantle Announces His Retirement from the Yankees." National
Baseball Hall of Fame, https://baseballhall.org/discover-more/stories/inside-pitch
/mickey-mantle-retires.

"Colt Stadium." Academickids.com (online encyclopedia).

Corbett, Warren. "Roy Cullenbine." SABR Biography Project, https://sabr.org/bioproj /person/roy-cullenbine/.

Costello, Rory. "April 9, 1965: Astros Beat Yankees in First Game Inside the Houston Astrodome." SABR Games Project, https://sabr.org/gamesproj/game/april-9-1965 -astros-beat-yankees-in-first-game-inside-the-houston-astrodome/.

———. "Sandy Amoros." SABR Biography Project, https://sabr.org/bioproj/person /sandy-amoros/.

Creamer, Robert. "Mantle and Maris in the Movies." *Sports Illustrated*, April 2, 1962.

DeVito, Carlo. *Scooter: The Biography of Phil Rizzuto* (Chicago: Triumph Books, 2010).

Dicker, Ron. "Mickey Mantle's Gross Move on Reporter Detailed in Her New Memoir." *Huffington Post*, April 23, 2020.

Drebinger, John. "Yankees Pay Tribute to Pitching Artistry of Braves." *New York Times*, October 11, 1957.

"Dugout Scene Yankee Stadium from That Touch of Mink (1962)." YouTube.com, https://www.youtube.com/watch?v=-nuEZAZyfGs.

Eisenhauer, Kelly. "The Evolution of Mickey Mantle's Signature." *Sports Collectors Digest*, January 12, 2020.

Elderkin, Phil. "'Tape Measure Homers' Were the Brainchild of Publicist Red Patterson." *Christian Science Monitor*, September 13, 1988.

Elliot, Steve. "Why Most People Don't Get High the First Time They Smoke Weed." Herb.co, August 21, 2019 (retrieved September 22, 2021).

Elson, Howard. "August 4, 1963: Mickey Mantle Returns to Yankees in a Pinch." SABR Game Project, https://sabr.org/gamesproj/game/august-4-1963-mickey-mantle -returns-to-yankees-in-a-pinch/.

Enders, Eric. *The Fall Classic: A Definitive History of the World Series* (New York: Sterling Publishing, 2007).

"Eulogy of Mickey Mantle." Jerrytuttle.com, www.jerrytuttle.com/the_mick.html.

Evans, Jeremy. "A Lesson in History: Mickey Mantle and Yasiel Puig." Dodgersnation .com (blog), https://www.dodgersnation.com/a-lesson-in-history-mickey-mantle -and-yasiel-puig/2016/08/08/ (retrieved June 30, 2021).

Falkner, David. *The Last Hero: The Life of Mickey Mantle* (New York: Simon and Schuster, 1995).

FBI Records: The Vault: Mickey Mantle, https://vault.fbi.gov/mickey-mantle/mickey -mantle-part-01-of-01/view (retrieved July 19, 2021).

Ferguson, Ryan. "How Mickey Mantle Embodied the Maturation of America." Ryan Ferguson.co.uk (author blog), https://ryanferguson.co.uk/blogs/pinstripe-galaxy /mickey-mantle-tribute-yankees-bio, June 20, 2020 (retrieved August 29, 2021).

Ford, Whitey, with Mickey Mantle and Joe Durso. *Whitey and Mickey: An Autobiography of the Yankee Years* (New York: Viking Press, 1977).

Ford, Whitey, with Phil Pepe. *Few and Chosen: Defining Yankee Greatness Across the Eras* (Chicago: Triumph Books: 2001).

"Former New York Star Joe Pepitone Sues Hall of Fame to Get Valued Bat Teammate Mickey Mantle Hit His 500th Home Run With." ESPN.com, July 10, 2021,

https://www.espn.com/mlb/story/_/id/31796334/former-new-york-yankees-star
-joe-pepitone-sues-hall-fame-get-valued-bat-teammate-mickey-mantle-hit-500th
-home-run-with (retrieved July 25, 2021).

Frey, Jennifer. "Bidding Mantle Farewell: A Day of Recollection." *Washington Post*,
August 14, 1995.

Friend, Harold. "Mickey Mantle Almost Gave Up Switch-Hitting in 1960." Bleacher-
Report.com, August 31, 2011, https://bleacherreport.com/articles/829154-mlb
-why-mickey-mantle-almost-gave-up-switch-hitting-in-1960 (retrieved August
11, 2021).

———. "Mickey Mantle's Courageous Ninth Inning at the End of His Life." Bleach-
erReport.com, https://bleacherreport.com/articles/912624-mickey-mantles
-courageous-ninth-inning-of-life.

———. "Mickey Mantle's Temper Made the Yankees Laugh and the Fans Angry."
BleacherReport.com, https://bleacherreport.com/articles/722499-mickey-mantles
-temper-made-the-yankees-laugh-and-the-fans-angry, June 3, 2011 (retrieved July
24, 2021).

Halberstam, David. "Curt Smith Shares Why Pioneer Red Barber Was Fired by Yanks
in '66, Costas Gets Frick Award Tomorrow in Cooperstown." *Sports Broadcast Journal*, July 27, 2018, https://www.sportsbroadcastjournal.com/historian-curt-smith
-shares-why-pioneer-red-barber-was-fired-by-yanks-in-66-costas-gets-frick-award
-tomorrow-in-cooperstown/ (retrieved August 18, 2021).

Hersom. Bob. "Like Father, Like Son: Mantle's Son Gets a Lot of Second Chances."
Oklahoman, June 28, 2005.

History.com.

Hoffer, Richard. "Legacy of Mickey Mantle, Last Great Player on Last Great Team."
Sports Illustrated, August 21, 1995.

Hochman, Stan. "Life Writes a New Ending to 'Ball Four.'" *Philadelphia Daily News*,
December 7, 2000.

"Home Run Derby S01E01, Mickey Mantle vs Willie Mays." YouTube.com, https://
www.youtube.com/watch?v=HaxrzW3aSrc (retrieved July 16, 2021).

Hulsey, Bob. "The Indoor Era Begins." Astrosdaily.com, https://www.astrosdaily.com
/history/19650409/ (retrieved September 4, 2021).

Hurte, Bob. "Bill Mazeroski." SABR Biography Project, https://sabr.org/bioproj/person
/bill-mazeroski/.

Justice, Richard. "Friend Says 'So Long, Mick': Baseball: About 1,500 Attend Funeral
for Hall of Famer Mickey Mantle in Dallas." *Los Angeles Times*, August 16, 1995.

Kaplan, Daniel. "Former Yankee Joe Pepitone Sues Baseball Hall of Fame Over Mickey
Mantle Bat." TheAthletic.com (online sports news), July 10, 2021, https://the
athletic.com/news/former-yankee-joe-pepitone-sues-baseball-hof-over-mickey
-mantle-bat/olhI5IICeeEH (retrieved July 25, 2021).

Kelly, CJ. "A Clean Sweep: The 1963 World Series." HowTheyPlay.com, https://
howtheyplay.com/team-sports/A-Clean-Sweep-The-1963-World-Series, January 4.
2021.

Kernan, Kevin. "There Is Spying in Baseball." *New York Post*, February 11, 2001.

Krell, David. "September 20, 1968: Mickey Mantle's 536th and Final Home Run Marks the End of an Era." SABR Games project, https://sabr.org/gamesproj/game/sep tember-20-1968-mickey-mantles-536th-and-final-home-run-marks-end-era/.

Krell, David, ed. *The New York Yankees in Popular Culture: Critical Essays* (Jefferson, NC: McFarland & Co., 2019).

Kreuz, Jim. "Tom Greenwade." SABR Biography Project, https://sabr.org/bioproj/per son/tom-greenwade/.

Kriegel, Mark. "DiMaggio Was Perfect Fit for My Song, Simon Says." *New York Daily News*, https://www.nydailynews.com/archives/sports/dimaggio-perfect-fit-song -simon-article-1.820331, November 27, 1998.

Leavy, Jane. *The Last Boy: Mickey Mantle and the End of America's Childhood* (New York: Harper Collins, 2010).

———. *Sandy Koufax: A Lefty's Legacy* (New York: Harper Collins, 2002).

Leventhal, Josh. *The World Series: An Illustrated History of the Fall Classic* (New York: Black Dog & Leventhal, 2001).

Lincicome, Bernie. "Welcome to Baseball and Gambling . . . with Apologies to Pete Rose." *Chicago Daily Herald*, August 22, 2021.

Liptack, Mark. "This Day in White Sox History: Base-Brawl." Chicagonow.com, https://www.chicagonow.com/soxnet/2016/06/this-day-in-white-sox-history-base -brawl/, June 13, 2016 (retrieved August 4, 2021).

Livacari, Gary. "The Yankees Infamous Copacabana Incident." Baseballhistorycomesalive .com (blog), September 15, 2019 (retrieved August 3, 2021).

"Malapropisms—The Insanely Successful Yogi Berra Technique of Humor." Almost anauthor.com, https://www.almostanauthor.com/malapropisms-the-insanely -successful-yogi-berra-technique-of-humor/, November 24, 2016 (retrieved August 16, 2021).

Mantle, Merlyn, Mickey Mantle Jr., David Mantle, and Dan Mantle. *A Hero All His Life: A Memoir by the Mantle Family* (New York: Harper Collins, 1996).

Mantle, Mickey. "Guideposts Classics: Mickey Mantle Honors His Father." Guideposts .org, https://www.guideposts.org/better-living/entertainment/sports/guideposts -classics-mickey-mantle-honors-his-father (retrieved June 30, 2021).

Mantle, Mickey, and Robert Creamer. *The Quality of Courage* (Lincoln, NE: Bison Books, 1999).

Mantle, Mickey, and Lewis Early. *The American Dream Comes to Life, Volume I* (New York: Sports Publishing LLC, 2002).

Mantle, Mickey, with Herb Gluck. *The Mick* (New York: Doubleday & Co., 1985).

Mantle, Mickey, with Mickey Herskowitz. *All My Octobers: My Memories of 12 World Series When the Yankees Ruled Baseball* (New York: Harper Collins, 1994).

"Mantle's Prodigious Blast Nearly Leaves Stadium." *New York Times*, May 23, 1963.

"Mantle's Transplant Raises Delicate Issues About Organ Allocation." *Journal of the National Cancer Institute*, Vol. 88, no. 8, April 17, 1996.

Margolick, David. "63 Years Later, a Confession in Legendary Yankee Scandal." *New York Times*, June 19, 2020.

Martin, Andrew. "Mickey Mantle's Forgotten Twin Brothers." Seamheads.com, March 2, 2018 (retrieved July 11, 2021).

Martinez, Michael. "Mays, Mantle Reinstated by Baseball Commissioner." *New York Times*, March 19, 1985.

The Match Game Series Page, Imdb.com, https://www.imdb.com/title/tt0055688/.

"The Match Game 10 September, 1965." YouTube.com, https://www.youtube.com /watch?v=qdqVvq2g8NE (retrieved July 15, 2021).

McCarron, Anthony. "Former New York Yankee Pitcher 'Bullet' Bob Turley Still Calls Them as He Sees Them." *New York Daily News*, June 19, 2010.

McGowen, Roscoe. "Dodgers Once Again Hear 'Wait 'Til Next Year.'" *New York Times*, October 6, 1953.

"Mickey Mantle Blasted Setbacks into the Cheap Seats." *Investor's Business Daily* (online stock market news site), https://www.investors.com/news/management/leaders-and -success/mickey-mantle-did-not-let-injuries-beat-him/, June 14, 2012 (retrieved September 8, 2021).

Mickey Mantle page, IMDb.com, https://www.imdb.com/name/nm0544144/.

Mickey Mantle Quotes Page, https://www.baseball-almanac.com/quotes/quomant .shtml.

"Mickey Mantle, The 1961 Home Run Race with Roger Maris." YouTube.com, https:// www.youtube.com/watch?v=U5Ew48mxTeU.

"Mickey's Quotes By Lewis Early." Stevetheump.com, www.stevetheump.com/themick .htm.

Molito, Tom. *Mickey Mantle Inside and Outside the Lines* (Castroville, TX: Black Rose Writing, 2016).

Mulder, Craig. "Mantle, Ford Headline Stellar Class of 1974." National Baseball Hall of Fame, https://baseballhall.org/discover/inside-pitch/mantle-ford-inducted-in-1974 (retrieved August 23, 2021).

Myerson, Allen R. "Mantle Receives New Liver as Donor Is Found Quickly." *New York Times*, June 9, 1995.

Neft, David S., Richard M. Cohen, and Michael L. Neft. *The Sports Encyclopedia: Baseball 2000* (New York: St, Martin's Griffin, 2000).

Nemec, David, and Saul Wisnia. *100 Years of Major League Baseball: American and National Leagues 1901–2000.* (Lincolnwood, IL: Publications International Ltd., 2000).

Newhan, Ross, and Douglas Shuit. "Gravely Ill Mantle Gets a New Liver." *Los Angeles Times*, June 9, 1995.

___. "Red Patterson Dies of Cancer." *Los Angeles Times*, February 11, 1992.

Noble, Marty. "Balk Defined 1961 All-Star Game, Stu Miller's Career." MLB.com, July 11, 2015.

Obernauer, Michael. "Merlyn, Widow of Yankee Icon Mickey Mantle, Succumbs to Alzheimer's Disease at Age 77." *New York Daily News*, August 11, 2009.

Oliveria, D. F. "Organ Donor Work Made Mantle a Hero." *Spokesman-Review* (Spokane, WA), August 16, 1995.

Ollave, Michael. "Too Much Too Soon and Far Too Often Biography: Book by Mickey Mantle's Family—and a Chapter by the Mick Himself—Gives Sobering View of the Dark Side of a Hero's Life." *Baltimore Sun*, October 14, 1996.

Peary, Danny. *We Played the Game: Memories of Baseball's Greatest Era* (New York: Black Dog & Leventhal, 1994).

Pietruscza, David, et al. *Baseball: The Biographical Encyclopedia* (Toronto: Sport Media Publishing, Inc., 2003).

Posnanski, Joe. "The Boudreau Shift." Joe Blogs, https://joeposnanski.substack.com/p/the-boudreau-shift, July 10, 2014 (retrieved September 12, 2021).

Precker, Michael. "Mantle's Widow Finally Steps Out of His Shadow." *Chicago Tribune*, October 27, 1996.

Ricks, Delthia. "Do Rich, Famous Get Preference for Transplants?" *Orlando Sentinel*, June 9, 1995.

Roberts, Randy, and Johnny Smith. *A Season in the Sun: The Rise of Mickey Mantle* (New York: Basic Books, 2018).

Roger Maris Quote Page. Baseball-Almanac.com, https://www.baseball-almanac.com/quotes/quomari.shtml.

Rothenburg, Matt. "Team Tours of Japan Bridged Cultural Gap Following WWII." National Baseball Hall of Fame, https://baseballhall.org/discover-more/stories/short-stops/team-tours-of-japan-bridged-cultural-gap.

Sandy Koufax Quote Page. Baseball-Almanac.com, https://www.baseball-almanac.com/quotes/quokouf.shtml.

Seideman, David. "Mint $2.5 Million Mickey Mantle Card Nearly Dumped in the Atlantic." *Forbes*, https://www.forbes.com/sites/davidseideman/2018/04/18/mint-2-5-million-mickey-mantle-card-nearly-dumped-in-atlantic/, April 18, 2018.

Silva, Drew. "Bob Sheppard: The Voice of God." NBCSports.com, https://mlb.nbcsports.com/2010/07/11/bob-sheppard-the-voice-of-yankee-stadium-1910-2010/, July 11, 2010.

Simon, Andrew. "Ted Williams: Last to .400, Among the First to Face Shifts?" MLB.com, https://www.mlb.com/news/ted-williams-faced-defensive-shifts-in-1940s-c191605204, July 29, 2016 (retrieved September 12, 2021).

"Simon and Garfunkel Lyrics, Mrs. Robinson." A-Z Lyrics.com, https://www.azlyrics.com/lyrics/simongarfunkel/mrsrobinson.html.

Smerconish, Michael. "Telling the Stories They Once Could Not." *Post Star* (Glens Falls, NY), April 20, 2011.

"The Spook Light." Joplin, Missouri, website, www.joplinmo.org/575/The-Spook-Light (retrieved July 11, 2021).

Sternman, Mark S. "The 1951 World Series." Society for American Baseball Research, https://sabr.org/journal/article/the-1951-world-series/.

Stewart, Wayne. *Wits, Flakes and Clowns: The Colorful Characters of Baseball* (Lanham, MD: Rowman and Littlefield, 2000).

Stone, Larry. "The Quest—Roger Maris." *Seattle Times*, July 6, 1997.

Stout, Glenn. *Yankees Century* (New York: Houghton Mifflin, 2002).

TheMick.com.

ThePeopleHistory.com.

Thorn, John. "Remembering Mickey Mantle." Our Game (official Major League Baseball blog), https://ourgame.mlblogs.com/remembering-mickey-mantle -17c9a65845db, August 15, 2016 (retrieved August 29, 2021).

"Throwback Tulsa: Oklahoma Native Mickey Mantle Became a New York Yankee 70 Years Ago Today," *TulsaWorld.com* (online news site), https://tulsaworld.com/news /local/history/throwback-tulsa-oklahoma-native-mickey-mantle-becomes-a -new-york-yankee-70-years-ago-today/collection_f2689533-0409-5e47-9a43 -d1ca07a45886.html#2, April 17, 2021 (retrieved July 11, 2021).

Trafford, Abigail. "Mickey Mantle: Tough Call." *Washington Post*, August 8, 1995.

Turbow, Jason. "The Complete Guide to Tipping Pitches in Baseball." TheBaseballCodes .com, https://thebaseballcodes.com/2021/01/27/the-complete-guide-to-tipping -pitches-in-baseball/, January 27, 2021 (retrieved September 6, 2021).

"Uses and Risks of Amphetamines." MedicalNewsToday.com, https://www.medicalnews today.com/articles/221211 (retrieved July 25, 2021).

Viglioti, Jake. "10 Sordid Stories of Baseball's Greatest Switch-Hitter." Listverse.com, https://listverse.com/2015/09/18/10-sordid-stories-of-baseballs-greatest-switch -hitter/, September 18, 2015.

Vitty, Cort. "Ripper Collins." SABR Biography Project, https://sabr.org/bioproj/person /ripper-collins/.

———. "Switch-Hit Home Runs: 1920–1960." Society for American Baseball Research, https://sabr.org/journal/article/switch-hit-home-runs-1920-60/.

Vorperian, John. "Ralph Houk." SABR Biography Project, https://sabr.org/bioproj/per son/ralph-houk/.

Wancho, Joe. "Rocky Colavito." SABR Biography Project, https://sabr.org/bioproj/per son/rocky-colavito/.

Warnick, Ron. "Spook Light Legend Was Debunked More Than 70 Years Ago." Route-66News.com, https://www.route66news.com/2018/12/17/spook-light-legend-was -debunked-more-than-70-years-ago/, December 17, 2018 (retrieved July 11, 2021).

"What's My Line?—Mickey Mantle" (May 17, 1953). YouTube.com, https://www.you tube.com/watch?v=ipU3xwSuQ3E.

"Why Mickey Mantle Walked Away from the Yankees." Retrosimba.com (Cardinals blog), https://retrosimba.com/2019/02/25/why-mickey-mantle-walked-away-from -yankees/, February 25, 2019 (retrieved August 20, 2021).

Williams, Roger. "Goodbye, Casey. Goodbye." *Sports Illustrated*, October 31, 1960.

Williams, Ted, with John Underwood. *My Turn at Bat: The Story of My Life* (New York: Pocket Books, 1970).

Wulf, Steve. "The Stuff of Legend: In 1957, Cincinnati Fans Stacked the All-Star Team Too." ESPN.com, June 29, 2015 (retrieved June 29, 2021).

Yogi Berra Quotes Page, BrainyQuote.com, https://www.brainyquote.com/authors/yogi -berra-quotes.

Young, Dick. "Young Ideas." *New York Daily News*, May 26, 1970.

Zminda, Don. "Home Run Derby: A Tale of Baseball and Hollywood." SABR .org, https://sabr.org/journal/article/home-run-derby-a-tale-of-baseball-and -hollywood/.

INDEX

CPSIA information can be obtained
at www.ICGtesting.com
Printed in the USA
BVHW050317220123
656764BV00006B/12